T0244511

# Memories of a Gay Catholic Boyhood

# Memories of a Gay Catholic Boyhood

COMING OF AGE IN

THE SIXTIES

..................

JOHN D'EMILIO

Duke University Press   *Durham and London*   2022

© 2022 DUKE UNIVERSITY PRESS All rights reserved
Printed in the United States of America on acid-free paper ∞
Designed by Courtney Leigh Richardson
Typeset in Garamond Premier Pro and New Century Schoolbook
by Westchester Publishing Services

Library of Congress Cataloging-in-Publication Data
Names: D'Emilio, John, author.
Title: Memories of a gay Catholic boyhood : coming of age
in the sixties / John D'Emilio.
Description: Durham : Duke University Press, 2022.
Identifiers: LCCN 2021050641 (print)
LCCN 2021050642 (ebook)
ISBN 9781478015925 (hardcover)
ISBN 9781478023166 (ebook)
Subjects: LCSH: Gay men—New York (State)—New York—Biography. |
Catholic gay men—New York (State)—New York—Biography. |
Catholics—New York (State)—New York—Biography. | Italian
Americans—New York (State)—New York—Biography. | Italian
American gays—New York (State)—New York—Biography. |
Bronx (New York, N.Y.)—Biography. | BISAC: SOCIAL SCIENCE /
LGBTQ Studies / Gay Studies | BIOGRAPHY & AUTOBIOGRAPHY /
LGBTQ | LCGFT: Autobiographies.
Classification: LCC HQ75.8.D44 A3 2022 (print) | LCC HQ75.8.D44
(ebook) | DDC 306.76/62092 [B]—dc23/eng/20220121
LC record available at https://lccn.loc.gov/2021050641
LC ebook record available at https://lccn.loc.gov/2021050642

*Cover art:* Photos of the author. *Front, top to bottom:* At an essay contest
award ceremony, 1962; playing with his brother, circa 1959; at his desk,
senior year. *Back:* His brother's first birthday, 1958 (*top*); with trophies,
1964 (*bottom*).

This book is dedicated to the memory of my parents,
Sophie Scamporlino D'Emilio (1925–2010)
and
Vincent Anthony D'Emilio (1924–2020)

# Contents

PART III

Everything Changes

*A gallery appears after page 116*

# Preface

For three decades, I taught undergraduate college history courses that covered the 1960s. When I first began teaching, many of my students were of an age where they had older brothers and sisters who had participated in the events of the decade and from whom they had heard many stories. By the time my teaching career ended, the sixties had become the experience of my students' grandparents. But over those decades, one thing remained unchanged. Across identity lines of class, race, and gender, students displayed a deep fascination with the events and movements of that era. The fact that young adults—many of them college students like themselves—were at the heart of the turbulence only made the decade more compelling to them.

Many of the histories of the 1960s highlight headline-making names, whether Presidents John F. Kennedy, Lyndon B. Johnson, and Richard Nixon or prominent leaders of social justice movements, like Dr. Martin Luther King Jr., Malcolm X, or Betty Friedan. But my students were most curious about the lives of young adults like themselves, youth who came from ordinary, not-privileged backgrounds and might best be described as "faces in the crowd"—those many individuals who sat down in the streets and blocked traffic, rallied in front of government buildings, and paralyzed campuses. How did so many young people move from the quiet of their family backgrounds to the social and political upheavals of this seemingly revolutionary era? What kinds of experiences provoked their shift in outlook? How did they become agents of change? And how did their lives change because of this? What kinds of life paths opened up for them?

As the sixties move farther into the past and as our nation lives through an era in which so many Americans seem to have outlooks at odds with the hopeful progressive vision of social justice that the sixties projected, the need to bring this period back to life through the experience of ordinary Americans seems more important than ever. In the midst of a Black Lives Matter movement against police violence, a #MeToo movement against sexual violence and abuse, a movement to save the planet from climate change, and an effort to challenge gender binaries with a queer vision of identities, it is worth recalling how a previous generation of young people moved from the routines of daily life into a new world of activism, dissent, and nonconformity.

. . . . . . . . . . . . .

I was one of those many faces in the crowd in the second half of the 1960s, when protest and dissent were at their height. But anyone who had observed my life growing up in the conformist decade of the 1950s would never have expected to find me in such a role just a few years later. At the height of the baby boom years, my large, multigenerational family of Italian origin was making every effort to be good Americans. We watched the benevolent family comedies that television networks were offering, celebrated Memorial Day and the Fourth of July with backyard picnics of hot dogs and hamburgers, and sang the praises of Dwight Eisenhower, our war-hero president who projected a calm, reassuring demeanor and promised to protect America from communism.

How does a boy from an Italian immigrant family in which everyone went to confession regularly and unfailingly attended Sunday Mass become a lapsed Catholic? How does a family who worshipped the politics of Senator Joseph McCarthy and whose members were loyal to Richard Nixon to the end of his political career produce an antiwar activist and pacifist? How does a multigenerational family in which the word *divorce* is never spoken and where no adults leave home until marriage raise a son who comes to explore the hidden gay sexual underworld of New York City? How does a politically engaged intellectual whose work, later in life, will help shape a historic Supreme Court decision, emerge from a family in which almost no one ever read a book?

In addressing these questions, I hope that this book sheds light not only on the life of an individual but on the larger baby boom generation whose experiences are still shaping the United States today. Its three parts will take you from the working-class neighborhood in the Bronx that I almost never left during my childhood, to the Jesuit high school for academically gifted Catholic boys that introduced me to the wonders of intellectual life and the culture of Manhattan, and finally to the Ivy League campus of Columbia and the political and social upheavals of the late 1960s.

Part I, "An Italian Boy from the Bronx," re-creates the flavor of my large, extended Italian immigrant family and the Depression-era housing project in which I grew up. I lived within the boundaries of "Big Grandma's house," where aunts, uncles, and cousins gathered every chance they could, where the adults spoke Italian, and Big Grandma was adored by all. Family, I learned, was everything, and it deserved an unbending loyalty. At the parish elementary school, nuns and lay teachers taught us catechism every day and imposed a firm discipline upon us. I learned to be a good Catholic boy, or else pay the price, on earth now, and later in hell for all eternity. Relief came from the occasional teacher who treated us with kindness and, most of all, from the school and neighborhood friendships that formed among the boys. We ran wild together through the neighborhood in the hours after school, until this band of boys came to seem more important than my Italian clan.

Part II, "A Jesuit Education," covers the adolescent years of high school, which took me out of the boundaries of family, parish, and neighborhood. I won admission to Regis, a Jesuit high school located on Manhattan's elegant Upper East Side. Regis brought together academically gifted Catholic boys from the greater metropolitan area. Its Jesuit and lay male faculty introduced us to the world of classical learning and held out high expectations for our future mission in life as committed Catholics. I was chosen to be mentored in the speech and debate society, and soon I was traveling throughout the city and across the country to tournaments, where I won state and national championships. I had friends to die for, and together we explored Manhattan—its museums, its parks, its grand old movie palaces. A boy who had almost never left the Bronx was suddenly enveloped by a world of intellectual engagement that my family could scarcely appreciate.

Meanwhile, these years also saw this good Catholic boy drawn into an underground world of male homosexual desire. On the subways of New York and the streets of the theater district, I found men who had sex with men. In subway restrooms, along the edge of highways in the Bronx, in the bushes by railroad tracks, and in tenement buildings in Manhattan, I had sex with men whose names I never learned and whom I never saw again.

Part III, "Everything Changes," revolves around the campus of Columbia University on Manhattan's Morningside Heights in the second half of the 1960s. Black Power activists, antiwar protesters, and student radicals committed to overthrowing "the system" were holding rallies, marching through campus buildings, disrupting classes, and frequently shutting down the university. Almost immediately, the campus had an impact on me. During freshman orientation, I learned from the campus Protestant minister that "God is dead." In my Western Civilization course, I found myself unable to challenge the logic of the great philosophers who proved that God did not exist. I encountered radical priests and nuns who believed that war was always evil and needed to be opposed as a matter of conscience. My rejection of Catholicism and embrace of pacifism provoked intense conflict with my conservative Catholic parents. Meanwhile, as I struggled with the draft, declared myself a conscientious objector, and counseled other young men on how to avoid military service, I was slowly discovering a hidden gay social world on the streets of Greenwich Village, in the standing-room section of the Metropolitan Opera, and among some of the pathways in Manhattan's parks. I met a man who became my lover and introduced me to New York's secretive gay life. I came out to a small circle of friends.

The political radicalism and emerging sexual revolution of the late sixties led me to reject the professional career options that an Ivy League education held out. Instead, I landed an entry-level job in a Brooklyn library, continued my activist work against the war, and maintained my ties to New York's gay geography and the safety it seemed to provide for exploring my forbidden desires and developing a gay social world. When my work in the library exposed me to a new radical literature on American history, I realized that my intellectual abilities and my activist impulses had found a place where they could come together. Rather than return home, as a good unmarried Italian boy was expected to do, I embarked upon a life path that nothing in my family background and upbringing could have prepared me for. The sixties had changed profoundly the direction that my life was meant to take.

. . . . . . . . . . . . .

Recounting one's life story a half century or more after the events occurred can offer challenges. Fortunately, my training as a historian impressed upon me early the value of preserving evidence from the past. My personal archive of correspondence with friends, especially from my college years, allowed me to reconstruct both events and my responses to them. As an adult, I preserved connections with some elementary school, high school, and college friends, and we have exchanged many reminiscences over the years. I also reread the *Columbia Spectator* from my years on campus in order to capture the range of activities and protests during my time as an undergraduate.

The culture of the Scamporlino and D'Emilio clans has also been a great resource. From the time I was a child and into my decades of adulthood, family members never failed to tell over and over the stories that I grew up hearing about as well as those that I was a part of. And my mom, Sophie, who appears in many of the pages of this book, was meticulous in preserving materials from the family—and my—history. She carefully put together photo albums, treasured the home movies, and collected and saved local news clippings about my victories in speech and debate tournaments as well as in other student competitions. I hope I have done her justice in retelling some of those tales from the past.

PART I

# An Italian Boy
# from the Bronx

.............

# 1

.............

## An Italian Family

In 1977, in his first year in the White House, President Jimmy Carter made a celebrated trip to the Bronx to prove that a peanut farmer from Georgia cared about our cities. Images of crumbling buildings and rubble-strewn lots flashed across television screens. A corner of America looked remarkably like a devastated war zone. Soon after that, I began to notice a new line dividing native New Yorkers from everyone else. If I told someone I was from the Bronx, a New Yorker said, "Oh! What neighborhood?" Everyone else said, "Oh" and looked at me sadly.

To me, the Bronx where I was born after World War II was special. It had the biggest zoo in the world, with its own pair of Chinese pandas. It had the Yankee Stadium of Joe DiMaggio and Casey Stengel. On the Grand Concourse, the Loew's Paradise stood with star-spangled vaulting so spectacular I could forget the movie I was watching and just stare at the ceiling. We had the best Italian ices this side of Naples. On warm summer evenings, you could stroll forever along Pelham Parkway or ride a roller coaster on Bruckner Boulevard. Bronxites knew we were the best. Had you ever heard anyone say "the Brooklyn" or "the Manhattan"? But the Bronx: it just rolled off the tongue.

My part of the Bronx was the best of the best. I grew up in Parkchester in the 1950s. Parkchester claimed the distinction of being the world's largest housing project. More than forty thousand people filled its twelve thousand units, making our two hundred acres among the most densely populated in the world. The buildings were brick, seven or twelve stories tall, with one-, two-, and three-bedroom apartments. The halls were well lit, the elevators always ran, the apartments were painted every three years, and everything—from the grounds outside to the floors inside—was immaculately clean.

Parkchester opened in 1940 so that, when I was a child, it still possessed a spanking new quality. A product of the Great Depression, it was built, owned, and operated by the Metropolitan Life Insurance Company to provide decent housing to working people—as long as they were white. For those privileged to live there, it was the best of corporate paternalism, even if no Parkchesterite ever called it that. The housing was as good as New York offered for the money. With New York's rent control program, you could live there for decades and never see your rent increase. Good citizens that they were, my parents voluntarily signed a new lease every three years and accepted a modest rise in rent. To them, living in Parkchester was a gift, and they were thankful for it.

They had reason to be. Each had spent their first two decades in the South Bronx, my dad by way of a few years on the Lower East Side. The tenements they lived in were built to turn a quick buck at the expense of immigrant families. Mom's family had left the old neighborhood just before the war ended, but Dad's sisters and mother ("Small Grandma," to distinguish her from "Big Grandma," my maternal grandmother) still lived on 147th Street.

Every couple of months, we visited on a Saturday and always took a cab. It made the trip a great adventure because nothing else ever caused Mom and Dad to splurge on anything as extravagant as a taxi. The block Small Grandma lived on was lined with an unbroken row of tenements several stories high. Only the fire escapes interrupted the old brick fronts. They hung so precariously, ready to fall at any moment on anyone foolish enough to linger under them. As soon as Mom had me out of the taxi, I slipped my hand out of hers and ran as fast as I could into the building to avoid so grisly a fate.

But inside wasn't much better. The hallways were dark and narrow. The climb to the third floor was steep and scary. There was no elevator. The two-bedroom apartment was smaller than our one-bedroom. The floors tilted. The walls were lumpy and rough. The bathroom had a tub but no shower fixture. A chain attached to an overhead tank made the toilet flush. It rumbled so much I was sure it would collapse on top of me.

And then there was Small Grandma. I knew I was supposed to love her, but to a little boy she was very scary. She looked older than Methuselah. She dressed completely in black. Not quite five feet tall, she was thinner than any living human being I had seen. Her arms were nothing but bone, the skin stretched so tight that her veins almost popped out. Small Grandma didn't speak English, but words crackled out of her as her bony fingers reached for my cheek and pinched it sharply in greeting.

These visits always happened on a Saturday when everyone was likely to be home. Small Grandpa died when I was an infant, and Small Grandma moved out of her own apartment, a few buildings down the street, into one with Anna, her eldest daughter, and Felix, Anna's husband. She occupied a tiny bedroom just off the kitchen, having displaced my cousins Donald and Johnny, who now slept in the living room on a sofa that opened into a bed at night.

Johnny was the saving grace of these visits. He was a year older than me, which, at age three or four, seemed a big deal. Our best times came when we hid in the bathroom. Above the tub a window opened into the kitchen where the adults sat and talked. By standing on the edge of the tub and stretching our small frames, we could almost see over the window ledge and secretly listen. At some point, someone was sure to say something that struck us as funny, and we quickly slid down into the tub and held our mouths shut to keep from laughing aloud and being discovered.

Mom's father—Big Grandpa—still owned a store a few blocks away on Morris Avenue. Sometimes we strolled there from Small Grandma's apartment before hailing a cab to take us home. We knew he'd be there. He worked in the store 365 days of the year. His only concessions to leisure were the half days he took off on Sundays, Christmas, New Year's, and other holidays.

Big Grandpa sold olive oil and tomatoes, anchovies and cold cuts, macaroni (what "pasta" was routinely called back then), and other staples of an Italian family's kitchen. Everything canned or boxed was imported from the old country, which is to say, Sicily. Much of the time Grandpa had a simple display in the window: boxes of rigatoni or cans of peeled tomatoes stacked pyramid style. But if he was between displays, he let me climb onto the built-in window seats. It was so different from the view out of our sixth-floor Parkchester apartment. I could hear the noise of the buses and delivery trucks and watch the small dramas played out among pedestrians. Sometimes my presence in the window would elicit an "Oh, what a cute little boy" look from an adult passing by.

Grandpa opened the store every day in part because his signature item was the mozzarella he made each morning. It kept customers returning, even after the war when the ranks of Italians in the South Bronx were dwindling. More than thirty years of shaping the curd into mozzarella and twisting the end until it made a nice head had mangled the shape of his right hand. Grandpa could always extract fright from me by calling me over, holding out his left hand, the palm facing me and the fingers spread, and then whipping out his right hand from behind his back. The tendons and muscle joining the thumb to the rest of his hand had worn away, eroded almost to the wrist. I'd scream in terror while he, laughing, reached out to draw me close in a big hug.

The grocery store allowed Big Grandpa to weather the Depression, and by the war years, he had saved enough to buy a house in the northeast Bronx. Its twelve rooms, plus basement and attic, must have seemed like a mansion to my mom and her sisters. It was large enough for three generations of the family to live there. Big Grandma quickly planted a fig tree in the backyard, a reminder of Sicily. Every fall, when the chill in the air turned steady, she lovingly wrapped the tree in layers of cheesecloth to keep it alive through the winter. The tree never produced more than a handful of figs each season, but to Grandma they were as precious as gold.

The house was less than a mile from Parkchester. Just out of high school when the family moved to Silver Street, Mom managed to get a job as a book-keeper in Parkchester's main office. This meant she could leapfrog over the hundreds of families on the waiting list for an apartment. She and Dad had been engaged for three years. They timed their marriage for when an apartment became vacant. With the housing shortage after the war, this was a real coup. Mom also wrangled a janitor's job for her brother-in-law Phil, and soon Aunt Lucy, Uncle Phil, and my cousin Paul were also living in Parkchester.

I grew up thinking I lived in the closest thing to paradise this side of Eden. Parkchester was made for kids. Its two thoroughfares intersected at the dead center of the housing project, creating four large quadrants. There were play-grounds and ball fields and handball courts, lawns and grassy fields and winding paths, and benches where older folks sat and young mothers rocked their baby carriages. Protected from the dangers of traffic, young children played and ran without ever having to cross a street. With my short four-year-old legs, it seemed like I could run forever without ever reaching the borders of my kingdom.

Since Mom defined the essence of overprotective, it's a sign of how different New York was in those years that, even before I started kindergarten, she let me go to a nearby playground without her. One of my earliest vivid memories of childhood is of racing down the hill behind our building, a big smile on my face, my short legs straining and my arms pumping to get me there as quickly as possible. The playground was a wealth of delights, and I remember having the time of my little life, feeling strong and full with the freedom Mom was giving me. There were swings, slides, and monkey bars, a basketball court, and a tetherball. By age five or six, my favorite game was tetherball. I took to this game quickly and was pretty good at it—so good in fact that the older kids who dominated the playground let me line up to play with them. I gave them a run for their money as I strained and stretched and jumped, pounding the ball with all my strength. The bigger kids cheered me on, and sometimes I actually triumphed.

..............

When the weather was rainy or cold, the playground was not an option. On those days I stayed home. Mom often had laundry to wash or carpets to vacuum. She dusted and polished furniture, scrubbed countertops, and kept the windows sparkling clean. In the lingo of the day, her floors were clean enough to eat off them. When not doing housework, she was on the phone. She talked every day with Big Grandma and with her sisters Lucy, Anna, and Jenny. During those hours I kept myself busy in the bedroom. I had a wooden puzzle of the forty-eight states, and long before I understood what Minnesota or Wisconsin was, I knew that they fit together along the top edge. I had a set of wooden blocks and built forts and skyscrapers. I had Smokey the Bear and a stuffed panda as playmates. Panda was as tall as I was. I would drag him onto my parents' bed, lie on top of him, and rub my nose in his face.

But Panda and the forty-eight states held my attention for just so long. Eventually I made my way to the living room or kitchen to find Mom. If I caught her between tasks, I would climb onto the sofa and sit next to her.

"Read to me," I said, with a puppy dog eagerness that I hoped was irresistible.

Mom never read on her own. She sometimes opened the Bible and stared at the page for a long time. Or she looked through a cookbook, seemingly considering recipes, but never making them since our weekly meal schedule was as dependable as the sun rising and setting. But when I spoke my plea, she responded. She had decided early on that school was my future, and so our small apartment was filled with children's books that she stocked for me.

Fetching one—Aesop's Fables, Hans Christian Anderson, a children's version of the Bible—she pulled me close so I could see the illustrations. She took me to a world where donkeys spoke back to their masters, little boys who were bad had their arms turned into flightless wings, and violent floods almost wiped out life on the planet.

But reading wasn't Mom's thing. She inevitably tired of reading before I tired of listening. I always fared better if I spoke the magic phrase.

"Tell me a story," I begged.

"What do you want to hear a story about?"

"Tell me about Grandpa and the store."

"Well, you know, Grandpa didn't set out to open a store."

"What did he want to do?" I asked.

"Grandpa wanted to be a priest. His family raised goats in Sicily, and they had a few olive trees too. But Grandpa didn't want to work in the fields. So, he set out one day with his clothes rolled in a sheet. The seminary was several towns away, but he never got there. And it's a good thing because if he had, he never would have met Grandma, and you and I would never have been born."

"Really?" My eyes widened.

"Really."

"How come he never made it?"

"He met a friend who was going to America. His friend told him, 'You're crazy to be a priest. Come to America. There's gold in the streets. My cousin is in New York; he will get us jobs.' So, Grandpa got on the boat and came to America instead."

"Then did he open the store?"

"Oh, no, he had lots of other jobs first. The one he liked best was as a delivery man for Sheffield Farms. They taught him to drive a truck, and he went all around the city. Oh, how he used to tell us stories about those days!"

"But what about the store?" I reminded her.

"Well, Grandpa was a good worker, and his supervisor was German and liked him, and he gave Grandpa the best routes. But he got promoted, and Grandpa got a new supervisor, an Irishman. He expected Grandpa to grease his palm. That's when Grandpa decided to open the store. He said to himself, 'I will never work for anyone else again.'"

This wasn't enough of a story, and Mom was on the edge of falling into one of her rants, so I pressed on. "How did he meet Grandma?"

"Grandma worked in a factory with Grandpa's sisters. Grandpa had brought Aunt Connie and Aunt Anna over, since there was no real work for young girls in Sicily. When Grandma came as a teenager, she got a job in the same dress factory as his sisters. They became good friends because they were all from Sortino."

"Did they know each other in Sortino?"

"Oh, no. They weren't from the same society. Grandma's family had nothing. They were so poor that her mother took her out of school when she was seven. She took care of her younger brothers and sisters and did all the housework, while her mother cleaned the houses of others. Grandma had a very hard life. She never learned to read or write. She had nothing before she came to America."

"How did they meet?" I wanted to know.

"Well, Grandma and Aunt Connie were walking back to Morris Avenue after work. He saw them and thought, 'That's the woman for me.' Grandpa was already over thirty. He needed to marry or else he'd be an old bachelor. Grandma was from the same town. She was a paisan. And she was beautiful. You should have seen the pictures of her in her wedding dress. She was thin, with long hair that she wound into a bun and—"

"Big Grandma was thin?" My eyes almost popped out in disbelief. Grandma was so heavy that when she laughed, the fat on her upper arms rolled steadily, like waves heading toward the shore. That was why she was "Big Grandma" instead of "Small Grandma."

"Oh, yes, she was thin, like Aunt Anna is now. But Grandpa told her she had to fatten up. She needed to be strong, like a horse, to work in the store and have children. And so he fed her eggs and macaroni and ricotta. Later it made her sad to look at those pictures from when she was younger, and she tore them all up."

Mom could talk like this about her family forever. She had a story about every twist and turn in the saga of Vincenzo and Jessica Scamporlino and the five daughters they raised in the old neighborhood. Mom's eyes lit up and a smile spread across her face as she described Grandma peeling tomatoes in the back of the store, where the family took its meals. Just like Mom did with me, Grandma bustled around as she told stories about the old country, about the donkeys that wandered through Sortino, about her own parents and the brothers and sisters she missed so much.

I never tired of Mom's stories, no matter how often she told them. There was the time her older sister Lucy came to the dinner table wearing lipstick and Grandpa shouted "Puta!" as he slammed his fist down and made the dishes rattle. I heard about the day Grandma took her daughter Vincenza to enroll in first grade. Unable to speak English, she was helpless when the principal said, "Vincenza? That's not a girl's name. We'll call her Jenny." I heard how Jenny, the daughter who never married, loved to dance and was popular with the boys. With her girlfriends she formed a club, "The Gay Teens." They sometimes skipped school and gallivanted around the city. Not to be outdone, Mom formed "The Debuteens." One time, they headed to Coney Island and met up with a group of boys from the neighborhood. They rode the Cyclone, feasted on cotton candy, and took pictures of each other smiling happily, the ocean in the background. When Anna, the eldest, later saw the pictures, she snatched them from Mom and ripped them to pieces. Anna knew there would be hell to pay if Grandpa found evidence of his thirteen-year-old daughter flirting with boys at an amusement park.

As someone who never put pen to paper except to write a shopping list or scrawl greetings on a Christmas card, these tales were Mom's way of doing history, of keeping alive the times and places that meant the most to her. And her storytelling had a purpose. She had lessons to teach, and she was not shy about making them explicit. She'd look up from the vegetables she was chopping, shake the knife in my direction, and announce: "Obey your parents and never speak back to them!" "Show respect for your elders." "Blood is thicker than water. Family is everything." She always insisted—and I mean *always*—that hers was the happiest family in the world, that she loved her Mama and Papa to pieces, and that they were the best parents a girl ever had. I should consider myself lucky to be growing up in the Scamporlino clan. Nothing was more important than family.

But there were also lessons she didn't intend. They lingered in the air, long after the telling, like the smell of Sunday's roast chicken when it cooked too long or Wednesday night's gravy if it scorched the pot. Sadness and tragedy, anger and resentment wafted through these narratives. There were the tears shed by Anna, Mom's oldest sister, when Grandpa took her out of school after ninth grade so that she could learn dressmaking and work in the garment industry during the early years of the Depression. There was the tragedy of Lucy, a year younger than Anna. Grandpa also pulled her out of school, but Lucy, who loved her movie magazines, used dressmaking school to learn how to make clothes in the latest Hollywood fashion. She wore her creations as she strolled along Morris Avenue, and she sold dresses to girls in the neighborhood. But then, struck with crippling arthritis that deformed her hands and made walking painful while still in her early twenties, she stopped going anywhere except to church on Sundays. There was Jenny, the sister with whom Mom was closest. By everyone's account Jenny was the pretty daughter, with an outgoing personality and lots of boyfriends. She too did well in school, winning oratory contests and excelling in dramatics. But when Grandma had a last child late in life, Grandpa forced Jenny to leave school before graduating. He needed Grandma to work in the store, and Jenny had to care for her infant sister. Mom told how Jenny cried and cried, begging to stay in school.

Mom, of course, never pointed the finger at her papa for any of the things that happened to her sisters. Instead, I learned through Mom's storytelling that the Scamporlinos were a "hard luck" family. Whenever good fortune came our way, someone cast an evil eye in our direction. I learned that I must keep my successes to myself because bragging would provoke someone's envy, and they would rain curses on my head. The wrongs done to us were many. Even so, in Mom's eyes we were still the happiest family there ever was, and I must always be thankful that I was born into it.

# 2

.............

## Big Grandma's House

Big Grandma's house was the place where that happiest of all families gathered with great frequency. A few blocks from Parkchester, her house on Silver Street was my second home. Every Sunday and holiday, every weekday during the summer when school was not in session, in fact any day Mom could manage it, was a day spent there.

"Family" never meant just me, Mom, Dad, and later my brother, Jimmy. It was the whole Scamporlino clan. Anna, the eldest daughter, and Tommy, her husband, lived on the second floor of the house with their children, Vincent, Sylvia, and Laura. Lucy, the next eldest, started married life there but then, with her husband, Phil, moved to Parkchester. Their son, Paul, was born a month after me. Jenny, never to marry, lived in the house too, as did Fran, the "baby" of the family. Five daughters, three husbands, six grandchildren: we were always together, it seemed.

Sometimes the crowd swelled to include the family of Grandpa's sister Conchetta, or Aunt Connie as we called her. She and her husband, their four daughters and husbands, and the grandchildren lived together in a three-story house, two neighborhoods away in Throgs Neck. For birthdays or wedding anniversaries, everyone came over. My uncles pushed the large dining table flush against the wall, and Grandma crammed it with plates of cold cuts, cheese, olives, eggplant, and roasted peppers. Dad put records on the phonograph. He played music from the thirties and forties when the big bands performed in Manhattan's ballrooms. Cousins Yonnie and Danny, who, as Mom put it, were "good on their feet," spun their wives around the living room. But mostly the women danced with each other, two sets of sisters who had done this in their teens more times than anyone could count.

Laughter is what I remember most from these gatherings. When the daughters were with Mama, troubles slipped from sight and everyone was happy. Anything might provoke fits of giggling. A favorite card game was "donkey." It lacked complicated rules and required little strategy. When the dealer said "pass," everyone passed a card to the left. The first person to get four of a kind raised a finger to their nose, and that set off a scramble among everyone to do the same. The last person to touch their nose got a letter—"D...O...N... K..."—until the word *donkey* was spelled out.

To the adults it was pure fun, and the best part was watching Mama. Inevitably, at some point, she started to laugh. Maybe she had four of a kind and was pleased by her success. Maybe she was the last to notice and, having gotten a letter, was embarrassed. But once the laughter started, there was no stopping it. First one daughter and then another saw Mama laughing, and it spread around the table until my aunts were wiping the tears from their eyes.

Often the laughter involved television, which to the adults was still new and thrilling. Sometimes wrestling matches were on. Mom and Dad said they were "fixed," everything done to put on a show. But Grandpa watched religiously. He winced, or raised his hands to protect himself, when one guy was the target of a particularly fierce attack. If someone landed with a thud, Grandpa's groan filled the room. And then his daughters would start to laugh, exiting quickly in order not to show disrespect, and hugging their sides in the next room as they enjoyed Papa's faith in what he saw on the screen.

Grandma, too, liked TV. She didn't need much English to grasp the antics of Milton Berle or Sid Caesar and Imogene Coca. But her favorite was women's roller derby. Like wrestling, a lot was show. Brawls were part of the game. An elbow jabbed into an opponent provoked another player to make a body slam that drove a third over the railing, and then all hell broke loose. The women were on top of each other, punching and slapping and pulling hair. Without fail, Grandma would start laughing, quietly at first but soon matching in its fullness the intensity of the fight. When she laughed hard, her whole body shook. Soon her flesh was jiggling up and down. If Grandma was watching roller derby, everyone knew this would happen, and we all watched in anticipation. Grandma's laughter was contagious, and soon the whole room was laughing with her, the television forgotten.

There was a reason her daughters loved her the way they did. This was a woman who wouldn't—couldn't—hurt a fly. She always projected a jovial mood. She smiled easily and wanted you to smile too.

Food was her instrument for keeping spirits high, her universal language of happiness. On summer days when Paul, Laura, and I were playing in the yard, Grandma would come to the back door and summon us to the kitchen. There she displayed large bowls with watermelon and cantaloupe, cut into perfect bite-size balls. Through her cooking magic, she even transformed the meatless Fridays of Catholics into feasts. Grandma sautéed garlic and onions in a pan filled with olive oil until the scent of garlic wafted through the house and the onions had turned yellow and sweet. She'd add mounds of escarole, stirring and stirring until it wilted. She pressed heaps of this mix into loaves of Italian bread and served us vegetable heroes for lunch. Or she fried thinly sliced potatoes ever so slowly so they became soft rather than crisp. She beat eggs together, turned the gas up high, and poured them in. The eggs crackled as they hit the pan, and soon the mix was on our plates, along with chunks of crusty bread to soak up the extra oil.

Every Sunday evening, the family of fifteen gathered around the dining room table, extended to its full length. No one was absent—ever. The food was always the same: ham, salami, pepperoni, and prosciutto; sliced cheeses and olives; lettuce and tomatoes. Once we were seated, Grandma came from the kitchen with two large brown paper bags and turned them over. As sandwich rolls spilled out, hands grabbed from every corner of the table, pulled open the rolls, and filled them with cold cuts.

From the time I was old enough to sit on my own chair, these Sunday meals were precious to me. At home during these years, I rarely had dinner with Mom and Dad, since Dad got home too late for what Mom considered an appropriate supper time for a young child. Instead, she cooked early for me and sat at the table as I ate. Later, when she and Dad ate, I might be watching TV or playing with my wooden blocks. But on Sunday nights, I got to be part of the big people's world. I heard what they talked about and, sometimes, even argued over.

During summer, the topic was often baseball. Mom was a rabid New York Giants fan. Anna's husband, Tommy, the "cut up" in the family, loved to provoke her into snapping at him—never a hard thing to do—by bad-mouthing *her* team and championing the Yankees. Politics, too, caused sparks. Maybe because he owned a grocery store and was his own boss, Grandpa became a dyed-in-the-wool Republican, and his daughters followed suit. The men who married into the family, like my Dad, took on their wives' affiliation. But not Tommy. A contrarian, he knew how to drop just the right remark to get things going. I didn't have much clue as to what was going on, but I learned at those Sunday dinners to hate Franklin Roosevelt and his wife, Eleanor, and to love Senator Joe McCarthy, the rabid anti-communist whose name became symbolic of those Cold War years. Communists inspired everyone's hatred. Mom was overjoyed when Joseph Stalin, the Russian dictator, died. She took credit for his demise, since she had prayed for it to happen for years.

Occasionally on Sunday evenings, after the meal, Dad lugged a heavy 16-millimeter projector into the living room. Because Dad worked as bookkeeper at a small camera store, he got free film and didn't pay to have it developed. So he bought himself a movie camera, and now and then Mr. Berkey, his boss, let him bring home a projector for the weekend. It was the one luxury our family had, and the one thing that made Dad seem special, since he was the keeper of the family movies and the projectionist. As I got older, there were more reels of film to choose from, and family members shouted out their favorites: "dancing around the Christmas tree" or "the Fourth of July barbecue" or "Laura's first birthday party." Watching these films at age six or seven and seeing myself in some of them, I experienced the thrill of being in the movies. These were the Scamporlinos' version of Hollywood.

My favorite was Mom and Dad's wedding. They had hired someone to film it, from the wedding at St. Raymond's Church to the reception afterward at the Hunts Point Palace on Southern Boulevard. Mom was beautiful, her wavy, black hair in a pompadour style. Her wedding dress had a long train that her sister Jenny carried from behind, and it made her look glamorous, like the movie stars of the 1930s with their floor-length gowns. Her deep brown eyes, high cheekbones, sharp-edged nose, and the smile on her face suggested the beauty of Barbara Stanwyck, whose old movies played on television. Every time the camera found Dad, he was beaming. Almost paper thin, with hair much lighter than one expected among Italians, he projected the sense that in marrying Sophie, he had received a miraculous blessing from God. Meanwhile, around them, my aunts and uncles and their cousins were dancing across the floor. Every time the family watched the film together, the same scenes provoked laughter, and none more than the moment on the receiving line when Nicky, a friend from the old neighborhood whom Mom had once dated, leaned in to kiss her and wouldn't stop.

Meals and home-movie time aside, the grandkids were pretty much on our own. As the adults did whatever it was that adults did together, and the teenagers were out with their friends, Laura and Paul and I were inseparable. We filled our time as best we could. Laura knew where her sister Sylvia kept her James Dean scrapbooks, and we took them out when no one else was upstairs.

Sylvia had photos of Dean with Natalie Wood and Liz Taylor, photos where he looked tough and mean, and others with a smile so big it melted your heart.

We shared forbidden things from the adult world. We smoked cigarettes from a pack of Chesterfields that Uncle Phil left unguarded and drank from a beer we found on the kitchen counter. Laura showed Sylvia's bras to Paul and me and explained that they covered big lumps on Sylvia's chest. I refused to believe that they were anything more than a fashion, like high heels and skirts, to keep us from confusing men and women, but Laura insisted that, yes, women really did have lumps on their chest.

Summer was the best time of all. We made excursions out of the neighborhood. Restaurant eating was not a common thing. Dad took Mom and me out on Mother's Day, and a couple of times a year we walked to our neighborhood Chinese restaurant. But for the most part, restaurants were a luxury. Why spend money when we could eat more cheaply at home? And so there were all those Sunday meals and parties at Big Grandma's to celebrate one birthday or another.

Except in the case of Grandma and Grandpa. Their birthday Sundays in June and August were the two times a year when, as a clan, we all made a trip to a restaurant. When the day was bright and clear—and the sun always seemed to shine for Big Grandma—the family made its way to Amerigo's in Throgs Neck. The waiters sat us at a long table in the center of the room. At first the mood seemed somber, as the adults stared long and hard at the large menu. But once the ordering was done, the tone brightened, and it was like Sunday dinner at Grandma's, with conversation jumping from topic to topic and frequent explosions of laughter.

But the best days were the Sundays when the adults said to me, Paul, and Laura, "We're going to Bruckner Boulevard." Bruckner Boulevard was the setting for a children's amusement park. Though nothing like Coney Island in Brooklyn, it had enough rides to keep us squealing with joy. We got strapped onto one of the pony seats on the merry-go-round. There was a children's roller coaster that pulled the screams out of my mouth. But best of all were the bumper cars, where Paul and I could smack into others at full speed and have it be considered fun rather than making trouble.

Trips like this, whether to an amusement park or restaurant, were unusual. They cost money, and in our family every penny got counted and every expense carefully calculated. But even when we stayed close to home, summer was the best because Paul, Laura, and I could be outside. We could make as much noise as we wanted and run ourselves ragged. One summer Grandma bought a rubber wading pool. On the hottest days she filled it with water from the garden hose, and we splashed around until we tired. Every Memorial Day, Fourth of July, and Labor Day, Tommy dragged a small grill up from the basement. As the coals turned red-hot, I waited expectantly for the hamburgers and hot dogs—American food for American holidays—that the family never cooked otherwise. On these days when everyone was outside eating, Laura, Paul, and I put on little theatricals. The adults applauded as we enthusiastically sang "How Much Is That Doggie in the Window?" and "What Did Della Wear?"

The Brucker family lived in the house next door, with a daughter, Ingrid, about our age. The four of us ran back and forth between our yards, screaming at the yellow jackets that buzzed around what we called the "bumblebee tree." We had many hours of fun with Ingrid, who was skinny as a stick and, even in summer, unnaturally pale. The Bruckers were Lutheran, a fact that always got mentioned with slightly lowered voices, so that early on it seeped in that this was not good. Once, Laura told me that Ingrid had fed her dirt pies. I was outraged. Marching into the yard, I flung in her direction the worst thing I knew to say: "You're going to hell! You'll burn forever!" Ingrid bravely threw back, "I am not," but without much conviction, and soon tears were flowing.

Grandma was outside in a flash. She shooed me back into the house and offered Ingrid one of the biscuits she always seemed to carry in her apron pocket, wiping Ingrid's tears until the sobs were just a whimper. I was mortified by what I'd done, less for how it made Ingrid feel than that I'd provoked Grandma's displeasure. But when she came inside, she drew me to her. In a voice so patient, she repeated, "Giovannin', Giovannin'," the diminutive of my name, with the final vowel clipped in Sicilian fashion. She pulled me close, played with the head of blond hair that she couldn't quite believe belonged to one of her grandchildren, and then extended to me a biscuit that told me better than any words could, "We are family. No matter what you do, I will always love you." It was a message that echoed through her house every hour of every day.

# 3

..............

## School: Becoming a Big Boy

With its church and elementary school, St. Raymond's was familiar to me for as long as I can remember. We passed it every time we walked to Grandma's house. The church was a big, impressive building standing back from the road, with a parish cemetery in front of it where priests who had served in earlier times were buried. Two tall, rounded towers stretched toward the sky, and a large stained glass window shone above the entrance.

Mom and her older sisters had gone to public school in the old neighborhood. But when the family moved to Silver Street during the war, the kids—Aunt Fran and my older cousins, Vinny and Sylvia—were enrolled in St. Raymond's. Perhaps it was a step, along with homeownership, that signified upward mobility? Perhaps Anna and Lucy picked up from the Irish families in the neighborhood that this was the thing to do? Whatever the reason, the parish school became the place where my cousins and I got our education.

When the family arrived in the parish, the school was housed in a dark, three-story brick building, dating back several decades. It was a grim, primitive place. The hallways were long and narrow. There was a twisting staircase protected by a floor-to-ceiling metal-linked fence. Presumably the fence was meant to save young ones from tumbling over the banister to an early death, but it seemed more like a cage intended to secure a pack of wild animals. All the toilets were in the basement, with its concrete walls and floors and with water pipes visible.

By the time I started kindergarten in 1953, the parish had constructed a brand-new building to house the expanding enrollment of baby boomers. The "new school," as everyone called it, was everything the "old school" was not. The halls were wide and full of light. There were bathrooms on each floor. It had a huge auditorium and a gymnasium large enough for a full-size basketball court.

The summer before I turned five, Mom began preparing me with tales of how wonderful school was going to be. I would learn to read and write. I'd make lots of friends, learn my catechism, and be a good Catholic boy. By the end of summer, school was sounding like heaven on earth. When the first day arrived, I was dressed and ready before Mom was. We headed along Unionport Road toward Tremont Avenue, me holding Mom's hand tightly and trying to pull her along to get there faster.

As we got closer to the school, a group of women approached, talking excitedly, and Mom stopped to ask them something. Suddenly she was pulling me. Mom, who was never late for anything, apparently had the time wrong for when school began. Sure enough, no one was assembled outside when we reached the building. She found the room I was assigned to and stood outside, looking hesitantly through the glass-paneled door.

The woman who came to the door introduced herself as Mrs. Utsinger. As she and Mom talked, I peeked inside. There were maybe forty boys and girls, sitting at long tables in groups of six or eight. They were busy doing something, but I couldn't tell what. As I looked around the room, I noticed picture books spread open on top of low bookcases that were pressed against the walls, and stuffed animals perched on tables.

Suddenly I realized Mom was leaving. She had her worried-smile look on her face and waved to me as Mrs. Utsinger took my hand and led me to a table with an empty seat. All the kids had paper and crayons and were busily drawing and coloring. Mrs. Utsinger told me to draw whatever I wanted and then moved to another table to see how her new pupils were doing. I reached for some paper, but there was not a crayon around. I could feel the worry in my tummy, and tears were starting to well up when the long-haired girl sitting across from me said, "Here, take some of mine." She pushed two or three crayons in my direction, smiled, and went back to coloring. It felt like the nicest thing anyone had ever done for me.

...........

I liked kindergarten a lot. Unlike my neighborhood playground, where I never knew who might be there and the cast of characters kept changing, at school the same kids showed up every day and we each had our assigned seat. Before long we had become familiar enough to recognize each other as we walked to school with our moms. We became this steadily growing pack of kids heading toward the corner of Purdy Street, where we obediently waited for our moms to catch up and take us across the street. When the day ended, the process was reversed. We poured out of the building, shouting and running to our moms, and then the pack made its way through Parkchester. Mom and I were always the last of the group since we lived farthest from the school.

The time in kindergarten was fun too. The supply of crayons and paper never seemed to run out. Every day, Mrs. Utsinger read us a story in a voice so soothing that I felt like she was cuddling me in her arms. We played games: musical chairs; red light, green light; pin the tail on the donkey. And unlike in the playground, we were all the same age. In Mrs. Utsinger's classroom I didn't have to compete with kids twice my age.

Fun as this was, the rules of kindergarten seemed to elude me. At the playground I could run around and jump up and down whenever I wanted. But now we all had to start and stop according to Mrs. Utsinger's wishes. When she told us to go to our seats, we did. But a few seconds later I might run to another table to pin the tail on Tommy Porter or tag Vincent Gallela, or squeeze into a seat with Marilyn Martin. Mrs. Utsinger's face never betrayed anger. But she made it plain that I wasn't following the rules, and I spent a lot of time standing in a corner, facing the wall as punishment.

Unlike Mrs. Utsinger, Sister Perpetua Mary, who taught first grade, never cracked a smile. She looked the age of Big Grandma, but instead of the warmth and laughter that Grandma brought into every room, Sister Perpetua stood glaring at us in her nun's habit. As a Sister of Charity, she was covered from head to foot in black, as if dressed for a funeral. The skirt reached to just above the ground. Her top stretched up to her neck and down to her wrists. She wore a black cap, tied to her head with a long, thick black ribbon, so that only the front of her face showed.

Religious instruction was woven into every day of class, but since we were just learning our alphabet, it came not in the form of a catechism but through Bible stories that Sister Perpetua read aloud. In her grim voice, she took us through the Old Testament. Snakes slithered about and spoke to people. Older brothers murdered younger ones. Rain poured from the sky until all the people and animals drowned except for a few lucky enough to squeeze into a big boat. After people filled the earth again, an army of soldiers drowned when a sea closed over them. A young boy named Daniel was trapped in a cave with an angry lion.

Mom had been reading to me from a children's version of the Bible for years. I snuggled next to her on the living room sofa and looked at the illustrations as she spun out what seemed to be wonderful adventures of another time and place. I must have carried her version of these stories with me as Sister Perpetua spit out her tales, because they didn't make much of an impression. But that was not the case, apparently, for my classmates. Soon I was hearing Mom telling Dad over dinner how the other mothers were all talking: their children were having nightmares, and it had something to do with Sister Perpetua and the Bible.

But even Sister Perpetua couldn't dampen the excitement of learning to read and write. Mom had taught me some letters to prepare me for school. Now, at school, we went through the alphabet from start to finish. Sister Perpetua had us copy letters over and over until we knew them by heart. Soon we progressed to readers and spelling books. There was a dog named Spot, a cat named Puff, a boy named Dick, and a girl named Jane. We copied each lesson until we could recite the spelling of every word in it.

I took to reading and writing like I had taken to the playground a couple of years earlier. Mom went through the lessons with me, and soon I was racing ahead of my classmates. Before long, when Sister Perpetua began a new lesson, I already knew the story by heart and had memorized every word on the page. All this made for very good grades on the report cards that became a regular feature of life. But it also made me "antsy," as Mom put it, sitting at my desk with the assignment already done. Sometimes I leaned across the aisle, to see how another student was doing. I showed my sheet of paper, with all the words neatly printed on it, to my neighbor. My strong performance protected me from the worst of Sister Perpetua's wrath, but when I heard her announce, "Turn around and sit quietly, young man," I knew I needed to obey.

One morning, I went too far. Sister Perpetua was having us line up, an aisle of students at a time, to show her our homework. As I sat waiting for my row's turn, I saw Jane Halligan standing on the line. Jane was among the group of classmates I walked home with every afternoon. She had long brown hair and a sweet smile. As I watched her, a wave of love washed over me. The next thing I knew I was running over to where Jane was standing. I planted a big kiss on her lips. She looked back, surprised at first, but when she saw it was me, she began to giggle. I kissed her again.

By this time the class had noticed, and some kids were laughing and clapping. That's when I heard Sister Perpetua roar, "What are you doing, young man? You should be ashamed of yourself! Jane! Don't let him do that! Slap him on the face like he deserves!" Jane's eyes had widened, and she was starting to cry. She looked at me, confused about what to do. She raised her hand to slap me; her face seemed to say "I'm sorry." Meanwhile, Sister Perpetua was approaching me and still shouting. "Get back to your seat," she screamed, "and don't get up until I tell you to!" I walked back, but the screams kept coming. "You should be ashamed, young man, ashamed! I will teach you never to do that again. I'm keeping you after school. You'll be locked in the basement overnight where the rats will eat you!"

The room had quieted. Not a sound was coming from anyone. Sister Perpetua returned to the front of the room and gestured for the next student to approach with their homework. The morning continued. When the lunch bell rang, we made our way outside to our waiting mothers. As I looked for Mom, I was aware that many of the kids were looking at me as they took their mothers' hands and began the walk home for lunch. Mom collected me and my cousin Paul, who was in a different first-grade class, and we walked as usual to Paul's apartment in Parkchester, where Aunt Lucy had prepared our lunch.

I couldn't tell Mom what had happened. Sister Perpetua was a servant of the Lord. If she said I had done something wrong, then God was speaking through her. If I told Mom, she might add to the punishment, though it was hard to imagine what she could do after the rats had eaten me. As we ate lunch, I looked up from my sandwich and blurted out, "I don't feel good. I'm sick."

"What's wrong?" Mom asked, a look of concern on her face. "I don't know," I moaned. "I don't feel well." She touched my forehead. "Your forehead isn't hot," she said.

"No, I'm sick," I continued. "I can tell. I'm getting sick."

Mom got up and headed toward Lucy's bathroom. I could see the annoyance on her face. She returned with a thermometer and stuck it under my tongue. "Normal temperature," she announced. "Finish eating so I can get you back to school." I tried to protest, but she was having none of it. She got my coat on and practically pulled me out of the building, and we began the walk to St. Raymond's.

I was holding on tight to Mom's hand, trying to pull her in the other direction, away from school. Soon I was crying and tugging at her, saying over and over, "I won't go back to school, I won't. Take me home." As we turned onto Purdy Street, I could see mothers and students gathered by the schoolyard. By now I was kicking and screaming, as Mom dragged me along. If there was anything she hated, anything that worked her up, it was public embarrassment. She did not want to look foolish to the "outside world," as all except family were called, and here I was, creating a scene that made everyone stare.

When we reached the schoolyard, Sister Perpetua was standing there, hands tucked inside her habit. I quieted down immediately, and Mom pushed me into the yard as she started to talk to Sister Perpetua. "I'm sorry, Sister. He's usually not like this," I heard her saying, while I tried to vanish among the students in the yard. As they continued talking, Mom threw glances in my direction.

Then she left, the bell rang, we marched to our classrooms, and the afternoon went on. The bell rang, signaling the end of the school day, and I left with all my classmates. No basement, no rats. The incident was never mentioned again.

I survived my year with Sister Perpetua. I adapted to the discipline expected in a St. Raymond's classroom. But never completely. I still found myself with time on my hands, since I did my assignments quickly. Before the fall ended I often had worked my way entirely through our reader and the lesson books we got each year. I learned to hold still until our teacher left the classroom for a few minutes or was writing on the blackboard with her back toward us. Then I might slip from my desk and crawl quietly along the floor, sneaking up behind Donald Gallagher and untying his shoelaces, or lifting up the skirt of Linda Gokey. They knew not to make noise in response, because then they might get caught up in the wrath of our teacher.

Each year, the first weeks of school were the edgiest. I nervously tried to figure out what this person at the front of the room was like. They weren't all cut from the same cloth. Mrs. Utsinger had been warm but firm. Sister Perpetua embodied the wrath of an angry god. Miss Leahy, my second-grade teacher, was the kindest human on the planet. Third grade brought Miss McManus. Extremely grumpy, she seemed more interested in talking in the hallway with Mrs. Dunne, another third-grade teacher, while we sat at our desks endlessly copying words from our speller. And then there was Miss McGlynn in fourth grade. It was impossible not to love her. We all competed for her attention, each of us wanting to be the best student possible, doing whatever it took to make her smile grow even wider.

. . . . . . . . . . . . .

Besides the playmates and the pleasure of learning to read and write, school brought another change, but this one at home. At some point in second grade, Mom upgraded me to "big boy" status.

The first time I heard that phrase came one evening just before dinner. Ever since I had grown tall enough that she could dispense with the high chair and have me sit at the table, the routine was that soon after five o'clock, she called me to the table and served me dinner. While Mom was a wonderful storyteller, she was also a good listener, and dinner was my time to talk. In the years before I started school, I might babble about the kids at the playground or the games I had played in the bedroom. But once I started school, there was so much more to say. Mealtime was the chance to recite my lessons again, tell stories about other kids, or describe the "special activities" like art and music that occasionally broke the routine.

Mom always seemed to enjoy my stories, but eventually, my plate empty, she picked up the dish and glass and utensils and headed to the kitchen to prepare dinner for herself and Dad. I returned to the living room and lost myself watching Roy Rogers on television as he rode Trigger through the open spaces of a West I could only imagine existed.

At some point, the sound of a key in the door meant that Dad was home from work. Once, early on, eager to tell him about an adventure that day, I ran to the door and threw myself at him. But carrying a whole day of tension from his job, he roughly brushed me away. The next night, as Dad's arrival home approached, Mom made clear what I was not to do. "Don't bother your father when he gets home," she said. "He has his routines."

And so, when the key turned in the door, I knew to let Dad's routines unfold. He put his newspaper on the table. He put his coat and jacket in the closet. He went to the bedroom, changed out of his white shirt and tie, and walked through the apartment picking up the bits and pieces of the day's rubbish. He gathered them in a single bag and carried it to the building's garbage chute, where he dumped the bag. Then, back in the apartment, Dad was now officially "home" for the evening. He and Mom had dinner together and talked about the day. After eating, they retreated to the kitchen. Dad proceeded to wash the pots, pans, and dishes. Mom dried each item and put it away. Through it all, they talked. Once they emerged from the kitchen, Mom announced it was my bedtime. She, not Dad, helped me into my pajamas, led me through prayers, and kissed me good night.

Dad had other routines that kept me at arm's length. On weekends, his favorite place in the apartment was the living room sofa. There he sat, the *Daily News* in front of his face, reading every line of the sports pages. Then he shifted his position a bit and, his face down, did the crossword puzzle. Or he might listen to music, his one real pleasure. Dad had quite a collection of records, from the big bands of the 1940s to selections of classical music. With the album cover serving as a wall separating him from me and Mom, he read over and over the notes about the music.

Eventually, an edge of annoyance in her voice, Mom shouted from the kitchen, "Listen, DeMille! We have things to do!" Dad then roused himself and did what Mom had in mind—a trip to the dry cleaner or to Sid's Deli or, once in a long while, a trip with me to the local diner where father and son had lunch together. But these were temporary cracks in the wall he erected between him and a world, including me, that in his view existed only to bother him.

But now, as a big boy who was attending school, I got to sit every night at the dinner table with Dad as well as Mom. I listened to their talk about the day.

What Mom said was usually no surprise, since she was discussing the familiar—calls to her sisters, the doings in the neighborhood, my reports from school. But Dad? Everything he said was new. The mysterious world that he disappeared into each day was as unknown to me as the places described in the geography books that Mom and I brought home from the library.

Work was a source of deep anxiety for Dad. He often said that, if he didn't need to support a wife and child, he would have been content to remain a messenger, his first job out of high school, and buy himself a hamburger for dinner every night while he read the newspaper. More than once as a young child, I remember being awakened in the early morning by noises coming from the bathroom. It was not the sound of the shower or an electric razor. It was Dad retching into the toilet, throwing up his guts. From my crib, I could see Mom pacing in the bedroom, that familiar tightening of her jaw whenever she was upset, with a look on her face that was part worry and part anger. "Inventory," I heard her mutter. I had no idea what it meant, but I knew it couldn't be good.

Now I got to learn about inventory and many other things as he talked about his day at Peerless Camera. There was Mr. Berkey, who founded the business and whom Dad spoke of with reverence. There were the two friends with whom Berkey developed the business: Mr. Simon, who, according to Dad, was hard to work with, and Mr. Dunn, who was kind. There was inventory. It came with the "tax season." Each January, Dad had to count up everything—rolls of film, cameras, anything that could be sold—and then add up how much it all cost and report it to something called "the IRS." Dad's voice sank to a whisper when he said those letters.

Then there were the times, not nightly but often, when conversation would be interrupted. Dad might pause in the middle of a sentence and belch. Or he entwined the fingers of his two hands, pressed them toward his chest as his elbows pointed outward, and suddenly cracked his knuckles. Whether a belch or a crack, Mom's response was the same. "DeMille!" she spit out. The message was clear: do not do that at *my* table! And Dad's rejoinder was similar too. He forced out another belch or found another knuckle to crack. Mom made a face back at him, and Dad giggled as he turned toward me and said, "I guess I got the boss mad." And soon we were all laughing as Mom and Dad rose from the table, cleared the dishes, and began their washing and drying together. Just another night at the dinner table, where food brought the family together.

# 4

............

# Baby Jim

For years I didn't seem to notice that I was an only child. Among the cousins I played with, all of us were either the only child or the youngest. Our parents had stopped making babies after us, and I never gave it a second thought, until I started school. Now I had a set of friends whom I saw daily. I played with them, talked with them, and got to know them well. They were rapidly becoming part of my life and how I saw the world.

One Saturday during first grade, Mom and I were walking on Unionport Road. We had delivered some clothing to the dry cleaner. As we came onto the street, I saw a classmate, Eddie, and waved to him. He was holding the hand of a younger boy, while a woman, his mother, pushed a baby carriage. She and Mom introduced themselves and started talking.

With his hand on top of his brother's head, Eddie wheeled him around to face me and said, "Billy, this is my friend John." Then he pointed to the carriage. There was a little one, his eyes wide open and his tiny hands wiggling in jerky motions as if he was slapping away a horde of flies. Eddie waved his hand at the baby, who turned his head and laughed. "He had his six-month birthday yesterday," Eddie said.

I didn't know there were six-month birthdays, but I knew that I liked this little creature, and little Billy, too, who was tugging at Eddie's sleeve. They were so much better than stuffed animals. They moved on their own. They could talk when they got to be as big as Billy. You could play with a little brother forever, I thought, and by the look of things they played back with you. I decided I wanted one.

When we got back to our apartment, I told Mom, "I want a little brother."

Dad was sitting on the sofa, doing the crossword puzzle. He put the paper down and looked up.

"Well, it's not as easy as saying you want one," Mom replied. "It's not like a toy that you buy at Macy's."

"So where do we get one?" I asked. "Where did you get me?"

"We brought you home from the hospital."

"So, let's go now. Let's go to the hospital and bring home a little brother."

Dad came over to the table and sat down. "It doesn't work that way," he said. "Babies come from God. We prayed to God to bring us a baby and eventually He brought us you. A baby grows inside a mommy until it's big enough to come out, and then we go to the hospital where the doctor takes care of everything."

That night, I added a new wish to my bedtime prayers. I asked God for a baby brother. I asked him to make a baby grow inside Mom. Each night, I repeated the prayer. Now and then I asked Mom if a baby had started to grow. Even though Mom said that we couldn't buy one at a toy store, as Christmas drew near and I made my list for Santa, I put "baby brother" on it. After all, Santa was Saint Nicholas. Maybe he had some influence with God.

This went on for almost two years. Early one September, just as I started third grade, Mom told me I could invite some school friends to a party for my eighth birthday. This was a big deal. Non–family members rarely set foot in our apartment. Birthdays were family affairs, always celebrated at Big Grandma's. I came up with a list. Mom gave me envelopes with cards inside, and I passed them out to my friends. When the day came, they all showed up after school. The living room was decorated with a "Happy Birthday" banner that hung on the wall. A colorful crepe paper tablecloth was on the dinner table, which had been extended to its full length. Everyone brought me a present, and Mom had gotten my favorite cake from Lambiasi's Pastry Shop and topped it with nine candles, the extra one for good luck. After everybody sang "Happy Birthday," I closed my eyes, made a wish, and blew out the candles. You can imagine what I wished for.

That evening, after we had dinner and Mom and Dad had cleaned up, they sat back down at the dinner table and called me over. "We have something to tell you," Dad said. "We have a special birthday gift for you. Mommy is going to have a baby."

My joy was uncontainable. I leapt out of my chair, threw my arms around Mom, and began jabbering away.

"When, when? Should we go to the hospital?" I shouted.

"Now, don't get impatient," Mom said. "Dr. Manfredi thinks the baby will come sometime around the holidays. Maybe for the New Year."

"Are you sure? Maybe he's wrong. Maybe it's time!"

"No, no, calm down. The doctor knows. When a baby is inside, a Mommy's tummy starts to swell. Put your hand here. Can you tell? My tummy has to grow much bigger before the baby will come out."

"There's one more thing, though," Dad chimed in. He seemed worried. "We can't know if it'll be a boy or a girl until the baby arrives."

I had never given this a thought. But I knew what I wanted, and it didn't occur to me that anything else was possible. "Oh, it'll be a brother," I said, as if I was privy to the secrets of the universe. "I've been praying."

That Sunday, as always, we went to Grandma's house. The door had hardly opened when I raced through the hall and into the living room screaming, "I'm getting a baby brother! Mommy's having a baby!" Grandma came out of the kitchen, wiping her hands on her apron and laughing at my excitement. I found Laura and Paul, who were upstairs playing, and told them my news. "We already knew," Paul told me.

"It was a secret," Laura said. "We weren't supposed to tell."

Apparently, I was the last to learn. But what did it matter? I was in heaven.

............

Not long after the big announcement, Mom sat me down one afternoon for one of her serious talks. "I'm glad you're happy," she said. "But having a baby brother or sister isn't just fun and games. You're going to be the big brother. That means responsibility. Now you really are a big boy. You don't just get to eat at the dinner table with me and your father each night." Mom explained that, with a baby to take care of, she wouldn't be able to do everything she usually did. I would be in charge of food shopping. There was still time for her to teach me how to do it, but once the baby arrived, it would be my chore.

Thus began a training in shopping for food as precise as the multiplication tables I was learning in school. Supermarket shopping was like a science for Mom. As with everything, there was only one right way to do it, and she alone knew the right way.

Training began the next afternoon. She sat me at the table and began to print on the back of an old Christmas card a list of items. Next to each she placed a number that signified how many we were to get. We got the shopping wagon out of the front closet, went down the elevator, and walked on to Unionport Road. I had been to Safeway with Mom dozens of times, so I automatically turned left when we hit the sidewalk.

"No," she said. "You can't go that way."

"How come? Safeway's right there," I told her, as I pointed to where the store was located.

"That's the way you go with me," Mom replied. "But that way there's only a crosswalk, and you're small and the cars might not see you. I don't want you *ever* crossing that way! We're going to the traffic light."

I turned around and headed toward the traffic signal.

"Wait a minute, buddy boy," Mom called out. Being the big brother was getting more complicated by the minute. "When you start going to Safeway by yourself, you'll have to wheel the shopping wagon."

Mom handed the wagon to me. Its handle reached my shoulder. I almost bumped into a couple of pedestrians in my first effort to drag it along the sidewalk. Mom was trying hard not to laugh and, I have to say, was more patient than she normally was.

Once we got to Safeway, Mom showed me how to attach our wagon to the store's grocery carts. Then we began our trips up and down every aisle. I learned how to judge just the right proportion of yellow and green on a banana skin. I was to make sure there were no soft spots on each apple I picked. As we moved to the packaged foods, Mom gave me lessons in brand names. Among the cereals, Kellogg's yes, Post no. Among the breads, Arnold yes, Wonder no. Del Monte was the favored name in canned vegetables. For macaroni, it was always Buitoni.

There were other lessons to be learned about the science of shopping. On Thursdays and Sundays, Safeway took out full-page ads in the *Daily News*, the paper of choice in our family. The ads listed the sales that week; they also included coupons to save money and, best of all, to get extra Gold Bond stamps.

Gold Bond stamps were my reward for being a big boy. Whatever stamps I received on a shopping trip, I kept. I began applying my arithmetic skills to earn as many stamps from Safeway as possible. Sometimes an ad said "100 free stamps with $5.00 purchase." It was fine with me to make two five-dollar trips to the store.

It required a few trips to absorb all of this. But I got plenty of help. There weren't many eight-year-olds rolling carts in Safeway's aisles. Every clerk came to recognize me. They pulled down cans and boxes from shelves I couldn't reach. They weighed my produce and stood patiently as I tried to decide if I was buying too much. The checkout clerks knew me by name. They smiled as I counted out my money and helped load the wagon with the bags they packed.

...............

It turned out that Dr. Manfredi's prediction was almost exactly right. Early in the evening, the day after New Year's, Mom started feeling pains. Dad called Aunt Lucy and Grandma and packed a few things fast. We went downstairs to hail a cab to the hospital. Pretty soon Mom was being rolled away in a wheelchair, and Dad and I waited until Grandma arrived with Aunt Fran. Excited as I was, after a few hours I could not stay awake, and Grandma took me to her house to spend the night. All the next day I waited, playing with Laura, wondering when it would be over. In the evening a call from Dad gave us the news: I had a baby brother.

I was always told that the children of Italians were named for the baby's grandparents. I was named after Dad's father, Giovanni. That meant my brother would be named Vincent, after Big Grandpa. But Dad was also named Vincent, and so was a cousin, and Mom wasn't having four Vincents in the family. Jimmy was Big Grandpa's nickname, and Mom had the idea to name the baby James. Then, when we called him Jimmy, everyone would know whom he was named after. So there we were, John and James, the two brothers, the favorites of Jesus.

The first day Jimmy was home, Mom had me sit on the sofa and brought him to me, wrapped in a blanket. She told me to stretch out my arms to hold him. She showed me how she cradled his head against her upper arm. "Babies can't hold their heads up for the first few weeks," she said, "so you have to be careful. We don't want his neck snapping back." That was all I needed to know. I pulled my arms away quickly and shook my head back and forth. I wasn't going to be the cause of a snapped neck.

But that didn't stop me from showing my fascination with this tiny creature. He was the littlest thing I had ever seen, smaller than my Smokey the Bear. His face was red, his nose tiny, and all his features seemed scrunched together. That winter and spring, I didn't at all mind not going out to play. Jimmy was much more absorbing than anything the playgrounds in Parkchester offered. Each day with him was like a new adventure.

In those first months, when Mom wasn't holding him, Jimmy spent his time in a cradle. It will be a while, Mom explained, before he can see clearly and recognize us, but from the beginning he heard things. I stood by his cradle, shaking the little rattle that someone had given him. He turned his head to follow the noise. Every few days brought something new: the first time his eyes followed the finger I moved in front of his face; the first time he recognized my voice and smiled; the first time he grabbed my finger; the first time I was finally brave enough to hold him. Eventually, he graduated to a playpen. Soon Jimmy was crawling around and sitting up and eventually standing while he held on tightly to the bars. By the time we were celebrating his first birthday, Jimmy was making his way around our apartment, though one of us always followed nearby, ready to pull him up if he toppled over.

Once Jimmy was mobile, I created worlds of play that were all our own. On Saturdays, when I didn't have school and we didn't trek to Big Grandma's, we seized possession of Mom and Dad's bed. Around this time, a new cartoon series, *The Huckleberry Hound Show*, had premiered on TV. It set its title character in the Wild West among cowboys and cattle thieves. With the help of his sidekick, Quick Draw McGraw, Sheriff Huckleberry always outsmarted the bandits. Jimmy was transfixed by it. One Christmas, Santa brought him a stuffed Huckleberry and Quick Draw, and with them we improvised our own chase scenes and shoot-outs. If we got too loud, Mom came in to assert her own version of law and order.

Game time aside, Jimmy was mostly a quiet baby. He didn't howl or scream, and he seemed to go along with the program that Mom set out for him. But there was one big exception: he didn't like to eat. As the transition to solid food began, he became colicky. In his high chair, he'd throw his head back and twist from side to side as Mom raised a spoon with food to his mouth.

Mom wasn't good with any kind of "no," so Jimmy's refusals drove her crazy. Mealtime became an ordeal, with Mom insisting and Jimmy stubbornly resisting. Around the time he started to talk, Mom had the idea of distracting him as she tried to feed him. She took out an alphabet book that she had once used with me and opened it in front of him. A picture of a bright red apple appeared on the page.

"Look," she said. "A is for apple." She pointed to the *A* and then to the apple, as she mouthed the sounds in exaggerated fashion. Jimmy's eyes opened wide, and he stared at the page. Mom turned the page and repeated the routine with "B is for boy." She turned another page and said "C is for cat." By this time Jimmy was waving his arms as he reached for the page. Twisting his head back and forth, he looked quickly from the book to Mom and back again. Mom returned to the first page and repeated "A is for apple." This time, Jimmy pointed too, and fixated on the page, he began to imitate what Mom was saying. As he opened his mouth, Mom put a spoonful of food in. He swallowed without protest.

Mealtimes now became transformed into reading lessons. My two-year-old brother was learning to speak and read simultaneously. He moved through the alphabet and graduated to elementary readers. This was happening at the time that I started taking trips to the public library without Mom, and Jimmy now sat with me as I pored through the books that I brought home. He went through *Swiss Family Robinson* so many times that he must have committed it to memory. Before long he was reading at the same grade level as I was, and I was already several grades ahead of my classmates. At Grandma's on Sunday, Mom had Jimmy demonstrate his skills. This always provoked sounds of wonder.

Mom was eager to get Jimmy into school, but when she went to enroll him in kindergarten, she learned that St. Raymond's had changed its admission cycle since I had started eight years earlier. Now it was tied to the calendar year. With Jimmy's birthday on January 3, it meant she had to wait until he was almost six before he could start school. "Impossible," I heard her mutter in the kitchen, after she got back home. "What will I do if I have to keep him home another year?"

The following week, Mom decided to "take things into her own hands," as she was fond of saying. She gathered a couple of books and, with Jimmy and me in tow, went to St. Raymond's and headed to the principal's office. Mom explained the situation to Sister Helen. I could see the skepticism in her face as Mom recited Jimmy's achievements and made a case for letting him start school. Jimmy was small for his age, and having him be the youngest in class would only make him seem tinier.

Mom's prospects weren't looking good, until she noticed that Sister Helen had a globe on her desk. "It's not just reading," Mom said. "He knows geography too. You can test him. Really, he knows where everything is."

"Is that true?" Sister Helen asked. "Do you really know where everything is?" Jimmy nodded.

"Well, why don't we have a little test? I will spin the globe and point to different places, and you can tell me what country it is."

She spun the globe and pointed. "Brazil," Jimmy said. She spun again. "Egypt." She spun a third time. "Philippines." Mom was smiling, almost on the verge of laughter. I was excited too. "He knows the capitals of a lot of countries," I heard myself saying.

"My, my," Sister was saying. "You're a very impressive young boy. What do you want to be when you grow up?"

"A paleontologist," Jimmy replied.

For a moment, Sister Helen stared in disbelief. A four-year-old had announced his intention to be a paleontologist. Then, with the slightest smile on her face, she agreed that, yes, it would be appropriate for Jimmy to start kindergarten that September.

# 5

.............

## Change, and More Change

"He always was, always will be, and always remains the same." That's what our Baltimore Catechism declared about the nature of God, in one of its earliest pronouncements.

It was Mom's philosophy too, not just about God but about everything. She never quite said it outright, but how she lived her life—and wanted everyone around her to live theirs too—rested on the conviction that change was bad. It had to be resisted at all costs.

Everything in life could be reduced to a predictable routine. Take breakfast, for instance. Each morning, from the time I started school, she poured some hot coffee into a blender, added milk, cracked a raw egg into the mix, and turned on the blender. I had coffee-with-egg for breakfast every morning from the age of five until I left home for college. Or dinner: on Mondays she made lamb chops; on Tuesdays, meatballs and macaroni with Italian gravy; on Wednesdays, soup and chicken; on Thursdays, steak. Friday was our "no meat" night. Saturday dinner was predictable in its unpredictability. Each Sunday, it was soup and chicken again for the main midday meal, with the chicken delivered on Saturday morning by Uncle Felix, who worked at a poultry market nearby. Occasionally, Mom surprised us with a different weeknight meal, with pork chops or pot roast, but the change itself served as a reminder of the routine being broken.

Even newfangled things like television supported the view that life rolled along in unchanging fashion. *Lassie* and *The Ed Sullivan Show* were always there on Sunday evenings; *The Mickey Mouse Club* came on at the same time every afternoon. This was how life was, and I never thought to question it.

Then Jimmy was born, and everything seemed to change, in one short concentrated period of time. But it wasn't so much Jimmy's arrival, though that was certainly a big change, and a good one at that. Through the spring and summer of 1957, one event after another upset the rhythms and routines, the very feel, of everyday life.

. . . . . . . . . . . . .

Apartments in Parkchester weren't available in an open rental market. The Metropolitan Life Insurance Company kept tight control not only of who moved into the project but of moves within as well. Larger apartments were dispensed to deserving families. "Deserving" meant your children hadn't gotten into trouble with Parkchester's security force and that you paid the rent on time. It also meant that the family was growing and needed more space. So once Mom knew she was pregnant, she and Dad asked to be put on the list for a two-bedroom place. By May, when Jimmy was four months old, the application was approved and we moved into the larger unit.

In some ways the move hardly changed anything. The buildings in Parkchester all looked the same. The hallways and elevators were alike, as was the arrangement of the eight apartment doors on each floor. Our new apartment was even in the same location on the floor. The first time I walked in, I thought we hadn't moved at all. The entrance opened into a small foyer, with a closet to the right and a doorway to the kitchen. The foyer led into a living room of the same size and shape as our old one, and a door from the living room led to the bathroom and sleeping area.

But when I walked through that door, I might as well have tumbled into the rabbit hole of *Alice in Wonderland*. Beyond the living room were two bedrooms. I was given the smaller one, and for the next few years, until Jimmy stopped sleeping in a crib, I had a room to myself. To make this even more special, Mom and Dad bought me a desk. Now I could do my homework in private, instead of at the table where we ate. Or I could close the door (at least until Mom shouted, "What are you doing in there, young man?") and lie on my bed listening on my transistor radio to the current top songs.

But the biggest deal wasn't getting a room of my own. Our apartment on Unionport Road had been at the far edge of St. Raymond's Parish. When I walked home from school with Mom each day, one by one my schoolmates peeled away until I was the only one left walking.

Our new place was just a block from St. Raymond's. Suddenly I was living surrounded by schoolmates. Mom let me walk to school on my own. I started getting there early to hang out in the schoolyard, play tag, or trade baseball cards, until the bell warned us to line up for class. After school, my friends and I ran home as fast as we could, changed clothes, and met in the playgrounds in my new section of Parkchester. And since Mom had Jimmy to care for, she let me sign up for the school lunch program. Five days a week, nine months a year, from eight in the morning when I arrived at the schoolyard until five thirty in the afternoon when I had to be home for supper, I was surrounded by a gang of friends.

............

Before all this kicked in as a regular routine, school was out for the summer. Our new apartment cut the distance to Big Grandma's house in half. Now, not even the care of a five-month-old could keep Mom from seeing her mother. Every weekday that it didn't rain during summer, we had an early lunch and then Mom packed Jimmy into his carriage and we walked the six blocks to Grandma's place.

But the house on Silver Street wasn't as much fun as before. Sure, Laura, Paul, and I played in the yard or shared gossip about our moms and dads. And Sylvia, who was still in high school and hadn't started working full-time, was often around. She was always ready to teach us card games, like poker and rummy, which required more strategy than donkey. But now that I was living near St. Raymond's and within shouting distance of my school friends, I wanted to be with them. My impatience started to show. After a couple of hours, I'd start pestering Mom in the hope we might leave early enough for me to squeeze in playground time before supper.

One day that summer, I persuaded Mom to leave Grandma's early. No sooner did we get home than I was out the door. "Be sure you're home by five thirty," Mom shouted into the hallway as I got in the elevator. I raced from the building and headed to one of Parkchester's playgrounds. No kids that I knew were there that afternoon, but that didn't stop me from getting into a rotating tetherball match with a few other boys. It was easy to lose track of time. When I looked at my watch, it was just about five thirty.

Mom was a stickler for being on time. Ten minutes late could mean no playgrounds for a week. In a flash I was running home as fast as I could. To reach our row of buildings, I had to go up a set of stairs, stretched out on a gradual incline. Some kids were playing catch, and in trying to avoid them as I raced up, my foot clipped the edge of a step and I tumbled over. Before I could throw my arms forward to cushion the fall, I was on the ground, my left arm smashing into the edge of a step. The other boys rushed over and helped lift me to my feet.

When I held out my arm to see if it was bruised, I could hear gasps from them. Instead of stretching in a straight line from elbow to wrist, my arm was bent in the shape of a half moon. It scared me half to death. "Hurry up, go home," one of the boys shouted. I made my way up the rest of the steps, walking carefully, until I reached our building, my arm still held out as if I had to see it to believe it. Through the set of double doors, down the corridor to the elevator, and up to the fifth floor, I kept the arm stretched in front of me and rang the bell.

Mom was already talking as she opened the door. "You're late, young man," she was saying, as I held out my arm. "Oh, God," she cried. The worry on her face made me even more scared. If Sophie looked that upset, it had to be bad. This was why she had her routines and rules, to make life predictable so nothing like this ever happened. But now my running home because I was late had ruined all that. "What happened? What happened?" she kept saying. I tried to explain, but tears were now pouring out, and it was all I could do to hold my arm steady and not rush into her and be held until everything was better.

The next few hours were a blur. Mom started making calls. Dr. Manfredi was still holding office hours and promised to wait for us. She called Grandma and Lucy and Anna. She left a note for Dad, who wasn't home yet. Cousin Vinny picked us up in Uncle Tommy's car. Sitting in the back with me, Mom kept stroking my hair to quiet me as every bounce of the car over the cobblestones in the South Bronx made me wince. Finally, we reached Manfredi's office in the old neighborhood on Morris Avenue. I had never been there before, since the doctor always made house calls to us. He touched my arm carefully, pressed it a bit, and then told Mom that it was badly broken. "I'm calling Dr. Perrotta," he said. Perrotta was a surgeon with an office just a few blocks away.

Within a few minutes we were at Perrotta's office. Unlike Manfredi, who always seemed kind and calm, Perrotta was loud and brash. His words filled the office, and I got more and more scared as I tried listening to what he was saying. "Hospital . . . operation . . . gas . . . plaster cast" was all I could hear. The next thing I knew Mom was calling Dad from the office phone. "Meet us at Westchester Square Hospital," she told him. She called Anna and Lucy, too, before she led me to the car and Vinny drove us to the hospital. Over and over I heard Mom saying, "And on the feast of Our Lady of Mount Carmel," the patron of the village her parents had come from in Sicily. Now July 16 would forever be remembered in the family not as a religious feast but as the day Johnny broke his arm.

This was my only time in Westchester Square Hospital except for Jimmy's birth. In my family's phrasing, hospitals were not a place anyone in their right mind chose to go. Birth or death: that's what brought someone to a hospital. Two years earlier, Big Grandma had suffered a cerebral hemorrhage and spent many days in the hospital. Visiting hours were limited then, but the sisters did shifts in the waiting room, at least two of them always there until either the unspeakable happened or God intervened and Grandma came home, to everyone's relief.

Now it was my turn. Dad was waiting outside when we arrived, and so were Jenny, Fran, and Sylvia. As Vinny dropped us off, I held out my arm and, sure enough, fear washed over their faces. They took me inside, and we waited until what looked like a bed on wheels came rolling toward us. Doctor Perrotta was on his way, a nurse explained, and they needed to get me ready for the operation. As they rolled me down the corridor, the family stood huddled in a pack, feeble smiles on their faces as they waved goodbye, as if they expected never to see me again.

The nurse helped me undress and pulled a sheet up to my neck. When Dr. Perrotta finally came in, he was already talking. "We'll give you some gas to put you to sleep. When you wake up your arm will be in a cast, so you won't be able to move it or touch it." Someone put a mask to my face, and Dr. Perrotta told me to count back from a hundred. Good boy that I was, I obeyed. "100, 99, 98, . . . 97, . . . 96."

When I woke up, it was dark. I was in a room with several other beds. Everyone else was sleeping, and the room was quiet. Something pressed against the left side of my body. I touched it with my right hand, and it was hard and heavy, just as Dr. Perrotta said it would be. I lay there wanting someone, something, but didn't know whom to call for or whether anyone would come.

. . . . . . . . . . . .

The broken arm put an end to my begging Mom to leave Grandma's house early. There was no more running and playing that summer. Each weekday, Mom and I walked to Silver Street, as she wheeled Jimmy in his carriage and I kept the plaster cast tight against me. We stayed until it was time for Mom to get home and start dinner.

But Grandma's house wasn't the place it had always been. The laughter was muted. The adults talked in whispers. They had worried looks on their faces. Uncle Tommy, it seemed, was sick. It had something to do with his skin, I was told. He was always an "easy burner," as Mom used to say. One time long ago, he had gotten something called a third-degree burn. So in summer, while the kids ran around outside and the adults sat in the yard with faces turned toward the sun, Tommy sat under a tree, protected. The sun didn't bring him a tan. His arms were pink, and exposure to sun made it worse.

That spring, before the summer heat hit, he started making visits to the doctor. He began missing days at work and spent his time upstairs in bed, drained of energy. Paul, Laura, and I had to be quiet when we went up and down the stairs. We stopped running around the apartment upstairs because Tommy might be sleeping. Once, when I went up looking for Laura, I passed his bedroom. He waved me in and took my hand when I got to the bed. "Things aren't looking good," he told me.

In mid-June, Jenny and Fran, the two unmarried aunts, took a vacation to California, traveling cross-country by train. Two summers before, the whole Grasso clan—Aunt Connie and Uncle Carmine, their daughters, sons-in-law, and grandchildren—had sold the house in Throgs Neck and moved to Los Angeles. I didn't see them often—just a few birthdays and anniversaries each year—so their leaving meant very little to me. But Grandma was losing the only woman relative she had in the Bronx whom she could speak with in Italian, and Mom and her sisters were losing the cousins they had grown up with. The trip to California meant that Jenny and Fran could report back on that distant world. It was the only vacation either of them had ever taken, and it set Mom to talking for weeks beforehand about her honeymoon to California and the wonderful places she and Dad had seen.

In the three weeks they were gone, Tommy took a turn for the worse. He stopped going to work. He never left the house to play cards with the neighborhood guys, as he often did on weekends. He never even came downstairs to be with the family when we watched TV on Sundays or to sit at the table over dinner. Among the adults, the word *cancer* was spoken, almost in a whisper. I didn't know what it meant, but I could tell it was bad. The Saturday that Jenny and Fran returned from California, Dad went to Manhattan to meet them at Penn Station. When they got home, the rest of the adults were sitting in the living room, silent and grim. Jenny and Fran told stories about Aunt Connie and the cousins. I heard about palm trees and the big waves of the Pacific. A trip like this should have made the living room on Silver Street sparkle with excitement, but it wasn't happening. The mood was somber.

A week or so later I broke my arm, and two weeks after that Tommy made the dreaded trip to the hospital. Aunt Anna spent most of each day there, and Mom brought us to Silver Street every day so she could help Grandma take care of Laura. And then, one day in August—"unlucky 13," as Mom put it—it happened. Tommy died.

The morning after Tommy died, Dad didn't go to work. With Mom and Dad both dressed in black, we walked to Grandma's house early that morning, with Jimmy in the carriage. When we got there, I went upstairs to where Tommy, Anna, and my cousins lived. Sylvia, who taught me card games and shared every detail of James Dean's life that she had captured in her scrapbooks, was standing in the kitchen and, like my parents, was dressed in black from head to toe. I had no idea what to say or do. This was the first death I had experienced close at hand. Death happened in war movies on television. Before I could stop myself, I blurted out, "How does it feel not to have a father anymore?" Sylvia said nothing, but her eyes filled with tears as she turned away. I felt so stupid that all I wanted to do was run away and hide.

There was a routine to deaths that our extended Italian clan observed. The wake went on for three days at a neighborhood funeral parlor. Close family was there from morning to night, and everyone was expected to take those days off from work. More distant cousins, in-laws, and friends from Morris Avenue all came to pay their respects. Wakes and funerals were the one setting, other than watching a Hollywood tearjerker, where tears flowed. Each new person who arrived and knelt before the body provoked a new round of wailing. Then, after the funeral Mass and burial, after three days of shedding tears, everyone gathered at a restaurant, laughing and laughing as if sadness and grief were the last things anyone was feeling.

Except for that meal, held at Amerigo's, where we also gathered for Grandma's and Grandpa's birthdays each year, I did not experience the funeral ritual for another several years. As children, Paul, Laura, and I were considered too young to see a dead body in a coffin. We were kept at home. Grandma took care of us while everyone else was at the wake.

That meal at Amerigo's seemed to perform at least a little bit of magic. The deep sadness that had infested Grandma's house during Tommy's illness lifted somewhat. Life went on. But something was missing. Tommy brought irreverence to family gatherings. He was the one who got everyone laughing. Now, without him, there wasn't as much fun and joy on our Sundays together.

Tommy's death disrupted the household in other ways. Grandpa had retired the year before. After almost forty years running the store on Morris Avenue, he sold the business. At seventy-three, the grind of rising by 5:00 a.m. and making a daily supply of mozzarella was becoming too much. Besides, the old neighborhood was changing, and his loyal Italian customers were no longer there. But Grandpa had been subsidizing Tommy's family for years. Tommy's work in the pants factory did not easily support a family of three kids, and Grandpa never asked for rent. Now that Tommy had died, and Grandpa was retired, Anna had to find work to support herself and the children. She enrolled in a program for a high school equivalency degree so that, hopefully, she might not have to work in a garment factory, as she had before marriage.

Devoted daughter that she was, Mom spent more time at the house on Silver Street, so that Grandma and Grandpa wouldn't be alone and Mom might help care for Laura while Anna was out. And Mom worried, worries that she expressed to Dad as they washed and dried the dinner dishes. Would Anna get an office job? Would Anna's oldest child, Vinny, fill his father's shoes and help support the family? Was there a danger, God forbid, that Grandma and Grandpa might lose the house on Silver Street now that money was in shorter supply?

These were not topics for a child to listen to, even if I was her big boy. Mom spoke in the kitchen in hushed tones. But while she tried to keep these concerns shut off from my ears, it was hard not to notice the worry on her face. Between the mood at Silver Street and in our Parkchester kitchen, family didn't seem quite like it was supposed to be. When school started that September, I was more than ready to go, more than ready to be among my friends.

# 6

.............

## A Family of Friends

Friends didn't play a role in my family. Mom often told stories about her group of girlfriends in high school, their trips to Coney Island and the beach in summer, their ogling of boys when they were not in the line of vision of their parents. But those friends were nowhere to be seen. Once, long before I started school, Mom invited a couple of friends from the old neighborhood and their husbands to dinner. Dad disappeared into the bedroom before they arrived and never came out. Mom made excuses about how he wasn't feeling well, and the dinner went on, but that was the last, and only, time that friends appeared in our apartment. And Dad? Well, yes, he talked about guys from the office. But he never took Mom out to meet them and their wives, never invited them to our place. Dad was so friendless that the best man at his wedding was a cousin of Mom's whom Dad barely knew.

But friends were about to become the most important thing in my life, more important than Grandma's house. Fourth grade at St. Raymond's ushered in a whole new experience of friendship, where friends were more than kids I saw at school. Friends were everything.

.............

The first days of school in September were always a trial. St. Raymond's was so large that each grade had five classes with almost forty students each. In the four years from kindergarten through third grade, we were reshuffled each fall so that some classmates disappeared and I had to learn new names and new faces. And then, of course, there was the teacher. Would I get another Sister Perpetua and be terrified all year?

Fourth grade brought the biggest change in my time at St. Raymond's. It was the year the school separated boys and girls. We weren't just assigned to separate classrooms. From fourth to eighth grade we were in different buildings. The girls got the new building, and everything that came with it—spacious corridors, classrooms with large windows, an auditorium and gym, toilets on every floor. The school cafeteria was in their basement. At lunchtime, the girls went downstairs for their meal, whereas the boys trudged through rain or snow or cold to get there and back.

At some point that first morning, we heard the call of Brother William, the principal of the boys' school. He was a giant of a man, big and bulky, with dark hair, thick neck, and a booming voice. Something in that voice let every boy know that we must obey. Starting with eighth graders, he called out class numbers and pointed, and the students quickly gathered in a neat line in front of the teacher who was standing there. I found myself standing close to our teacher. Unlike my previous teachers, she was young, younger even than Mom. Her black hair was perfectly done, her bangs neatly trimmed, her lips painted a bright red, and her face powdered. Her skirt swayed gently as she moved. Best of all, she was smiling. Her face seemed to glow with delight as if she was happy to meet us.

As we entered our classroom, instead of assigning places she told us to find ourselves a seat. Such unexpected freedom! She introduced herself as Miss McGlynn, explained that she was new to the school, and proceeded to call attendance. She asked us each to stand as our name was called, and as we did, she gazed at us as if she would never forget who we were. When it was my turn, she saw the cast on my arm, stared for a moment, and then told me to come to the front and stand by her. When she finished the roll call, she looked again at the cast and asked what had happened. After I explained, she took her pen, wrote in neat letters on the cast "Get better," and signed her name. Then she turned to the class and said, "At lunch, I hope you will all sign John's cast." Sure enough, at lunch break my classmates swarmed around me. By the time Mom picked me up at the end of the day, the cast was a mass of names and messages. I was so happy. It was like having my classmates with me wherever I went.

Miss McGlynn's class was magical. She seemed to believe that we deserved to enjoy school. That first week, she collected our birth dates, and a couple of days later gave us each a note to take home. Apparently she was prepared to have a celebration for every one of us, because soon our moms started delivering large boxes on certain mornings, and cakes and candles and cookies became almost a weekly feature of our class.

But the fun wasn't just about singing "Happy Birthday" and eating sweets. Miss McGlynn made schoolwork exciting. She introduced us to spelling bees. Spelling became a way to win a game rather than an exercise in printing the same word over and over. Then there was reading. Other teachers had occasionally read aloud to us, but mostly reading time was organized around "point and stand." When the teacher pointed, you stood and began reading where the last student left off. Reading aloud became an exercise in humiliation for those who stumbled over new words. Miss McGlynn did it differently. She read aloud first. Then she had us recite it together. By the time she called on us to read in turn, there were far fewer mistakes.

Best of all, she read us stories. Her gentle voice spun out the tales that filled the pages. Unlike the nightmarish sagas of biblical punishments that Sister Perpetua spit out, Miss McGlynn read adventure stories. These stretched across many days of reading, keeping us wanting to know how they ended. "More, more!" we shouted when Miss McGlynn looked up from the page and closed the book. But there was reason behind her method. "You can find out how this ends," she told us. "I got this book from my public library. How many of you go to the library and take out books?" Not many hands got raised.

Every boy in that class was in love with Miss McGlynn. At one point a classmate reported that he had seen her driving down Castle Hill Avenue toward St. Raymond's. This began a competition that continued until the school year ended. Instead of playing in the schoolyard, an ever-growing group of us assembled on Castle Hill Avenue. We waited until we spied the car approaching, and then this group of nine-year-olds began shouting and waving and running on the sidewalk to keep up with the car. As she pulled into her parking space by the school, a crowd surrounded her. Miss McGlynn got out with her handbag and school materials for the day, and as some of us pleaded "me, me," she handed them to one of us to bring into the classroom. Even in this, she was wise. Every day, she gave her things to a different boy to carry, spreading the joy among us.

Miss McGlynn didn't stay more than another year or two at St. Raymond's. I don't know why, since she was my dream of the perfect teacher. Maybe the travel from Queens was too much? Or the pay, which Mom once said was fifty dollars a week, was too little? But maybe it was because a school grounded in fierce discipline wasn't willing to keep someone like her.

We had certainly become undisciplined. The next year, we were assigned Mrs. Hoctor, a kind, soft-spoken, white-haired lady. She expected us to sit in our seats and do the exercises she spelled out on the blackboard. But we were still in Miss McGlynn's learning-is-fun mode. Whenever Mrs. Hoctor asked a question, several of us jumped out of our seats and waved our arms. Sometimes answers came screaming from our mouths before she called on anyone. As some of us—me among them—unpredictably popped up and moved around, Mrs. Hoctor seemed at a loss. By the time the Christmas holidays arrived, we had driven her out of the school.

The substitute teacher we had that winter and spring, Miss Schretlen, was a German immigrant with the slightest hint of an accent. Young and energetic, she was also unflinchingly firm. She paced across the front of the room as she talked, a piece of chalk in one hand and a wooden pointer in the other. If we got unruly, she tapped the pointer on her desk, and we knew to sit quietly. One time, Stephen Jamieson was too rambunctious, and Miss Schretlen ordered him to the front of the class. "Bend over," she said. He shook his head to say "no." "Bend over," she repeated, this time shouting. As he leaned over the desk, she whacked his behind with the pointer. Just as it hit him, the pointer split apart. We all heard him scream, and suddenly Jamieson jumped up and ran to the far end of the room. Miss Schretlen ordered him to the front, but he just stood there, sucking his thumb like a two-year-old.

Sins, my catechism taught me, were punished by time spent in the fires of hell. The next year, our class received its punishment on earth for driving poor Mrs. Hoctor out of the school. We were assigned to Mrs. Hatton, who rivaled Sister Perpetua for meanness. She never smiled. She yelled a lot. But she was also clever. She never dispensed physical punishment. She gave us extra assignments to do at home, like copying the words in several spelling lessons over and over, so that our parents got the message that their son had misbehaved.

For those who still didn't settle down, she exacted revenge through our monthly report card. Because our class now had a reputation for being disorderly, our school principal came to hand out our cards. Academic subjects received number grades, but there were two letter grades, for "conduct" and "cooperation." Brother William said nothing about our number grades, but if we had Bs in conduct or cooperation—or, God forbid, a C—his wrath came down on us. A thick leather strap hung from the cloth sash that was tied around the waist of his black habit. If Mrs. Hatton's letter grades had marked someone as disorderly, Brother William dispensed a warning. But only once. Another B or C meant that you bent over the desk and he whacked you with the strap. One time, a classmate expressed resistance. Brother William reached toward him with one hand, grabbed the shirt collar and tie, and lifted him from the ground. "Don't ever speak back to me," he spit into the kid's face. We got the point.

As the year went on, our class quieted down. Miss McGlynn became a fading memory. We were now good Catholic boys, at least for the hours in class.

.............

Miss McGlynn aside, what saved those years, what makes them special in my memory, was not school. It was the friends I had.

Don't get me wrong. I liked school. Novels, history, geography, numbers: I ate it up. I loved getting good grades; I loved winning spelling bees; I loved how happy my report card made Mom. But I remember those years fondly less because of what happened in class and more for what occurred after school. The best thing St. Raymond's did was to keep us together, the same kids in class, from fourth grade through eighth. For five years, we all had each other. I was putting into my friendships the kind of passion and energy that, according to Mom, belonged only to family.

Way before fourth grade ended, each classroom had become a crew of its own. We played in the schoolyard before the bell rang. We sat side by side all morning, either bracing for punishment or seizing any chance we had for fun. We laughed on the cafeteria line and laughed as we ate our meals, except for the days when the food was so bad that we all groaned.

Friendships formed partly because we suffered in class together, but mostly because we played together. Something about the fourth-grade division between boys and girls served as another kind of marker. For the boys at least, our mothers seemed to disappear. They stopped walking us. Now, when we got to the schoolyard in the morning, we didn't have them watching, and we could run wild until the bell rang. At three o'clock we poured out of the building, free as birds. Without our moms to police us, in winter we could have snowball fights, one class against another. On other days, we flew from the building as fast as we could, raced home to change into playclothes, and then rushed to meet at an agreed upon place where we played until dinnertime.

Parkchester had big playgrounds in every quadrant. Besides swings, slides, and climbing bars, there were a basketball court, a concrete playing field set up for softball that was also used for touch football, and handball courts, too. The bigger kids—seventh and eighth graders—seemed to have claimed the courts and fields, and my friends and I knew not to challenge them. So we opted instead for running games that didn't confine us to a particular space. The best was foxes and hounds. The foxes had to run as fast as we could to get out of sight of the hounds. Sometimes foxes scattered in separate directions; sometimes they divided into groups. The smartest foxes snuck into a building undetected and hid in a stairwell until it felt safe to emerge. At some point that year, the larger group of foxes and hounds divided into smaller teams. For weeks, it seemed, Jimmy Rooney and I paired up against John Lameray and Tommy Burns. Those weeks of playing as a group of four created a bond that lasted through the next few years.

By fifth grade, we had found an alternative to the playgrounds that the older boys had captured. Just outside of Parkchester, the city had built a new junior high, PS 127. It had everything you could find in a Parkchester playground. And since the junior high kids scattered as soon as school ended, the playing fields were ours for the taking. By the end of fall term, going there had become the routine for a bunch of kids in my class. And because it wasn't in Parkchester, 127 was neutral territory. Kids from in and out of Parkchester played together.

Our play had a cycle that repeated itself yearly. Soon after school started in the fall, word went out to meet by three thirty at 127, where we divided into teams for touch football. Then, just after Thanksgiving, as if we all knew the time had come, when we showed up at 127, a couple of guys had brought basketballs. As the season changed and we discarded our winter jackets, the word went out: roller skates! For the next few days, we met up with skates clipped to our shoes and skated from one end of Parkchester to the other.

I loved play, but sports were something I had to figure out on my own. When I was still pretty young, Dad took me out a few Saturdays to Pelham Parkway. With ball, glove, and bat, he tried to teach me how to throw, catch, and hit. But Dad had no skills at all. He was a fan, not a player. Those few times happened, I'm sure, because Mom told him that's what a good father does. But while Dad could explain the rules of each team sport, he couldn't teach me how to play. I had to learn by imitating my more athletic friends.

Softball always remained a disaster. Even though it was a team sport, I couldn't hide among my team members and wait until I could seize a chance to shine. When it was my turn at bat, all eyes were watching and I was a wreck. I rarely got on base. And as a fielder? My lousy skills got me sent to the outfield, where I waited in dread for a ball to fly in my direction.

But touch football and basketball were different. For both sports, Peter Konrad and Ken Ferrarini were the pros. Konrad had height and bulk and strength. Ferrarini was short and thin. He sprinted faster than anyone. His small size and speed let him dodge in, out, and around groups of players. Konrad and Ferrarini always played on opposite teams. They flipped a coin to see who picked first and alternated until all of us were chosen. Burns and Lameray, two of my best buddies, who were each tall, thin, and fast-moving, got picked pretty quickly.

I was never great, never the team star. But as each year went by, I found myself creeping up the order in which teammates were picked until I had made it to the respectable middle.

Sometimes, and who knows why, sports were not the afternoon activity. A group of us—Lameray, Burns, Rooney, Eugene O'Rourke—just hung out. We visited the Oval Drug, sat at its counter, and slowly drank our egg creams as we chattered about everything that had happened at school. We played obnoxious-boy games. Lameray, who had a snarky sense of humor, had the idea to make anonymous phone calls to people whose names allowed for a play on words. We found ourselves a pay phone, each contributed a dime to the effort, and we went through the telephone directory and copied the numbers of people named Dunne. Then one of us dialed and, when someone answered, would say, "Are you Dunne?" If the person said yes, we all shouted, "Well, get off the pot so the rest of us can go!" At that point, whoever had made the call hung up quickly as we doubled over with laughter.

We also had more innocent pleasures. The public library allowed ten-year-olds to transition from the children's section to the adult division. It meant that Mom didn't have to come with me to check out books. Mom always encouraged my reading. I couldn't get into trouble if I was reading a book. In her view, it meant that I might someday make it to college and, as she put it, "get ahead." But she never picked up a book for herself, and when she took me to the library, she never browsed the shelves. Now, suddenly, I had been declared old enough to wander freely among the rows of books. Around this time, a brand-new library was constructed in the neighborhood next to Parkchester, not far from Big Grandma's. On some afternoons several of us visited the new library. I guess it says something about me and my closest friends that these trips were so much fun. We weren't in any way labeled "nerds." On most days we were playing football or basketball. But the library wasn't the place to find most of my other classmates.

Some of the books I have never forgotten. There was a young adult version of *The Iliad* and *The Odyssey*. To a Catholic boy who knew that God created the world in six days and on the seventh day He rested, that there was only one God and He was good and just, the notion of a world filled with gods and goddesses who fought and schemed and took different sides in earthly affairs fascinated me. I read both of these books so often that Mom finally bought them for me. Soon, Jimmy was reading them as well, and we talked at night about whether we liked Artemis or Athena more, and how it wasn't fair that Hector had to die.

Then there were the geography books. My life was pretty much confined to the Bronx. There were two or three trips a year to Manhattan. In the summer, there were occasional drives to Jones Beach on Long Island or to the amusement park in Rye. My tenth birthday came the same year the Giants abandoned New York and moved to San Francisco. For my birthday in September, Dad took me by train to Philadelphia to see them play the Phillies. The one great thrill was our only vacation; we went to see the cousins who had moved to L.A. The three-day train ride was like watching my map puzzle come alive, and I sat in the observation car riveted by the scenery. But that was it. My world was the Bronx.

The new library had a set of big geography books with bright red covers. They made visible the landscape of the map puzzle that I had played with so often. The books were filled with pictures of ranches and copper mines and cacti in the desert. And the regions were made concrete by the stories of families that populated them. I was especially fascinated by a Missouri farm family with a boy my age. He worked the fields with his dad, collected eggs from hens, and even milked cows. Suddenly, this kid who never had been on a farm and had never seen anything grow except the figs on Big Grandma's tiny tree was so excited that I announced at dinner one night that I was going to be a farmer when I grew up. Mom and Dad looked at each other, and then Mom replied, "Finish your macaroni."

.............

Family and friends existed in two different universes. I was with either one or the other. Except for the party on my eighth birthday, before Jimmy was born, my friends never came to our apartment. Friends were at school, at play, and on the phone after dinner, not at our table, or in front of the TV, or in the bedroom playing with me. And as far as I could tell, it was much the same with my friends. I didn't spend time in their apartments either.

But there was one exception. Many times during these years, sometimes because rain drove us inside, sometimes because we had run too much and were tired, a group of us found ourselves in the living room of Tommy Burns's apartment, sitting and talking with his mother. Mrs. Burns was a good bit older than my mom. Her hair was graying, and there were wrinkles around her eyes and across her forehead. She was also a smoker, something that Grandpa would never have allowed among the women in his family. While Mrs. Burns sat in the living room on her sofa, an ashtray on the coffee table in front of her filled with the day's butts, the group of us pulled up chairs, sat facing her, and babbled away. We talked about our game of tag in the schoolyard. We described the ice cream sodas we had just consumed at the Oval Drug. We discussed the books we were reading from the library. We went through the day at school from start to finish, even including whatever episodes of classroom disorder and harrowing punishments had occurred. Mrs. Burns sat and listened, nodding her head as she inhaled her cigarette, sometimes asking a question about why our teacher had done this or that. No matter what we told her—and as more of these days happened it seemed like we told her everything—no word of censure ever came from her. In a world where adults seemed to exist only to give kids orders and ensure our obedience, Mrs. Burns was an approving audience, a listener who welcomed what her son and his friends were telling her. During those hours when the group of us was with her, it seemed like my friends had become a family. We had found a place where all of us belonged and were welcomed.

# 7

............

## God Help Me!

Religion, or "the Church," as it was always referred to, was a powerful presence in my family. Mom and Dad went to Mass every Sunday and every Holy Day of Obligation. Once I started school, Mom also went to Mass every first Friday of the month, which promised to speed her time out of purgatory and into heaven. There was a thick, red-covered, gilt-edged Bible prominently atop the dresser in the bedroom, and statues of the Sacred Heart of Jesus and the Virgin Mary on display in our apartment. Mom read me Bible stories from an early age, and we had two collections of *Lives of the Saints*, one a massive volume, and the other smaller and directed toward the young. As soon as my reading level allowed, I pored through it, devouring stories of these servants of God and treasuring my favorites. Saint Anthony, Saint Francis, Saint Thomas: I wanted to live a life as holy as theirs and be eternally remembered because of it. A couple of neighborhoods from Grandma's house was a Catholic parish that had constructed a grotto near its church. A few times a year, the adults took Paul, Laura, and me to visit it. We walked through the cave-like structure, taking in the images and statues. We paused reverently before the statue of Saint Lucy. An early Christian martyr, Saint Lucy stood there, one hand holding out a Communion plate. On the plate were her two eyes. She had gouged them out rather than renounce her faith in Jesus, we were told.

At St. Raymond's, catechism was as important as any other subject. After Sister Perpetua, I only had lay teachers until the Brothers took over in seventh and eighth grade. But our lay teachers were as devoted to religious instruction as if it was their life's work. I learned to read as much through lessons in the Baltimore Catechism as I did through the adventures of Dick and Jane. Our teachers had us read the questions and answers over and over. "Who made us?" an early lesson asked. "God made us," it answered. "Why did God make us?" it continued. "God made us to show forth His goodness and share with us His everlasting happiness in Heaven." Religious teachings were part of the daily routine.

In second grade, our lessons took a new turn. Father O'Brien began visiting Miss Leahy's class almost daily. Like Miss Leahy, he could be described as kindly. He always seemed to be reaching out, as if he wanted to rest his hands on our heads and transmit God's blessing. He explained that he was preparing us for the most important day of our lives. As seven-year-olds, we had reached the "age of reason." We were old enough to receive Holy Communion, the Body of Our Lord. Father O'Brien's voice dropped almost to a whisper as he said this.

Reaching the age of reason meant more than the ability to receive Communion. It meant we were old enough to sin, to do things that could send us to hell forever. Father O'Brien took us through the Ten Commandments that God had given to Moses. We recited and memorized them just as we did our catechism lessons. Some were not a problem. I knew I wasn't going to worship "strange gods" or "covet" my neighbor's wife. But others? I didn't always obey my mother. And the eighth commandment, to "not bear false witness," meant that we couldn't tell lies. Did I always tell Mom the truth? But the church provided a way out through another sacrament, confession. A few days before Communion, all of us would confess to a priest, who would forgive our sins.

First Communion occurred in May, as the weather was warming. A Mass was held for all second graders and family members. St. Raymond's had us fitted in special clothes for the day, with boys and girls dressed in white from head to toe. Our teachers lined us up outside the church, one column of boys and another of girls. Holding our hands together as if in prayer, our faces slightly bowed, we marched up the steps, through the doors, and down the center aisle. Our parents occupied the back rows. They smiled broadly at the columns of children dressed in white. With Monsignor Tierney before the altar to greet us, we went into our respective pews. The organ played. The Mass began, the kneeling, the standing, the sitting, all of which I had learned by heart. Monsignor gave the sermon. Then came the moment when he raised the host toward the image of Jesus above the altar. He said his words in Latin, and the thin wafer was transformed into the Body of Christ. A row at a time, we made our way to the altar rail and knelt. As Monsignor Tierney reached me, I looked up, closed my eyes, opened my mouth, and extended my tongue. The wafer, the Lord Jesus, was placed on my tongue. I might as well have been ascending to heaven. Outside the church, Dad took a photo of me and my cousin Paul. The smiles on our faces made the sunny day even brighter.

Now that my classmates and I were able to receive Communion, weekly Mass became a collective experience. Students assembled outside the new school's auditorium every Sunday for nine o'clock Mass, marched in by class, and filled all the seats. Our progress through school was marked by how far we sat from the altar; each year, the distance grew, as younger boys and girls filled the front rows. Each Sunday, we marched in orderly fashion down the center aisle to receive Communion. In all my years of Sunday Mass, I don't remember seeing anyone not get up for Communion. To stay behind would have been a public admission of sinfulness without contrition.

"Contrition" was something I learned in our lessons about confession. Around the time I started school, Mom taught me to say bedtime prayers. At first, I repeated after her, a phrase at a time—"Our Father, who art in heaven . . . Hail Mary, full of grace . . . I believe in God, the Father Almighty." Eventually, when I knew them by heart, all Mom had to do was remind me to say them as she tucked me into bed. She also taught me to make special requests of God. "Watch over Grandma so she doesn't have to go to the hospital again," I pleaded. "Help Dad find another job," I begged, after his effort to get a Wall Street job had failed. Now, with my first confession and Holy Communion behind me, a new prayer got added, the Act of Contrition. It was the prayer that everyone recited in the confessional, after the priest had forgiven our sins. But it also could bring forgiveness between confessions in case, as Father O'Brien explained, "the Lord took you before you can make it to confession." All I had to do was say a "perfect" Act of Contrition. And so every night, I struggled to express the words just right. "Oh, my God, I am HEARTILY sorry for having offended thee," I recited, my eyes closed, as I imagined God judging my sincerity. "I FIRMLY resolve, with the help of thy grace, to sin NO MORE and to avoid the near occasions of sin, AMEN." I couldn't be sure I had passed God's test, but there was comfort in trying.

While Mom and Dad went to Mass every Sunday, going to confession was an irregular thing with them. But confession quickly became something I felt I *had* to do as often as possible. Was it the firmness with which Mom set out her rules for me? Her tone of voice when she called out, "Watch it, buster!" if I was doing something she didn't like? Or perhaps her demand that I not be a minute late coming home from play? Whatever the explanation, it didn't take long to convince myself that I was not the saint I hoped to be, but a sinner on the road to hell unless I begged God for forgiveness. Once we moved to the new apartment after Jimmy's birth and St. Raymond's was now just a block away, nothing could stop me from going to weekly confession.

There was something deeply reassuring about it. I waited near the confessional until it was my turn. Pulling aside the curtain, I entered a small, dark space, knelt, folded my hands together, and waited for the priest to slide back the wood panel. Once he was ready, I began: "Bless me, Father, for I have sinned. I accuse myself of." Convinced though I was of my sinfulness, I didn't have much to say. "I disobeyed my mother three times. I lied once. I was mean to one of my classmates." And then, as certain as the rising of the sun, the priest pronounced me forgiven, raised his arm to extend a blessing, and told me to say my Act of Contrition and one Our Father and two Hail Marys as penance. It was very predictable and comforting, until my level of sinfulness escalated dramatically.

............

One of the recurring features of dinner was Dad doing something that annoyed Mom. He might belch loudly or lace his fingers together and crack them. I was fascinated by the knuckle cracking. The older kids did it in the schoolyard, and it seemed another mark of being a big boy. So I tried until one day, in my bedroom, I succeeded. I couldn't believe it when I heard that first crack. I kept practicing until I was able to crack each knuckle. And then, one night at the dinner table, when Dad cracked his, I did the same. I was very pleased with myself and laughed. But Mom, who was cutting a piece of beef on her plate, pointed the knife in my direction and, with a glare on her face, said, "Listen, buster, I don't ever want you doing that again. Do you hear me?"

Well, the truth is, once she ordered not to, I couldn't stop myself from doing it. Of course, I wasn't stupid. I knew not to do it in her presence. But now it seemed I was cracking my knuckles every chance I had. If I finished my lesson in class and had nothing to do, I cracked my knuckles. If I was waiting for a friend, I cracked my knuckles. While teams were getting chosen for basketball, I cracked my knuckles. And every time I did it, I knew I was committing a sin of disobedience. It made my weekly trips to confession more pressing than ever. Now, instead of disobeying my mother three times, the number was reaching into the dozens, since I meticulously kept count of each time I cracked them. Saturday evenings and Sunday mornings were now torture for me, as I desperately tried not to crack knuckles between the time I went to confession on Saturday and Mass on Sunday. Soon, whenever I was walking somewhere alone, I found myself silently repeating holy phrases in order to accumulate indulgences that, I had learned, promised to reduce my time in purgatory. Every "Mother of Mercy, pray for me" cut three hundred days from my sentence.

Though I was feeling increasingly desperate, no one seemed to notice, including the priests in the confessional. Maybe I was reciting my sins so faintly that they didn't even hear me. Or, seeing a young boy kneeling with head bowed, maybe they hardly listened because, really, what sins could I possibly commit? But one Saturday, after months of this, I walked into a confessional booth that Father McGuire occupied. He had a reputation for being harsh; few smiles ever appeared on his face. I got on my knees and began as usual: "Bless me, Father, for I have sinned. It has been one week since my last confession. I accuse myself of." I then whispered, "I disobeyed my mother 130 times" and was about to list the next misdeed when, suddenly, Father McGuire began shouting. "Young man, how dare you make fun of the sacrament of confession! No one can disobey their parents 130 times in a week. Who do you think you're fooling?" I was mortified. I was shaking as I knelt there. I said to him, "No Father. You don't understand. I did disobey my mother that many times. She told me I mustn't crack my knuckles, but I can't seem to stop, and this week I counted 130 times. Please, Father. Help me." There was a moment of silence and then, in a tone of deep compassion, Father McGuire said, "Son, if your mother doesn't want you to crack your knuckles, of course you should try to do what she says. But you don't have to confess this. I promise you, it's not a mortal sin."

The relief I felt was indescribable. When I received Communion the next day at Mass, I almost started to cry, I was so happy. I felt new energy at school and at play. A few weeks later, we were told in class that St. Raymond's needed new altar boys to serve at Mass. I volunteered, and when I was chosen to be trained, I took it as a sign that, yes, I had come back from the gates of hell. Serving Mass brought me closer to God than I had ever felt.

. . . . . . . . . . . . .

I wish I could say that the relief lasted forever. I did get a good two years out of Father McGuire's intervention. But eventually, sin made its return, this time in the form of sex.

St. Raymond's taught nothing about sex. I never had a science class of any kind, even in the age of Sputnik and the space race, and I certainly didn't learn anything about biology. The subject of sex never came up once in class. Anything I learned, I learned from friends, though "learning" might be too much to claim. Once, in fifth grade, a group of us gathered in the playground around

Matthew as he told us how his older brother had explained how you made babies. "Girls," he said with assurance, "have a hole where we have a cock, and to make a baby, you put a finger up that hole." So much for the wisdom of the playground.

In seventh grade, my body began to change. Then, one afternoon a classmate—I'll call him "Mac"—invited me to his apartment on a day when it was too rainy to play outside. He had a copy of *Playboy* that belonged to an older brother. His brother had told him you could use *Playboy* to "jerk off," a phrase I'd never heard. Mac said we should try it, so we took down our pants and each of us started playing with our cock. It was the first time I had ever seen a classmate naked.

I'd had erections before this, sometimes at night, sometimes sitting in class, but didn't know what to do about it, other than hope my teacher wouldn't ask me to come to the blackboard while my pants were bulging. Now it was happening in front of someone else. Mac and I stood there, each stroking ourselves and watching the other, until I noticed it was getting hard to breathe. He told me not to stop, and suddenly a strange sticky goo was shooting from both of us. We never did it again together, but soon I started lingering in the bathroom at home longer than I needed to, playing with myself to see if I could make it happen. It didn't take much effort.

Not long after the time with Mac, on another rainy afternoon, a bunch of us retreated to Jimmy V's apartment, which was close to the playground where we hung out. His parents both worked, so no one was home. We went to his bedroom and spread out in a circle on the floor to play cards. Somebody suggested strip poker. Before long, most of us were down to our underwear, and soon that was gone too. Someone suggested a group jerk-off. We started, but before anything happened, Jimmy intervened. "We can't do this," he said. "This is wrong. We all have to go to confession. We have to tell the priest we had impure actions."

That's how I learned that playing with myself was a mortal sin. This started another round of weekly visits to confession, since by this time my lingering in the bathroom had become a habit I couldn't break. Fortunately, I didn't jerk off as often as I cracked my knuckles, so I wasn't in danger of telling the priest that I had impure actions 130 times. But no matter how fervently I pledged never to sin again, I couldn't keep my resolve for more than a few days. Saturday trips to the confessional became the rule once again.

............

The separation of boys and girls that began in fourth grade had been amazingly complete. By the time I started seventh grade, I barely remembered the names of the girls I had once walked home with every day. On Sundays at Mass, they were on the other side of the auditorium, but unless I happened to get a seat near the center aisle, I hardly noticed them. My friends were everything. Schooltime, playtime, phone calls after dinner: we always seemed to be together and on each other's minds.

Then, one day in April, Brother Kevin announced that the Knights of Columbus were holding a Saturday dance for seventh and eighth graders. The dress code was white shirt, jacket, and tie, and he encouraged us all to go. Everybody seemed excited at the idea. Mom said I could go, so when Saturday came, I headed to the building that housed the Knights, just across from St. Raymond's Church. Lameray, Burns, and I had agreed to meet outside, and we went in together. The Sisters and Brothers were there, too, to prevent shenanigans, though I didn't have any idea what shenanigans were likely to happen.

The first thing to catch my attention was the big open space for dancing. It was empty, except for a handful of boys and girls dancing quietly in pairs. Mostly, the girls were on one side of the large room, talking in small groups and sometimes looking in the direction of the boys, while all the boys were standing and doing the same thing, occasionally nudging each other to look at a particular girl. But then Lameray pointed to someone and took me and Burns over. He introduced us to Susie and Margaret, sisters who lived in his building, and they introduced us to Arlene, a friend of theirs. Soon we were talking and laughing as if it was the most natural thing in the world.

In the middle of this, the music changed. Chubby Checker was belting out "The Twist," and packs of boys and girls raced onto the dance floor. Lameray paired up with Susie, Tommy with Margaret, and I with Arlene. Chubby Checker had been on television's *American Bandstand*, and the hip-swiveling, arm-waving dancing associated with his song was the rage. Now the six of us were doing it surrounded by dozens of others, and we laughed our way through it. Even the Brothers and Sisters were smiling. Much as we shook and moved our bodies, at least the Twist kept boys and girls at a respectful distance from each other. But now that the Twist had broken the awkwardness, the next love song saw us all in pairs. I put my right hand around Arlene's waist, raised my left hand and held hers, and we slow-danced together.

The Sisters and Brothers, I noticed, strolled among the couples when the music was slow. If any pair was too close, if their bodies were rubbing against each other, a teacher made it quietly clear that some space had to be created. And I quickly understood why. Dancing slow with Arlene, touching her waist, having my pants make contact with her skirt: I felt that bulge in my pants. But what to do? If I pulled away, anyone near me might see what was happening. If I stayed close, something worse might occur.

That first dance opened a new world. My friends and I continued to meet for play at PS 127 after school. But on some afternoons, Burns, Lameray, Rooney, and others from my Parkchester circle now began hanging out in a play lot near the center of Parkchester, along with Susie, Margaret, Arlene, and a few of their friends. Or, more accurately, the boys hung out and the girls hung out at a respectful distance, with each group talking, laughing, and occasionally shouting something to the other. After a while, one of the boys or one of the girls walked the distance between us, and when lightning didn't strike, the others followed, and the talking and laughing occurred together. Before long, we might head to the Oval Drug, where each boy bought an ice cream soda or egg cream for one of the girls. Without talking about it, without making it a big deal, somehow we had all paired off. I never remember asking Arlene, "Will you go out with me?" or "Can I buy you a soda?" It just happened.

"Dates" were out of the question. At the age of twelve or thirteen, where would we have gone, and how would we have gotten there? But as the play lot afternoons continued and the pairing stabilized, a few of us took another step. We started "making out."

Besides elevators, each apartment building in Parkchester had a set of enclosed staircases that allowed for emergency evacuation. But there were never any emergencies, and so the staircases went largely unused. Lameray, who more than any of us pushed against the limits of what a good Catholic boy should do, suggested we use the stairwells to make out. It would be our version of the back seat of a car. So one afternoon Lameray and Susie, Burns and Margaret, and Arlene and I picked a building that none of us lived in, so that a neighbor wouldn't spot us. Making our way into the stairwell, each couple sat between a different pair of landings, out of sight, but not out of sound, of the others and made out.

Except I wasn't exactly sure what making out entailed, and I wasn't going to expose my innocence by asking. I figured it at least involved kissing, so I leaned toward Arlene and kissed her cheek. She didn't pull away, so I kept pecking at her cheek and then moved to her lips, and she kissed back. We kept kissing, and soon there was that bulge again that I hoped Arlene wouldn't notice. And then I heard laughter on the floor above us, and pretty soon all of us were laughing and running down the stairs and out of the building as fast as we could.

Kissing didn't seem wrong in the way that playing with myself in the bathroom did. People kissed on TV and in movies; I kissed Mom and Dad and my aunts and uncles; Mom and Dad sometimes kissed in the kitchen. But kissing Arlene only made me even more interested in playing with myself in the bathroom, and I knew for sure that God didn't want me to do that. Sex and religion? They did not go well together.

# 8

.............

# A Beginning and an End

I must have been about six when I first heard of Regis High School. The Baileys, a family who lived in our building, had a son starting high school there. In a conversation with Mom, Mrs. Bailey spoke of how prestigious Regis was. An all-boys Catholic high school, it provided full scholarships to everyone. Admission came through competitive exam. Every parish in the New York area could send a small number of eighth graders to take the test, and the top 175 got in. There were no other routes to admission. What made Mom's ears perk up, I'm sure, was Mrs. Bailey's revelation that every boy who attended Regis went to college, and all its graduates won scholarships.

That conversation fixed my fate. Throughout elementary school, whenever exam time came, the injunctions to study were accompanied by warnings that if I didn't do well, I would not be selected to take the exam and not have the chance of getting into Regis. When Kenneth Bailey graduated with scholarships to several Catholic colleges, the warnings intensified.

Higher education was not part of my family's world. The talk on the streets of the South Bronx did not often turn to college. But so many of Mom's family stories revolved around school-related decisions that had life-altering consequences. Anna and Lucy never went to high school because Grandpa sent them to sewing school so they could work in garment factories. Decades later, Anna was struggling to get a high school equivalency diploma, and Lucy had only been able to marry a janitor. Jenny was taken from high school to care for her baby sister; it affected the jobs she later held. Dad also had a story of educational hopes dashed. His older brother, Doc, the nickname a reminder of a dream unfulfilled, had to leave school to earn a teenager's wages during the Depression.

Both Mom and Dad graduated from high school, each learning bookkeeping in their high school's commercial track. By then it was the early 1940s, and the economic prosperity of the war years was beginning. With older brothers and sisters already working, I guess there was no need for them to drop out of school. As low-level white-collar workers in small businesses, their wages were likely not much higher than what my aunts and uncles made in the unionized garment industry. But the environment was cleaner and the work conditions easier. Mom never said it quite this way, but she had a street sociologist's sense of what made her life a bit better than her sisters'. She and Dad had a high school diploma. Her sons would get a college one. Regis was the pathway Mom had chosen for me. But first, I had to be selected to take the test.

..............

As eighth grade started, hopes looked good. For one thing, Ken Ferrarini, my strongest competitor for being chosen to take the exam, had moved with his family to Omaha, so I didn't have to worry about him. But even more, my homeroom teacher, Brother August, quickly began sending signals my way that, yes, I would be picked.

New to St. Raymond's, Brother August was unlike any teacher I had encountered. His very name suggested deep intellectual leanings, as if he hoped to follow in the steps of the great Saint Augustine. Tall and thin, with pale skin and dark hair, he had a deep voice, almost somber in tone. He often stared intently in class, as if pondering decisions of great magnitude. He treated us like we were men-in-training, soon to be out in the world with a mission to do good and spread the word of Jesus. He seemed so much like a man I should aspire to be.

As my classmates and I discovered that fall, Brother August was also great on the playing field. For all his appearance of maturity, he was only a dozen years older than us, in his midtwenties. He must have spied our gang playing football at PS 127 while he walked in the neighborhood because one afternoon, unexpectedly, we found him and Brother Robert, another teacher, stripped of their clerical robes and running onto the field to play with us. Taking a position on opposite teams, they ran and blocked and caught passes with all the enthusiasm that we displayed. When our play shifted to basketball, Brother August joined in that too.

Brother August took to me right away. He nurtured my intellect. He arranged to meet me one afternoon at the public library and guided me through the fiction shelves. Besides my young person's version of *The Iliad* and *The Odyssey* and some basic books like *Treasure Island*, geography books were my chief reading. Now Brother August was pointing me toward Charles Dickens and Thomas Hardy and Emily Brontë. I soon found myself racing through the pages of *Great Expectations* and *Wuthering Heights* and then running back to the library to replenish my stack of novels.

Brother August also chose me for a series of competitions that the archdiocese sponsored for eighth graders: mental arithmetic, spelling, oratory, and essay writing. I didn't last long in the mental arithmetic contest, and I stumbled in the semifinal round of the spelling bee. But oratory and writing allowed me to shine. I was surprised that Brother August chose me for oratory. I was short and lacked the impressive stature that one associates with distinguished public speaking. I smiled and laughed all the time, in contrast to the seriousness reflected in the speeches that students gave—orations by Patrick Henry and Abraham Lincoln, or monologues from Shakespeare. The text Brother August had me memorize reflected the personality he displayed in class. It began like this: "In a man's eyes there can at times be glimpsed something of the vast unsearchable abysses of the soul—his ideals, his desires, his fears. But in his hands can be read what that vast unsearchable soul has actually wrought in his life." It then described the struggles of a working man to support his family, make a mark in his world, and live a noble life despite lack of fame or fortune. It was an essay, I learned from him years later, that he had composed for a college writing class.

Oratory demanded much more than either spelling or mental arithmetic. It wasn't one word or one problem at a time, but a whole speech during which I must not stumble once. Each sentence had to be perfectly memorized. I had to project confidence, convey the appropriate emotion, and combine gesture, facial expression, and delivery into a compelling whole.

Still, I acquitted myself well. In the contest for boys from across the archdiocese, I made it to the finals. Unlike the preliminary stages, which involved only contestants, teachers, and judges in a classroom, the final round was scheduled for an evening in the giant auditorium of St. Nicholas of Tolentine School, near the Grand Concourse in the Bronx. The location symbolized the seriousness of the venture. Brother August told me that family members could come, and so it became a major excursion. I didn't win, but it was exciting to see those faces looking at me, listening to my every word.

Then there was the Mooney Essay Contest, another archdiocesan competition. Until eighth grade, Miss McGlynn was the only teacher who had us write regularly. Even though I hadn't done much writing in the succeeding years, this contest seemed easier to cope with than the others: no speaking before an audience, no room filled with other contestants who saw you get eliminated. Instead, I sat at a desk as I did every day, surrounded by other students, and did my assignment. The topic was whether the federal government should provide aid to Catholic schools. It had surfaced the year before as a political debate, when John F. Kennedy's presidential candidacy had unleashed a torrent of anti-Catholicism. Would he take orders from the pope? Would he end the separation of church and state? Would tax money be given to priests and nuns? Die-hard Republicans that they were, my parents would never have voted for Kennedy. But they bemoaned the attacks on our religion. Why shouldn't Catholic schools receive government money? They were educating young ones and saving the public schools tons of money. And so, loyal son and good Catholic that I was, I composed a piece arguing that funding Catholic education would not compromise the separation of church and state.

Much to my shock, I learned a few weeks later that I had won first prize. The announcement was featured in the *Catholic News*, the archdiocesan newspaper. It was so flattering to see my name and a summary of my essay. The prize winners were invited to a reception in the main offices of the archdiocese, by St. Patrick's Cathedral in Manhattan, and Mom, Dad, and Brother August accompanied me. Cardinal Spellman greeted us all. When my name was called, I walked up, bent to kiss the ring on his hand, and received his blessing. It was a day beyond what I could even fantasize.

. . . . . . . . . . . . .

I did get selected to take the Regis exam. Mom accompanied me to the school on a Saturday morning. We took the subway into Manhattan to East Eighty-Sixth Street. We walked down Park Avenue with its towering apartment buildings and along Eighty-Fourth Street to the school's main entrance. On the corner was St. Ignatius Church, which the Jesuits staffed.

A few weeks later, I learned that I had won admission. The day I got the news was as happy as any that I can remember in my family. Mom was standing at the door when I came home from playing that afternoon, smiling as she held out an envelope she had already opened. It wasn't her style to praise me highly, but I knew from the way she was humming in the kitchen as she prepared supper that she was pleased. And I was, too. I didn't know it then, but Regis would set me on a path of intellectual exploration that, with twists and turns, I'm still on.

. . . . . . . . . . . . .

As acceptance letters came from other high schools, my classmates were sorted into different groups. Lameray decided on Fordham Prep. Most of my closest buddies chose to stay in the neighborhood and go to the parish high school.

As June arrived and graduation approached, the talk suddenly turned to parties. Everybody, it seemed, was having a graduation party. Having people to our apartment was not a family practice. But as I came home from school each day announcing a new invitation and asking if I could go, Mom and Dad must have talked between themselves because one day Mom said, "So, would you like a party too?" By that point, more than half a dozen were already on the docket, stretched across the two weeks after graduation. I added mine to the list and began inviting all the guys who had invited me and telling them to bring their girlfriends.

There was something magical about those evenings. Anywhere up to twenty of us, half boys and half girls, arrived at an apartment that many of us had never been to before, but that was familiar because, after all, it was Parkchester. Food was laid out, parents greeted us and then disappeared into a bedroom, and for the next several hours we played records and danced. We did fast dances to Chubby Checker and Bobby Vee. We did slow dances to the lyrics of Paul Anka and the Shirelles. At some point, usually around eleven, the parents reappeared, the lights came on, and the music was turned off. I walked Arlene, my date for these parties, to her apartment, which was just a couple of buildings from my own.

The high point of the party nights came when a group of us made our way to Tavern on the Green, an outdoor restaurant in Manhattan's Central Park. The party was Pete Cleary's graduation gift from his parents. When Mom and Aunt Anna took me and my cousins to FAO Schwarz to see displays of Christmas toys, Central Park was in sight of the store. But I had never gone to the park, never spent an afternoon at its zoo or along the edge of its ponds. Now, suddenly, I was going to dine there.

The evening was different from the other parties. We sat outside on a warm June night. Around us were tables filled with people out on the town, virtually all of them adults. Music played; people danced. Our table was beautifully set, with a tablecloth and large cloth napkins, wine glasses filled with sparkling water, soup bowls on our plates, crisp rolls at both ends of the table. I had never experienced anything like this. A photograph survives of the evening, all fourteen of us at one end of the table, half of us sitting, the other half standing. The boys are in jackets and ties. Our girlfriends are wearing beautiful dresses, and each has a corsage attached to a wrist. The fun we were having is written all over our faces.

The rest of the summer had a quality all its own, different from summers before. Yes, there were days I went with Mom and Jimmy to Grandma's house, but that summer, when I was there, I spent all my time reading. Regis had provided a long list of books that it encouraged entering students to read, all of them the "great" novels of the nineteenth and early twentieth centuries. That summer I took the walk from Grandma's house to the Glebe Avenue library almost every week, checking out the books I could find and hunkering down with them on Grandma's front porch, sitting near Grandpa as he stared out the window at the street traffic. In the evening at home, I continued to read. I was already settling into the mode that would characterize my Regis years. But there were some days each week that summer when Mom said I didn't have to go to Grandma's. I could spend the afternoon with my friends. I happily took advantage of this new freedom from the daily summer routine.

. . . . . . . . . . . . .

When school started in September, it was very strange not to be in a classroom with the guys I had sat among for five years. No flipping baseball cards in the schoolyard before class, no hearing Brother William's booming voice telling us to line up. Instead, every face was new, every name someone I didn't know. The walk to the subway and the ride into Manhattan made for a fifty-minute commute each way. By the time I had gathered all the books from my locker at Regis and said farewells to my new classmates, it was close enough to dinnertime I couldn't roam Parkchester looking for my old friends. Plus, from the first week of classes, the workload was huge. When I got home from school, I told Mom a bit about the day but then immediately started my homework. Mom had no trouble reminding me that how I did at Regis would determine whether I got scholarships to college. So in those first weeks, my days were filled with the new and unfamiliar, and my evenings devoted to an almost frantic course of study. Except for an occasional evening phone call, there was little time to think about Lameray, Burns, Rooney, and the rest of my Parkchester gang.

Six weeks into the semester, St. Raymond's held a Columbus Day weekend dance. I knew my friends would be there, and with a three-day weekend ahead, maybe I'd be able to get together with them a second time as well. It took no time to find them in the gym where the dance was held. Some of the girls that we had dated were there too. I was so glad to see all of them, and they seemed happy to see me. I listened as they talked up a storm about this teacher and that class, this afternoon out together, the game they had played at PS 127, the movie they had seen. They weren't intending to exclude me, but there was nothing I could add. I hadn't been part of anything they talked about. I felt like a complete outsider. The dance ended, we said our goodbyes, and I came home with the feeling that I didn't belong here anymore, that I had stopped being part of the gang. Was Mom right, that you could only count on family, that friendships were something that came and went?

As it turned out, that dance proved to be the last time I ever got together with this group of friends who had been my life for the previous five years.

PART II

# A Jesuit Education

..............

# 9

..............

# A Whole New World

Bruce Springsteen has a tough-sounding, bittersweet song laced with irony called "Glory Days," about a group of working-class guys who, when they see each other, always recall their high school years. I can't lay claim to the hard times and shattered hopes of the characters in the song, but it does always remind me of my time at Regis. Sure, parts of those years involved intense struggle that made me feel as if I was teetering on the edge of a cliff and might tumble to my doom. But even so, I think of those years as glory days, a golden time when my mind was challenged, I had friends to die for, and new worlds spread out before me.

..............

Much of the exuberant sense of expansiveness that carried me through Regis rested on something solid: my world had expanded. Except for one vacation to California, an excursion to Philadelphia for a Giants game, and trips to the Planetarium and Museum of Natural History, I had barely ever left the Bronx. Now I was traveling to Manhattan every day. Manhattan was the real New York. It was the source of the global reputation that gave New York its cachet.

My daily subway ride began a brief period of intimate contact with Dad. I was riding the same train he took to work, and those first weeks became a tutorial in how to ride the subway. He may not have been able to show me how to hit or catch a baseball, but he described the ins and outs of riding the train with the precision that he applied to keeping the books at Berkey Photo. As we reached the Parkchester station that first day, the instruction began.

"Buy a week's supply," he told me, as we approached the token booth. "It will save you time."

"Walk to either end of the platform," he directed as we climbed the stairs. "The first and last cars are the least crowded."

When the train pulled in and the doors opened in front of us—and the doors always opened where Dad was standing because he knew exactly where the train stopped on the platform—he sped to the empty seats faster than I had ever seen him move. "If there's a seat at the end of the row, run for it," he said. "You'll be near the door, so it will be easier to get out." On days when the train was especially full, he showed me how to snake my way through the mass of bodies to a hand strap that I could barely reach. "Above all," he emphasized, "avoid standing by the poles. People will shove you to get in and out at every stop." With Dad as instructor, subway riding became a test of my skills rather than a dreaded commute.

Riding with me made Dad uncharacteristically talkative. Almost every stop provided an opening for a lesson about the city or a story from his and Mom's life. At Soundview Avenue, he pointed to the large apartment buildings that rose nearby. "This housing project is newer than Parkchester but not as nice," he said with assurance. At Hunts Point Avenue, he reminisced about his and Mom's wedding party at the Hunts Point Palace. One Hundred Forty-Ninth Street brought the observation that Big Grandpa's store had been nearby, and at Brook Avenue he reminded me that his sisters lived just a few blocks away. As we pulled into Eighty-Sixth Street, he always nodded toward the door and said, "Here's your stop."

These morning rides together continued for only a few weeks. Dad soon ran out of riding lessons and was repeating his stories. But more to the point, it didn't take long for Regis to become so appealing that I found myself leaving home earlier each morning. The building opened at seven thirty, and I wanted to get there as soon after that as possible to be with these guys who were fast becoming a new set of friends.

. . . . . . . . . . . . .

Regis was in the midst of an imposing neighborhood. Massive apartment houses rose up on both sides of Park Avenue, ten or more stories, red and gray brick, all built before the Depression. Doormen stood by the entrances, greeted residents as they entered and exited, and opened the doors of taxis when they pulled up to the building. This did not happen in Parkchester. The Regis facade on Eighty-Fourth Street was as impressive as the neighborhood. Its gray stone pillars soared to the top of the building's five stories, and the facade was capped by a carving that read, "Deo et Patriae," for God and country. Of course, as we all learned from the first day, the front entrance was only for faculty. Students entered from Eighty-Fifth Street through a tunnel that snaked its way to an interior courtyard and was filled with trash bins. "The garbage entrance" is how Regians affectionately described our path into the building.

My fellow students came from a wide geographic radius. They arrived from every borough of the city, from northern suburbs, and from Long Island and New Jersey as well. I knew that something called "suburbs" existed. Some of my first friends at St. Raymond's had left for the suburbs after second grade. But once there, they disappeared forever, as if they had moved to a distant land. Now, suburban kids were standing beside me in the courtyard and sitting in the same class. Some spent upward of three hours a day commuting. Some had fathers who were lawyers or business executives. Some had so many brothers and sisters that it made Mom's family seem small.

That first year, homeroom classes were set up alphabetically. Teachers came to us for their respective subjects. It was a new experience to find myself with seven teachers. Some were priests. Others were scholastics in training for the priesthood. The scholastics were young, in their midtwenties, and assigned to Regis for three years before returning to seminary to complete their religious instruction. There were also many lay teachers, but unlike at St. Raymond's, where every lay teacher was female, at Regis they were all male.

One of the first things Father McCusker, the school principal, communicated to the freshmen was that to succeed at Regis, we should expect to do three hours of homework every night. He wasn't kidding. There were books to read in history and English. Algebra introduced me to ways of calculating and solving problems that I had never encountered. General science left me lost most of the time. And on top of all that was Latin. Nouns came in five "declensions," and verbs had to be "conjugated." By our second class, I was memorizing the ten forms that first-declension nouns came in. And that still left four more declensions to memorize.

Even though schoolwork had been easy at St. Raymond's, Mom always made a point of checking my homework. At Regis, I was on my own. What did Mom know about the use of $x$ and $y$ in an algebra problem? How could she tell if a Latin noun was in the ablative case? Homework now sent me to my bedroom, before and after dinner. I sat at my desk and memorized Latin forms, read plays, and solved algebraic problems. When it was Jimmy's bedtime, I moved my books to the dining table, and Mom and Dad went to their bedroom to watch TV. In those first months, as I adjusted to these demands, I thought myself lucky if I finished in time to watch a ten o'clock TV series with them.

I suspect that what I've described has something of a nightmarish quality to it. An adolescent boy, accustomed to spending afternoons playing basketball or foxes and hounds, now was chained to his desk for hours each day. It *was* a lot of work; it did stress me out. But from the beginning, it was also exciting. The teachers at Regis wanted me and my schoolmates to think for ourselves. Most classes involved discussion. Our teachers sought our opinion; they provoked debates. It was OK to argue about a play's meaning or why something happened in history.

It wasn't long before I was seizing the challenge. Mr. Murray, a Jesuit scholastic, was my freshman English teacher. He assigned a five-page typewritten essay, longer than anything I had ever written, on any work we read that semester. I chose Shakespeare's *Merchant of Venice*, whose heroes and villains are clear. Antonio, Bassanio, and Portia are meant to command our admiration and sympathies; Shylock, the Jewish moneylender who demands a "pound of flesh" for a loan that's defaulted, is the evil villain. I titled my paper "Justification for the Hatred and Villainy of Shylock towards Antonio" and proceeded to argue that his behavior should be seen as a legitimate response to the anti-Semitism he faced from Christians. Jews were "unjustly maligned and slandered"; they were "persecuted and humiliated"; they encountered an "unjustifiable prejudice" every day. The vengeance Shylock sought was brought on by mistreatment. "The real villain" of the play, I concluded, was Antonio, not Shylock. Mr. Murray's only comment on the paper was "An unorthodox view." But he gave me an A and affirmed the sense I got from many teachers at Regis that every one of us needed to speak out and stand up for what we believed.

With all the classes I've sat in as a student and all the classes I've taught over a stretch of thirty years, perhaps I shouldn't be surprised that I can't recall many specific moments in my Regis classes. But I do hold before me a picture of many of my teachers, an image of what they projected in class. There was Mr. Rapisarda, my French teacher. He spoke French with a joyful lilt to his voice and a bounce to his step as he moved between our rows of desks. He communicated so much pleasure in the way he spoke that he made me want to learn French so that I could sound like him. There was Mr. Marasco, a Latin teacher. Full of boundless energy, he raced around the classroom as he taught us Caesar, making me feel as if I were on the battlefields Caesar described. There was Mr. Connelly, a history teacher. Himself a Regis graduate, and only recently arrived as a teacher, Mr. Connelly seemed to love history. He took us to faraway places and distant times; he urged us to enter into these worlds that no longer existed but that shaped the world of today. There were others as well, too many to describe.

It seems almost unfair to single out any one of them. But there was a teacher who looms especially large in my recollections and whom I came to appreciate even more in the years after high school. Father Owen Daley was my sophomore homeroom teacher and theology instructor. Short, with a round face, he exuded an intensity that I found almost intimidating. The year he taught me coincided with the assassination of President Kennedy. The fact that Kennedy had been shot was announced to the school through the intercom system. Even to me, from a Republican family and already rooting for Senator Barry Goldwater, who I hoped would defeat Kennedy the following year, it was a shock to hear. But Father Daley was visibly shaken when he came to class that afternoon. The color seemed washed out of his face. I remember him grasping the desk at the front of the room for support. He seemed to be having trouble speaking, and he had us take a few minutes to pray silently.

That same semester, the Catholic Church was in the midst of the upheavals provoked by Vatican II, the Ecumenical Council that Pope John XXIII had convened. A church claiming to be the bearer of an unchanging theology was debating everything. The very fact of the council's discussions acted as a signal permitting reform-minded and social justice–oriented zeal to be released in dioceses around the globe. This coincided with the high tide of the civil rights movement in the United States. Just before sophomore year began, the March on Washington was held. The protest received so much media coverage that it was impossible not to be aware of it, whether on the all-white streets of Parkchester or in the neighborhood of luxury apartment buildings where Regis was located.

Father Daley seemed to wrap these two developments together. There was passion in how he taught theology. He insisted we think about how we live each day in order to make these moral principles a reality. He acted on that injunction by initiating a Community Action Program. Regis students learned about an after-school tutoring program on the Lower East Side. A tenement neighborhood long associated with immigrants barely making ends meet through factory work, it was experiencing a turn toward a largely Black and Puerto Rican population. The students I tutored were in the earliest years of school; they were the age of my brother, Jimmy, or perhaps a year or two older. The work was straightforward—helping first, second, and third graders with basic reading and arithmetic. But Father Daley had a way of communicating that it mattered. It was the kind of thing God expected from each of us.

Regis prided itself on the unique education it claimed to provide its students. For decades, instruction in Latin and classical Greek was the heart of its curriculum. In the years after World War II, to keep abreast of a changing economy, it expanded its science and math offerings. At the end of freshman year, students chose whether to pursue a track that emphasized languages or one centered on science and math. Regis had also recently added a "double majors" class in which students took both sets of courses. Selection for double majors was an implicit award for superior performance.

When I learned I had been picked for double majors, it naturally satisfied the instinct to excel that Mom had instilled in me since first grade. It was a sign I was doing well in this best of all Catholic schools. But as the semesters passed by, I could hardly claim that double majors was right for me. I sat through chemistry and physics never understanding why I needed to know this. With trigonometry, I was lost to math forever. What grabbed me most, what captured my heart and soul, were the classics. I loved Latin; I adored Greek. They so excited me that the four years of Latin and three of Greek were not enough. I signed on for extra work that was the equivalent of an added year of study in each.

What made me love it so much? Some of it, I admit, was an intellectual snobbishness. Who in my world knew Latin or Greek? On Sundays, everyone listened with bowed heads as the priest spoke the words of the Mass in Latin. But who in those church pews understood what they were hearing? Now, week by week, more of those Latin words were becoming mine. At home in the evening, I was reading whole sentences and understanding them. And then there was Greek. The letters of the alphabet didn't even look like anything familiar. To the untaught, they were indecipherable. To me they were now as clear as *A*, *B*, and *C*.

There was also something more. Once our teachers took us beyond the basics, I threw myself into this ancient world. Caesar, Cicero, Ovid, Virgil: their work spun out the history, mythology, glories, and tragedies of a long-gone world that shaped the one in which I lived in ways I only dimly understood. I felt like the privileged possessor of buried knowledge. The study of Latin brought a special pleasure. It exalted the history of the Italian Peninsula, the homeland of my grandparents and their ancestors. It was the setting for one of the great empires. It produced an orator like Cicero, whose words I was now reading. The gods themselves ordained the greatness of Rome when they guaranteed that Aeneas, a survivor of the destruction of Troy, would make it safely there. The writings and history that Latin class put before me were things to be treasured.

And the Greeks! I could not get enough of Homer. My child's version of *The Iliad* and *The Odyssey* had opened my eyes to this world of strange gods and goddesses who didn't behave like God at all. I was swept up by their conflicts and plots, the love affairs with humans, the way the gods intervened in human affairs. I loved the heroism of the battlefield, the mayhem and slaughter that angry gods and goddesses provoked among humans. I was moved by the tragedy of good men unable to escape the wrath of the gods. Line by line, I watched the destiny of Hector and Achilles play out. And amazingly, I now had a bevy of friends as eager to talk about the machinations of Zeus and Hera as they were to talk about the Yankees and the Mets. How many teenage boys could claim that?

. . . . . . . . . . . . .

Regis did more than stimulate my mind and intellect. It gave me a whole new world of friends.

Regis had an autumn tradition that let upperclassmen reconnect after a summer apart and threw all the freshmen together for a day of recreation. On a Friday morning in September, we boarded buses at the school and were transported to Bear Mountain, a state park along the edge of the Hudson River fifty miles north of the city. It had a handsome lodge where one could sit and eat and talk forever, a field for playing touch football and doing sprints, and basketball courts as well. There was also a long row of gently inclined wooden stairs. Following them led to a trail that snaked its way through the trees and up the side of the mountain.

I wasn't about to embarrass myself playing sports with classmates I barely knew, but a trek to the top of the mountain was appealing. With Damiano and Ferraioli, two boys in my homeroom, I started climbing. At some point, we arrived at the road that cars took to the top and followed it. The view was spectacular. I had never walked on hillsides flush with green. Damiano and Ferraioli both also came from working-class Italian families, and from the way they stared at the landscape, I suspect it was a revelation to them, too.

Eventually, we had to make our way down to get back for the bus trip home. But as strangers to mountains and state parks, we couldn't remember where we had left the trail. It didn't occur to us, novices that we were, to follow the road all the way down. So at some point we saw what looked like a pathway through the woods, climbed the rocks separating the road from the forest, and began to descend. Within minutes it became clear that we weren't on a trail. We were in the middle of trees and stretches of rock, nothing we could easily walk on. We were almost tumbling from tree to tree as we let go of one, tripped forward to the next, and desperately grabbed hold. Eventually we reached a place where there was nothing ahead except a stretch of almost sheer rock. Behind us, the terrain was too steep to retrace our steps back to the road.

Damiano said we should sit down and, one at a time, slide until we reached a small clearing below. He volunteered to go first. I watched as he extended his hands out to the sides, placed his palms against the rocks, and pushed forward. Within seconds, he was sliding fast, his butt bouncing as he hit jutting rock, until he landed with a thud at the bottom of the stretch of cliff. "Are you OK?" Ferraioli shouted. After a few seconds he turned toward us and, in a not very convincing way, nodded yes. Ferraioli then lowered himself to the ground and prepared to go. As he was about to begin sliding, I heard him say, in a despairing voice barely above a whisper, "I wanted to be a priest."

The three of us did make it to the lodge. Bouncing back and forth between exuberance at our adventure and terror at what seemed like total foolishness, we laughed knowingly together while keeping silent about the details of our activities. But on that bus ride back to Manhattan, the whole crew of us tired from a long day of activity, I felt like I belonged. I knew we were all in this adventure called Regis together.

. . . . . . . . . . . . .

When I think about my years at Regis, my mind conjures up a set of scenes that happened again and again.

It's Friday afternoon. No homework is due the next day. A bunch of us float out of the building, giddy with a sense of freedom, ready to explore Manhattan. Jim Kuntz, Tim O'Connor, Vinny Hevern, Mike Dragovich, other friends: we head toward Fifth Avenue, where the Metropolitan Museum of Art rises before us. There are times when the museum is our destination, when our study of the ancient Mediterranean world or the cultural flowering of Renaissance Europe might be enriched by a museum visit. But most often Fifth Avenue simply offers the best route for racing south to Midtown. It borders the eastern edge of Central Park. With few cross streets or traffic lights to slow our progress, we run and jump our way to Fifty-Ninth Street, our schoolbags swinging at our sides. Sometimes we point at one of the mansions along the other side of Fifth Avenue, mansions so luxurious it is hard to imagine life inside them. Or we reach the square at the edge of Central Park at Fifty-Ninth Street and stare at the Plaza Hotel. Taxis and limousines pull up. We watch in awe at the people getting out, the staff in coats and top hats helping guests into the hotel and carrying an impressive collection of luggage for them. Or if it's near the holiday season, we may cross Fifth Avenue to FAO Schwarz, the most glorious toy store in the world, and share stories about the favorite toys of our childhood.

Sometimes we head to the Donnell Library on Fifty-Third Street, New York's research library for the people, a place where high schoolers can feel at home. Donnell makes my library branch in the Bronx seem like small potatoes. Besides a huge collection of books available to borrow, it has a research area filled with more encyclopedias and reference works than I knew existed. I will spend many afternoons there, especially as my involvement on the Regis Hearn Society debate team grows and I have to research new topics each year.

But the afternoons I love the most, the ones that bring the broadest smile when I recall them, are the Fridays when a Manhattan movie theater is our destination. Sometimes we go to theaters on the East Side along Third Avenue, where serious films are shown: *To Kill a Mockingbird* or *Darling*, the movie that made Julie Christie a star. I become so captivated by her that a fellow Regian can always provoke laughter by offhandedly asking me in the cafeteria or a hallway, "How's Julie?" In the holiday season, when Rockefeller Center sports a gargantuan Christmas tree awash with lights, we patronize Radio City Music Hall. We stare at the Rockettes as they kick and dance and wiggle their bodies before the movie begins. But most often our excursions take us to the theater district, where massive film palaces line Broadway. There the fare is more likely an epic adventure tale, like *Lawrence of Arabia*, or hilarious comedy, like *It's a Mad, Mad, Mad, Mad World*. Best of all are the musicals. *The Sound of Music* leaves us in ecstasy. Its message speaks directly to the heart of our Regis training, to live a life of moral purpose and integrity. I remember our leaving the theater, holding out our arms as if we are with Julie Andrews, and spinning in circles as we head down Broadway. I may not know which mountain to climb, but I know that something like that is expected of me. Julie Christie, Julie Andrews: they each make my heart sing, and I share these moments with a group of guys that I spend the better part of my time with.

Sometimes a few of us follow this afternoon movie with dinner. We discover Luigino's, a restaurant east of Seventh Avenue, and become loyal patrons. It serves food like I knew from Big Grandma's kitchen or Amerigo's in Throgs Neck. Except I'm here without the Scamporlino clan, among friends, eating in a Manhattan restaurant as if it is the most natural thing for this kid from the Bronx to be doing.

. . . . . . . . . . . . .

Then there is the Regis basement. Here is the locker room where we leave our coats and store the books we won't need until afternoon. Here also is the "old gym," available before or after class to students who want to shoot baskets or play a quick game. Most of all, the basement is home to the cafeteria. Before freshman year is far along, I find myself coming to school early in the morning, long before the bell rings at 8:55. With guys from my class, we make the cafeteria our study hall. We translate the Latin and, later, the Greek we will cover in class that day. We review algebra problems. We roll our eyes trying to make sense of Mr. Mahern's science lesson. Those sessions aren't all work. We make light-hearted screw of each other. We laugh about some of our teachers. We talk about the TV shows that are the rage. But our studies provide the steam that powers these gatherings. They become an oasis of safety where we face together the academic challenges of Regis.

When I think back on those mornings, what most stands out is how we helped each other. Class rank was important at Regis. We are told it will make a difference when we apply to college. But none of that factors into how those study sessions play out. If anything, we each revel in the ability to be the one who comes up with the best translation of Cicero or solves a geometry problem. If we are competing at all, it is with, not against, each other.

By sophomore year, lunch becomes the pivot that keeps the day moving and creates close friendship circles. Stable groups of four emerge at table after table. Mine consists of Vinny Hevern, Jim Kuntz, and Bob VerEecke. Stout and with a sense of humor that leans toward the snide, Vinny quickly becomes, like me, a debate society stalwart in freshman year. We find ourselves working together on cases and, as the years go on, spending a good part of many weekends together at tournaments. VerEecke has a Hearn connection as well, participating in oratory competitions. But with his blond hair and exceptionally handsome looks, he achieves fame at Regis through his work in the Dramatics Society, which culminates in a lead role in *Oedipus Rex*.

Besides Hearn Society activities, Vinny, Bob, and I share the experience of the double majors track. Kuntz, the fourth at our table, is neither in the Hearn nor in double majors. But he and Vinny were in homeroom together as freshmen, and they quickly learned to play off each other's humor. Tall and thin, with curly hair and hands that seem always to be flying in every direction, Jim projects a humor that is nothing short of wacky. When *Lost in Space* premieres on television, it becomes his obsession. He seems capable of memorizing the script after hearing it only once, and he often acts out scenes in the zaniest way. It is impossible not to laugh when Kuntz is around. Over my time at Regis, he becomes my best friend in a world where friendship overflows.

Near us is another table of four regulars. Jack Collins lives in Westchester County and is the oldest of eight siblings. John Fox and Tommy Gaye live on Long Island. Gerard Hackett lives in Greenwich Village, that world of beatniks and street musicians with such a magical aura attached to it. Quickly labeled "the clique," the four spend every possible moment together. Their laughter seems to betray a "we know things you don't" quality, and they have many of the rest of us wondering what is going on among them.

.............

The pizza shop. Located on Eighty-Sixth Street by the subway entrance, it is a pizza-by-the-slice place where you buy New York–style tomato-sauce-and-cheese pizza for a quarter and then leave with it wrapped in a sheet of wax paper. We hang out on the sidewalk eating slices and talking until it is time to get on the train, a few of us to the Bronx, the rest downtown to everywhere else, so that we make it home for dinner and begin our three hours of homework.

The exceptions are the days when there are home-court basketball games. Regis doesn't have a great team, but considering that no one was recruited for athletic prowess, the school performs respectably. Once I get to sophomore year, I never miss a home game. Kuntz and I always go together, screaming our lungs out as the teams race across the court. The most dramatic moment comes in junior year, when Regis plays Power Memorial. The star of their team is Lou Alcindor, a senior who already has the makings of a professional and will later take on the name Kareem Abdul-Jabbar. Over seven feet in height, he is the tallest human being I have ever seen, and he is leading his school to record-breaking championships. But that night Regis manages to stay ahead for the first several minutes. For a little while at least, it is the stuff of miracles.

On days when there is an afternoon home game, the pizza shop becomes our dinner joint. Especially for the guys who commute to Long Island or Westchester, it is too late to get home for a meal, so a bunch of us extend our day into evening as we eat a second and sometimes a third slice. Ten or twelve hours in a factory might make for a backbreaking day from which everyone wants to escape as fast as possible. But ten or twelve hours a day with my new family of friends? There isn't anything better.

# 10

...........

## Striving to Win

Besides the injunction to spend three hours a night on homework, Father Mc-
Cusker offered a second piece of advice during orientation. "You don't want to
be a two forty-two boy," he informed us. Two forty-two was the time when the
bell announcing the end of classes rang. At that moment, we were free to return
to our neighborhood and family lives. No one could stop us from doing that,
he said, but he strongly urged an alternative: extracurricular activities. The way
Father McCusker said "two forty-two" made me know instantly that I didn't
want to be tarred with that label.

That same week, our homeroom teacher told us that Mr. Cook, the Jesuit
who directed the Hearn Society, the school's speech and debate club, would visit
class and have us each read a selection from a speech. The Hearn had experienced
a revival under his leadership, winning more tournaments than it had in recent
memory. Mr. Cook was determined to keep that momentum going by recruiting
the most talented freshmen. My delivery of Brother August's speech made him
actively pursue me. Before the first month of high school was over, I made my way
to the Hearn meeting room to learn what was expected.

That decision changed my life perhaps as much as winning admission to
Regis. The skills that I developed as a public speaker during my years at Regis
would be deployed for decades in my role as an activist historian. But more
immediately, over the next four years, the Hearn became my home away from

home. The faculty directors during those years—all of them Jesuit scholastics—served as mentors and guides. The upperclassmen on the varsity team became my models of success. My teammates in speech and debate—Hevern, Bob Thoms, Mario Rizzo, and VerEecke—became buddies with whom I worked harder and more persistently than I had ever experienced. Shared research projects, cooperative case building, listening to each other, and providing feedback: all of this was new to me. As the Regis team went on to ever-greater levels of success in my years there, the Hearn opened the door to travel. Boston, Washington, Miami, Omaha, Albuquerque, and Denver were destinations. By car and train and, for the first time, airplane, I traveled the country and won awards that filled not only the trophy case at Regis but the apartment in Parkchester as well.

............

From the beginning, Mr. Cook pointed me toward both extempore speech and debate. While different, they shared a focus on current events. An extemp contest required participants to give as many as six speeches, five to seven minutes in length, each on a different topic. A contestant picked a topic out of a bowl and, half an hour later, stood before three judges and a few other observers and delivered—ideally—a flawless, well-organized, and convincing speech. Topics could be on any subject related to contemporary politics and economics.

Mr. Cook imposed a structure on these speeches that I obediently followed. At its heart was the notion that every speech should be divided into three parts—an idea that provoked laughter among us when we learned in Latin class that, according to Caesar, Gaul had been divided into three parts. Every speech also needed an opening, and since, as Regis students, we were immersed in the study of Latin and Greek, a defining characteristic of a Regis speaker became our opening with an ancient myth. But ancient myths and a three-part structure only worked if I became so well versed in contemporary issues that, no matter the topic, I could speak persuasively. Extemp spurred a four-year habit of following the news to a degree that I had never imagined. The daily *Herald Tribune* and the weekly *U.S. News and World Report* became my companions on the subway ride to school each day.

By contrast, debate required a team, and the topic remained the same all year. It was framed around a contemporary policy issue. Once the topic was announced in summer, research began. At the Donnell Library in Manhattan, I learned to use the *Readers' Guide to Periodical Literature*, which provided a listing of every magazine article written on a subject. I methodically went through the *New York Times Index* and read the relevant articles on a microfilm reader. I searched for government reports on the subject. Then, from everything my teammates and I read, we copied quotations on index cards. By early fall, the cards were already surpassing a thousand, and the numbers grew as the year went on.

Freshman year was a time of discovery. I watched the practice debates of the varsity team whose members awed me with their skills. They projected confidence. They smoothly spun out an argument and seamlessly integrated reading a quotation into the flow of their speech. It didn't take me long to realize that I wanted to be that confident, that fluent, and that powerfully logical.

As sophomore year started, Mr. Cook informed me that I would be a varsity extempore speaker. The opening tournament was the first weekend in October, at Mother Butler High School, not far from Big Grandma's house. Dressed in white shirt, blue tie, dark pants and jacket, I walked down Eastchester Road and arrived before my teammates and coaches. I could feel the nervous energy crackling through the room as speakers gathered in our meeting space. My first-round topic, the first speech I gave that was more than practice, was "What are the prospects for the US strategic hamlet program in Vietnam?" Several speeches later, I learned that I had made it to the finals. I received honorable mention, the only sophomore to be so named. Three years of tournaments were launched.

My success as an extemp speaker initially surprised me. The skills and traits required went completely counter to how I was raised. The message that the Scamporlino grandchildren received was that we must not "show off." Calling attention to ourselves invited the jealousy of others. As Mom put it, "Someone will point the evil eye at you and put a curse on your head." Now, as a speaker and debater, I was most definitely calling attention to myself. The whole point was to be better than everyone else. I had to carry myself with confidence, assert my intelligence, and win the judges over by the power and logic of my presentation.

As far as I know, in all my tournament years, no one cast an evil eye at me. But there was a different price to pay. I became anxious in a way that I never had before. After just a few tournaments, the tension began to show on my face. Whenever there was a weekend tournament, I woke on Thursday morning with an eruption of acne. Through Friday and Saturday, the pimples grew in size and number. Then, as if by magic, by Monday my complexion began to clear up. The next time there was a tournament, the process began again.

Sometimes, pimples were the least of it. After the Mother Butler performance, I continued to place well in local tournaments and acquired my first trophies. In the spring, I qualified for the Catholic national tournament, the only sophomore in extemp and the only Regis sophomore in any category to win a place in the nationals. The tournament was held in Denver. Whether because it was my first plane flight or because of the panic I could barely contain, I vomited as the plane started its descent.

The Denver trip was the first time I was away from my parents and my first time in a hotel. To me it seemed pure luxury. Maids cleaned the room, made the bed, and delivered fresh towels each day. Who knew such things happened? I was eating three meals a day in a restaurant. The hotel was located downtown, not far from the state capitol. All of it was beyond anything I had experienced. And so was the tension. There were students from across the country. They were competitors trying to beat me. As I went through the six preliminary rounds, the stakes grew. The moment was approaching when those qualifying for the semifinals would be announced and I would learn whether I was contributing to a Regis national championship or was part of the reason we lost.

I experienced a moment of relief when my name was among the qualifiers. But it was for a moment only. I barely slept that night. I rose early on Saturday and, before the semifinals began, walked through downtown toward the state capitol. As I took in the grandeur of the building, I prayed silently in a way at least as desperate as when I begged God to forgive my sins. As I walked and prayed, I promised God more and more—a daily rosary for the rest of the school year, Mass every day during the summer. As it turned out, I made it to the finals and placed fourth, a more than respectable outcome for a lowly sophomore.

............

Summer provided an opportunity for adventure in pursuit of success in debate. As a junior, I would be adding varsity debate to my responsibilities. Mr. DeLuca, who succeeded Mr. Cook as head coach, encouraged me and Bob Thoms to enroll in a summer debate camp held at Georgetown University. That July, Mom, Dad, and Jimmy accompanied me by train to Washington, DC. We spent a weekend taking in sights as we walked the Mall, climbed the steps of the Lincoln Memorial, and stared through the gates of the White House. On Sunday, they took me to the campus, where I checked into a dormitory along with dozens of other debaters.

Despite the hard work that was required, the three weeks were wonderful. Except for the trip to Denver, I had never been away from my family. I missed them, but it was also liberating. Instead of mostly sitting and reading at Big Grandma's house each day, I plunged into intense research for the new debate topic: whether nuclear weapons should be controlled by an international organization. Two years earlier, the Cuban Missile Crisis had been a terrifying moment in the Cold War; the possibility of nuclear war seemed real. Nuclear weapons remained in the news, since the crisis provided impetus for a treaty banning atmospheric testing. Now the National Forensic League was encouraging high school debaters to delve into the issue, to argue over whether nations should surrender their nuclear arsenals.

Evidence on both sides existed in abundance, and Washington, DC, was certainly the place to find it. On some afternoons, Thoms and I made our way to Capitol Hill. Dressed in jacket, white shirt, and tie, and each carrying a briefcase, we walked the halls of Congress looking for the offices that could provide copies of the congressional debates over the test ban. I looked at those passing us in the corridors and wondered if these were "important" men, the senators and representatives who carried on the business of government.

The time at Georgetown was freeing in another way. Though Thoms and I had to put cases together and engage in debates with others at the camp, none of it counted in the way that a tournament usually did. Schools weren't competing. Instead, the debating was actually fun, and I could share the fun with guys from across the Northeast whom I was to encounter many times over the next two years. Perhaps because Georgetown was the setting, there was a core of boys from Jesuit schools who became buddies for the rest of my time in debate.

............

Junior year brought lots of success. At the opening tournament at Mother Butler, I jumped to second place in extemp. I did it again at the next competition. Over Christmas, the team flew to Miami for a tournament that brought together schools from the entire eastern half of the United States. With Vinny, Bob, and others, at the end of each day we walked along the beach and saw the ocean's waves, an unheard-of experience in late December for a Bronx kid. As the first tournament in which I participated in both extemp and debate, it was more demanding than anything I had ever done. But the reward was that Regis won the trophy for best school performance. As the year went on, each tournament offered another cause for celebration as victories accumulated.

The stress accumulated, too. I was going to many more tournaments than the year before. Debate demanded much more than extemp. The research never ended, as each tournament brought out new arguments. Every day, I was in the Hearn office until Regis closed at four thirty. Staying at school longer, doing more homework as a double major student, and having Saturdays taken up with a tournament: I was becoming more of a visitor to my Parkchester apartment than a member of my family.

Then there was Richard Merz, who had won the national tournament the previous spring. I was his debate partner that year. Working closely with him all year and being by his side at tournaments from October through May made the year almost unbearable.

Merz was a prodigy. He was a contestant at varsity extemp tournaments from freshman year and became a varsity debater as a sophomore. Short in height, he made up for his size with an aggressive personality. No one was going to bully him. In a debate, he gestured with such force that it seemed as if each piece of evidence had the power of a physical assault. If he found something flawed in my speech, he scrawled a critical comment on an index card and passed it to me. His ordinary way of relating to others was with insults delivered in a mocking tone. Eruptions of anger were common. Such behavior was completely foreign to me. Whatever angry impulses I may have harbored as a child, Sister Perpetua and Brother William had driven out of me. By the time I entered Regis, I didn't even know how to get angry.

Merz's anger reached its apex at the Catholic national tournament. He approached it with fierce determination, expecting to win in extemp. But as winners were announced at the final banquet, he wasn't among them. As the first-prize winner walked to the podium, an angry diatribe burst from Merz's lips. I was shocked, as were all of us at the table. I saw on Mr. DeLuca's face a look of disapproval. A few days later, he met with me and Thoms and told us that Merz would not be going to the national tournament in Omaha the next month. Regis had won it the year before, and Merz had been gearing up for a repeat. But his behavior at the banquet led to his removal from the team. Thoms replaced him as my partner. I was relieved to be free of him. But it only created tension of a different sort for the national finals and didn't prove the best ending to the year.

. . . . . . . . . . . . .

Mom was proud of my successes. Soon after the first Mother Butler tournament, a neighbor had congratulated her on my performance. Mom was puzzled, until the neighbor explained that she had seen my name in the *Catholic News*, the archdiocesan weekly. Mom didn't realize that the paper covered these speech contests. Now she began buying it every week, and she clipped and saved articles that mentioned me and Regis.

But I could also tell that she wasn't happy with how Regis swallowed up my time. On a Sunday after a tournament, I often asked if I could stay home to catch up on homework rather than go to Grandma's house. Mom would "get a look on her face," as Dad might have phrased it. Her teeth clenched, her jaw tightened, and she turned away. Nothing mattered more to her than family. It had always come first and always would. But after a few seconds she muttered, "OK." Regis represented the possibility of a better future for me. My teachers and coaches were representatives of the church. How could she contest the demands they placed on me?

The most heartbreaking example of this conflict and of Mom's and my inability to confront it came in February of my junior year. At Georgetown there was a weekend-long debate competition. The fact that it was held at a Jesuit university guaranteed that every Jesuit high school in the East attended, which made it especially important that we excel. The experience of debate camp made me eager to return. Here was an opportunity to show those I had trained with that, yes, I had made the grade. For weeks, I had been talking up the tournament at home.

We were scheduled to drive to DC on a Thursday. On Wednesday morning, while I was sitting in class, there was a knock on the door. I was summoned into the hallway and informed that I should go downstairs to see Father McGuire, the school counselor. Nothing like this had ever happened, and of course I started to worry about what I had done wrong. Father McGuire, who always showed kindness in his interactions with groups of us, had me sit down. Saying that my mother had called a few minutes earlier, he told me that my grandmother had died. Father McGuire said I should gather my books and go home to my family.

The news was a shock. Big Grandma had been sick before. Ten years earlier, she had suffered a cerebral hemorrhage. But she recovered and went back to what she always did: making the family happy with her food and laughter. Now she was gone. I couldn't imagine what it would mean. Grandma *was* the family. How would it survive without her? What would this do to Mom? A day never passed without her calling her mother. She saw Grandma several times a week. I felt numb as these thoughts passed through me. Father McGuire must have sensed it because he extended his hand to mine and had us pray together before sending me home.

Mom was dressed in black, no makeup on her face, when I got home. She had already picked up Jimmy from school. Dad was on his way home from Berkey and would meet us at Big Grandma's house, she said. I heard the words—*Big Grandma's house*—and wondered if any of us would ever call it that again. But what else could it ever be?

Mom explained what had happened. Grandma hadn't gotten up at her usual hour. Jenny and Fran had already left to go downtown to work. Anna was about to leave for her job in the neighborhood when Grandpa mentioned that Grandma hadn't come downstairs yet. The way Mom described it, Anna panicked. Screaming, "Mama! Mama!" she raced up the two flights of stairs to the bedroom where Grandma slept. Grandma was lying in bed, not moving, not breathing. The doctor later told Anna that a blood clot likely caused her heart to stop and that she died quickly and peacefully in her sleep. It was small comfort for her daughters.

The wake that evening mostly included the Scamporlino clan. Over the next couple of days, neighbors from Silver Street and friends from the old neighborhood came to pay their respects. The funeral on Saturday drew many people who had known Jessica Scamporlino from her days behind the counter at the family store. Tears flowed, hugs were exchanged, and then the big meal followed where memories were shared.

Or so it was described to me later. That first night, after we returned from the funeral parlor, Mom and Dad told me to pack my suitcase so that the next morning I could go to Regis, meet my teammates and coaches, and drive to DC for the Georgetown tournament. I didn't know what to say. This was probably the most important moment in the life of my family, and I spent it debating the merits of nuclear policy. But Regis was calling, and though Mom and Dad didn't quite say this, their decision made it apparent that, no matter how Mom might have felt about it, Regis and what it promised me—and *not* family—had to come first.

# 11

.............

## My Sexual Desires

It took me years to realize that I threw myself into speech and debate so completely because I needed something to focus me and absorb all my energy. The Hearn certainly demanded a lot, but it also provided sanctuary, an escape from a struggle far more anxiety-producing than a debate tournament could ever be.

.............

It was in high school that a sexual yearning, a longing for men's bodies, began to take hold of me. I know that Lady Gaga has proclaimed we were "born this way," and it seems to be the official line among those who support equality for gays: we always were gay, it's natural, so accept us as we are. But I can't claim I was drawn only to men for as long as I can remember. In first grade, Jacob Apuzzo and I took turns one Saturday lying on top of each other in the back of his dad's car. But that same year I raced across Sister Perpetua's classroom to kiss Jane Halligan. Yes, I masturbated with Mac one afternoon. But I also made out on a staircase with Arlene and felt the bulge in my pants when I did so.

Something shifted in high school. Maybe it was the freedom to feel forbidden things now that I was leaving the neighborhood each day. Perhaps these feelings were so taboo that I could never let them surface when I was in home territory. Or was it just the fact of entering those postpuberty years when sexual urges assert themselves so strongly? Whatever the explanation, the feelings were there. They were powerful and undeniable.

Interestingly, they were not directed at my peers in school. I can't remember ever looking at a fellow Regian—in the cafeteria, the gym, or even the shower room when we stripped naked—and feeling sexual desire. My teachers did not elicit sexual longings, even though some were certainly good-looking. No, it was always directed at strangers, and always at adults. I seemed to understand instinctively that these feelings—unnamed, forbidden, and deeply sinful—had to be separated completely from any connection to people who were part of my life.

New York's subway system was the place where these longings unfolded. After Dad and I stopped taking the train together, I still followed his instructions to get on a front or back car in order to find an empty seat. But now, alone, I didn't rush to any empty seat. Instead, I looked for a place next to a man who struck me as attractive. Then, as the train grew crowded and the space on the long row of seating got taken, my neighbor and I inevitably found ourselves scrunched together. I subtly tried to have my leg press against his. I took advantage of the lurching of the subway as it pulled out of a station. I held my leg firmly in place as his shifted unintentionally against mine. I let my leg and body lean into his when the train stopped at a station. I straightened my body up, moving away from his, but kept my leg steady, ever so slightly invading his space. It was such a meager physical connection that I doubt these strangers noticed it. But for me it was unbelievably exciting. It always provoked an erection, and I often found myself short of breath as the train made its way to Eighty-Sixth Street.

Why was I doing this? How did I explain it to myself? I had no idea, no explanation, no words to give it meaning. Except, of course, my Catholic training. If I was getting an erection, it must be sinful. So now, besides confessing impure actions with myself, I added impure thoughts to my catalog of infractions. Since this happened almost daily, the pull to confession became more compelling. I tried to make a firm resolve, as my Act of Contrition specified, and this might last for a while. But inevitably a morning arrived when a guy that I found appealing had an empty seat next to him, and the cycle began again.

This continued for a year. Then, in sophomore year, something happened that changed my perspective forever. Mr. Ridley, a Jesuit, was my teacher in a course on American literature. In the spring, as we approached the works of the mid-twentieth century, he asked us to write a report on a contemporary novel of our choosing. I had no experience with current fiction, and so after class one day, I stayed behind to ask his advice. He looked at me, his index finger and thumb touching his lip as he reflected, and then he said, "Try James Baldwin's

*Another Country*. It was a best seller and just came out in paperback. I'd describe it as a novel for mature audiences, very contemporary in its concerns."

*Another Country* was unlike any novel I had ever read. It lacked the propriety so central to the nineteenth-century novels I had consumed. Sex was everywhere, and Baldwin mixed it with emotions that spattered across every page. Love and anger, sex and despair, yearnings and loneliness: his characters were riding roller coasters of feeling that drove them into relationships and then tore those relationships apart.

At one point in the novel, describing a character, Baldwin wrote the line "Love was a country he knew nothing about." He might as well have been writing about me. Nothing that I grew up with suggested anything like what happened in those pages. There was a humdrum quality to the marriages in my family. Grandma and Grandpa, Mom and Dad, Lucy and Phil, Anna and Tommy: there was no drama. Sure, Dad might disappear into the bedroom one evening in a "mood," but Mom just rolled her eyes and the next night they were back to washing the dishes after dinner and talking about the day. Television gave me *The Donna Reed Show* and *Father Knows Best*, where a happy togetherness reigned.

Did Mr. Ridley see something in me that I hadn't yet identified? It couldn't have been an accident that, of all the novels he might have suggested, he chose one in which homosexual relations played a major role. On the very first page, Rufus, the character around whom much of the novel turns, is in a Times Square movie theater. A man sits next to him and soon is reaching over to grope him. For Rufus, who is down-and-out and struggling to survive, the experience is not a happy one. To me, it was a shock. Were there such men? Did they do things like this? In the darkness of a movie theater, was it possible to go beyond pressed-together legs on a subway? Should I be going to movies alone, instead of with my Regis friends? As the novel progressed, a geography of male encounters emerged: Times Square and Forty-Second Street, Washington Square Park, bars near the Hudson River in Greenwich Village. But it was a geography of danger as much as anything. Feelings for men left characters tormented. Vivaldo and his friends beat a queer boy practically to death. Rufus commits suicide. One character who acknowledges his homosexuality flees to France. Yes, the novel ends happily. On the last page, a male couple separated by geography is reunited, and Baldwin says about one of them, "His fear left him, he was certain now that everything would be all right." But that isn't what registered for me. The conflict, the torment, the inability to stop oneself from stumbling down the trail of one's emotions: all were seared into my brain.

. . . . . . . . . . . . .

My feelings and attractions continued, though nothing came of them. The summer provided relief from the daily subway rides. But once school began, I was back to my subway-riding routine, reaching for even the tiniest connection to an adult male body.

As happened every year, all the students boarded buses one Friday in September and headed to Bear Mountain. Riding the subway home that evening, it was easy to find a seat, since rush hour was over. A couple of stops later, a husky blue-collar guy sat next to me. It had been a warm day, and he was wearing a short-sleeve shirt, revealing muscular, hairy arms. I felt a rush of excitement, and I soon began that slight pressing of my leg against his.

But this time, suddenly, I felt him pressing back. I caught my breath. This couldn't be happening, I thought. But it was, unmistakably. The train arrived at Parkchester, but he wasn't moving, so I didn't get off either. What am I doing, I thought? How will this end up? As we approached the Westchester Square stop, his leg suddenly pushed hard against mine. He stood up, walked toward the door as the train pulled into the station, turned toward me, and stared. The meaning was clear. I got up, too, and followed him off the train. We had been sitting in the last car, and he walked slowly toward the stairs so that, by the time we got there, everyone else was off the platform and heading to the street. He stopped on the staircase a few steps down so that we couldn't be seen by those on the other side of the platform. He was touching himself and reached over to touch my crotch, which was already bulging shamelessly.

"I'm Joe," he said. "You have a place to go?"

My eyes widened. The very idea made me gulp. I shook my head no. He thought for a moment, nodded slowly, and said, "Come with me."

We walked on to Westchester Avenue. We were just a few blocks from Grandma's house. Jenny or Fran or Sylvia could easily be doing an errand and spot me with this stranger. Fortunately, the sun had set and it was turning dark—less chance that a family member would notice me. But where was he taking me? Joe didn't talk, and I was too scared to open my mouth. After a couple of blocks, we reached the overpass for the Hutchinson River Parkway. An opening in the fence led down to the river and highway. He pushed through it and headed down the grassy slope, turning toward me with a look that said, "C'mon! Whaddya doin' standin' there?" We hit a stretch where the bushes were high enough to hide us and made our way through them until we were at the river's edge. He looked at me, grabbed his crotch with one hand, and grabbed mine with his other. The feel of his hand was strong. He pulled me closer, unzipped his pants, and pulled out his cock. Glancing down at it, he looked at me and said, "Blow me."

My heart practically stopped. This was a variant of a phrase teenage boys used all the time. "Go blow yourself," someone might spit out, as a way of dismissing what somebody else had said. I had used it among friends often. But I had no idea what it meant, and I was never going to expose my ignorance by asking. Now, here was a guy looking at his cock and telling me to blow him. I was in a total panic. I felt him put his hand on my shoulder and push me down. I got on my knees, looked at his cock, which he was holding up toward my face, and did what I thought he was asking: I sucked in my breath and then blew out all the air onto the head of his penis.

Years later, safely into adulthood and moving in a world of gay friends, I often recounted this story. In the seventies and eighties, and maybe still now, it was common among gay men, as we got to know each other, to describe our first sexual experience. I would go through the details, as I have done here, getting me and Joe to the bushes along the river's edge and his telling me to blow him. I'd then say, "So, I blew him," and in the most exaggerated fashion, I'd suck in my breath and blow it out as loudly as I could. It was always good for a roomful of laughs, and of course, I laughed too. But at the time it wasn't funny. It was terrifying and humiliating. I knew I was showing myself to be an idiot, a pathetic kid who wanted something badly but didn't know what it was or how to get it. That evening, when I "blew" him, Joe didn't say anything, but he must have instantly figured that he had ended up with an innocent. He lifted me up, held onto my arm as he played with himself, and in not much time let out a sound as sperm shot from his cock. He breathed hard for a few seconds, shook more sperm off, and then put his cock back in his pants and zipped up. "C'mon," he said, as he headed back through the bushes and up the slope to Tremont Avenue. He gave one last nod and then walked away, in the direction opposite to where I needed to go.

I knew I had to get home. Mom would be holding dinner for me. I walked to the bus stop, oblivious to everything around me. When I got home, Mom asked about the trip to Bear Mountain, and I started blathering. I was afraid that even a moment of silence would expose something in my face and reveal the evil I had done. But Mom just went with the flow, encouraging me to tell her more about the day.

The next morning, Saturday, I occupied myself with Regis homework, of which there was plenty. But my mind was on the trip to confession I would make in the afternoon. I thought about how to describe my sin. I certainly wasn't going to confess I "blew" a guy or played with a man's cock. "Impure action with another man" was the phrase I decided on, and I let it slip from my mouth as quietly as possible, waiting for the priest's response. But of course there was no commentary, only the formulaic announcement that my sins were forgiven and I should say an Our Father and a Hail Mary as penance.

One might imagine that the experience with Joe would have propelled me away from sexual searching. But humiliating and scary as it was, it didn't stop the pull to find other men. Two weeks later, I was riding home from Regis during rush hour, standing amid a mass of passengers packed together around a pole. Suddenly, I felt a man pushing against me and his arm sliding across my legs. He did it in a way that escaped the attention of other passengers, whose eyes were all staring vacantly through the crowd. I glanced at him to be sure I wasn't imagining it, and he stared back. And then, on the other side of the pole, I saw another guy whose eyes darted between the two of us. He obviously had figured out that something was going on. As the train pulled into 125th Street, he gave head signals to us to get off the train. The guy next to me squeezed my leg and started to exit. I had no idea what could happen in a crowded subway station, but I followed.

As it turned out, neither guy spoke English. One of them pointed upstairs while the other tugged at my elbow. My strong but undefined wanting and my fear of a scene developing led me obediently to follow them up the stairs and to the men's room that, in those decades, was a feature of subway stations. I had never used one before. But I followed them in, only to discover that the space was crowded with over half a dozen guys. I was already scared out of my wits; now I wondered what could possibly happen. But before that thought even registered, the man who had pressed against me on the train got down on his knees and unzipped my pants, while the other one pulled up close and began kissing me, his tongue pressing into my mouth. Everyone else stopped what they were doing and watched the scene unfold. I tried to pull away but couldn't. What would I have done? Start screaming? Start a fight with guys older and bigger than I was? I held on tight to my book bag and, after barely a couple of minutes, I came, and it ended. All the others went back to whatever they were doing (I didn't yet understand that all of them were looking for sex, that New York's public restrooms were hunting grounds for men wanting sex with men). The two who had worked me over each smiled, gave me a pat on the arm, and left, while I zipped up my pants and pulled myself together before continuing my trip home.

This second experience provoked terror of a different sort, a terror not of being found out but of being endangered, being vulnerable to what a stranger might do to me if I wasn't careful. Those few minutes remained so painful that I put every ounce of will into not repeating the experience, into not making body contact in the subway. My efforts were helped by the intensity of the

MY SEXUAL DESIRES 89

new demands that speech and debate were making on me as a varsity member. Through the rest of the fall and winter I managed to keep the sexual pulls at a distance. Sure, I noticed men who aroused my sexual desires, and some of them noticed me. But I turned my eyes away, and if I sat next to a man who attracted me, I did it in the morning on the way to school, when there could be no opportunity to act on my urges.

My restraint didn't last forever. As spring arrived and the weather warmed, as the trees and bushes filled out and provided places to hide, my search for sex resumed. But now, it was as if those first two experiences had left me better equipped to identify men for sex. The pattern was almost always the same: coming home from school at the end of the day, staying on the train beyond Parkchester, exiting at Westchester Square and finding a place to go together. Sometimes, as with Joe, we walked to the highway and hid in the bushes. Sometimes we went into the men's room at the station. Once, after dark, we snuck into a nearby junkyard filled with the wreckage of old cars. Wherever we ended up, we unzipped our pants and played with each other. Sometimes a guy bent down and blew me. Once, a guy turned me around and pressed his cock up against me. I couldn't understand what he was trying to do and turned back around after a few seconds.

Always these were blue-collar guys, identifiable as such because they weren't wearing the white shirt, jacket, and tie that was the universal uniform of office workers. We never exchanged information about ourselves. One guy did start talking. He asked if I had friends whom I did this with, but I just shook my head no. Occasionally they told me their first name, but I was too scared to say anything back. This was come (literally) and go, as fast as possible.

After my arrival home, I had to act as if nothing unusual had happened. I covered my tracks by talking about all that I had done at school, how I had stayed late because of a practice debate or a basketball game. If I was learning anything beyond that there were men who wanted to have sex with men, it was about how easy it was to lie, to invent stories so that *no one* ever knew what was going on. Parents, teachers, friends at school—all remained ignorant. This was all the more remarkable because, when I returned home after an encounter, I felt completely raw and exposed. I felt as if my whole body was shaking and the guilt painted on my face. Sadly, it was also a relief to realize I could cover my tracks completely and make my experiences invisible to everyone. How could it have been otherwise? How could I have described it except as shameful? What might help have looked like in those years, when I had never heard homosexuality mentioned other than in a novel that no one else I knew had read?

Summer brought new opportunities. Since Grandma's death in February, Mom had been going to Silver Street every day, so that Grandpa wouldn't be alone while Laura was at school and everyone else was at work. She continued during the summer, taking Jimmy with her, but she only expected me to come a couple of times a week, since I had a lot to do that summer. I had signed on at school for advanced work in Latin and English and had been selected for the Homeric Academy, a prized honor at Regis. And September always brought a new debate topic, for which research started in the summer.

All of this provided a reason for trips to Manhattan to do research at the Donnell Library and borrow books I couldn't find at my local branch. But my visits there were always much shorter than the time I was away from home. What I was really doing was exploring the geography of homosexual New York (the word *gay* was unknown to me). Following the trail laid out by Baldwin in *Another Country*, I wandered through Washington Square Park in Greenwich Village. I looked at the men gathered around musicians strumming guitars and wondered if any of them were looking for another male. I walked the length of Forty-Second Street from Lexington to Eighth Avenue and then back to Times Square. Was there something besides subway sex? If I found it, would I dare to participate?

Four or five weeks of such trips produced nothing. But then, one afternoon in July, after walking around Times Square, I headed to the subway entrance at Forty-Second Street. As I started down the stairs, I noticed a guy standing there, unshaven, with the look of a street bum. We caught each other's eye for a split second, but I kept heading down. As I reached the bottom and was about to disappear into the station, I looked up toward the street. He was still there, staring at me and touching his crotch. The look of him scared me, but I stopped and stood for a second or two. Then, when he moved his head as if to say, "Let's go," I came back up the stairs. "Want to come to my place?" he asked. "I live just a couple of blocks away." He put his hand on my shoulder as if to guide me, and we began walking down Seventh Avenue.

He introduced himself as "John" and commented on the books I was carrying. "Looks like you read a lot," he said. "Where do you go to school?" I don't know what possessed me to tell him, since I had never revealed anything about myself in previous encounters, but I said, "Regis. It's a Catholic school."

"No kidding," he replied, with a smile on his face. "I went to Brooklyn Prep. Two Jesuit boys, huh?"

That simple piece of information changed everything. It suddenly seemed safe to be with him. What bad thing could happen with a guy who had graduated from Brooklyn Prep? We kept talking as we walked to his place and climbed the stairs to his apartment. He was living in what New Yorkers called an SRO, a building of single-room-occupancy apartments with the barest elements of a kitchen in each unit and shared toilets on each floor. He had a single bed and dresser, a table and a couple of chairs, and not much else. Clothing was scattered around, and the bed was unmade.

Despite the rough edges in his appearance and apartment, there was a kindness to John that made my wanting even stronger. Almost as soon as he closed the door, he pulled me to him. Taller than I was, he put his hands on the sides of my face, bent down slightly, and began kissing me. I felt his tongue pushing against my lips, but unlike my earlier time in the subway men's room, when the tongue kissing was like a forced invasion, with John my mouth opened willingly and we drew as close as two bodies can be. Soon, he was undressing me and himself, and for the first time I experienced another man's naked body against mine, his arms wrapped around my back and drawing me into him. The hair on his chest tickled as we rubbed against each other, but rather than causing me to pull away, it only made me want to sink in closer. John moved me over to the bed and held my hand as I lay down. Both of us had erections. He lay down on top of me, his legs in between mine. The kissing went on. Holding himself up a bit as he leaned on one elbow, he ran his other hand up and down the side of my body, sending tingles of excitement from head to toe.

At some point, John raised himself onto his knees and looked down at me. He lifted my legs into the air and pulled me closer against him. The move was unexpected, and I had no idea why he was doing it. His action must have sent a look of fear across my face, because he put my legs down. He stared at me for a moment, stroked my body again, and then lowered his head and gave me a blow job. Within no time at all, I ejaculated, and John plopped down next to me and drew me in close. He didn't say a thing, and I had no idea what to say. A few minutes later, we were dressing. "I don't have a phone," he said, "so I can't give you my number, but if you're ever down here again, just ring the bell. You're welcome anytime."

. . . . . . . . . . . . .

A day or two after the encounter with John, I started reading *The Brothers Karamazov*, one of the many novels on my list of summer readings. Set in mid-nineteenth-century Russia, it detailed the dramatic conflicts and emotional confrontations between a father and his sons over money and, especially, women. The father is a despicable human being, and his behavior especially leaves its mark on his eldest son, Dmitri, whose life is spinning out of control.

As I made my way through the hundreds of pages Dostoyevsky devoted to this family drama, what stood out to me, what touched my soul, was not the main plot but an accompanying story of Alyosha, the youngest son. Alyosha attempts to escape the chaos of his family by entering a monastery. A young novice when the novel begins, he is especially attached to the elder of the monastery, a saintly monk who has the love and respect—the adoration, really—of almost everyone. Alyosha has absorbed the holy aura that emanates from the elder to such a degree that those who encounter him, whether in the monastery or in his forays into town, seem to notice. Alyosha communicates love and kindness in everything he does. He sees his mission as bringing light and goodness to the world. He seeks to calm the excesses of sensuality that have driven people like his father and brother to such destructive behavior. Sweet, cherub-like, saintly, Alyosha jumped out from the pages of the novel and grabbed my heart and soul at a moment of desperate need. I saw in him the total opposite of what was propelling me to walk the streets of Manhattan, of what had driven me into the bed of John. I felt as if the model of Alyosha might rescue me from a world of sexual sin, if only I could keep him in front of me to help me with my resolve.

When John had told me that I was welcome to return, I nodded. But now, just days later, with this larger-than-life fictional character before me, I prayed that I never would. Special and exciting as the sex with John had been, there was no way I could choose to go back. The conflict between the wants that propelled me into John's bed and the shoulds that I believed I needed to live by remained as strong as ever. Yes, I probably would sin again. But no, I couldn't plan to do it. I stopped my wanderings in Manhattan for the rest of the summer. If I wasn't going to sin again, then I had to be firm in my decision.

# 12

..............

## Another Ending

I was raised to be a good boy, in the best and worst senses of the phrase. Mom taught me to do the right thing, be respectful of the adults around me, and treat my friends well. The model of the saints seeped into my consciousness, and I wanted to be like them. But from Mom also came injunctions to "Behave yourself, young man!" Sister Perpetua and Brother William made it abundantly clear that I was to obey—or else. A fear of hell propelled me never to do anything to anger those in authority. Instead, I must not only do what I was told but anticipate what others expected so that I did not even need to be told. The result: it often became impossible to distinguish between what I ought to do and what I wanted to do, between what was expected and what I enjoyed.

Those tensions became almost unmanageable in senior year. Schoolwork was even more time-consuming. The Hearn demanded more. And of course there was the unresolvable conflict between my sexual urges and my religious leanings. Through most of it, I kept my "good boy" smile. My classmates could count on my laughter. I did what was demanded of me, which had become what I demanded of myself. But there were times when I felt my only options were to collapse or explode.

..............

Senior year offered more academic choices than previous years, and good boy that I was, I signed up for everything I could. I took Advanced Placement classes in history and English. In the English course, I read novels thicker than anything I had ever seen. Then there were the classics. The apogee of academic accomplishment at Regis was Homeric Academy. Working closely together, ten seniors translated both *The Iliad* and *The Odyssey* and read deeply in the critical literature about them. Toward the end of senior year, members mounted the auditorium stage for an evening and, facing an audience of parents, teachers, and fellow students, fielded questions from a panel of scholars. I was thrilled to be selected, but the workload was immense. As if that wasn't enough, I sought a special tutorial with my Latin teacher, who required me to translate the entire *Aeneid*. Three hours of nightly homework no longer described my responsibilities.

............

The Hearn, too, demanded more. As a senior, I was named president of the debate team. Hevern, Thoms, Rizzo, and I—the starting lineup—were a tight-knit gang, so being president did not add more tasks. But the idea weighed on me. If we lost a tournament, the responsibility felt like mine.

The year started well. At the opening tournament, I came in first in extemp. More victories followed. But even though the team and I were doing well, we kept coming up against the superior performance of St. Brendan's, a girls' high school in Brooklyn. As with so many other Catholic League teams, we hung out at tournaments, laughed and joked together between rounds, and mixed easily over lunch. I even had a crush on one member, Kathy Jones, and took advantage of every chance to be around her. But if we met them in a semifinal or final round, the odds were that we would lose.

St. Brendan's had a high-energy coach named John Sexton, who, many years later, became the headline-making president of New York University. He took up as much space as he could at tournaments, glad-handing anybody who would stop to talk and currying favor with judges. His coaching methods were very different from those at Regis. We researched and prepared our own cases and then received feedback from our coaches. But Sexton himself did much of the research, built the basic case, and then taught his team how to argue it.

The topic in senior year was "Resolved: that all labor disputes be settled through compulsory arbitration." After a couple of losing encounters with St. Brendan's, I became obsessed with the evidence they used to bolster their case and demolish our arguments against it. They kept referring to the "common law tradition" and to something called *Black's Law Dictionary*. So, compulsively responsible as I was, I made my way to the Donnell Library and over several afternoons read every one of the dictionary's thousand-plus pages. After days of poring through it, I came upon an entry that made me almost scream with excitement. *Black's Law Dictionary* was saying exactly the opposite of what St. Brendan's claimed! At the next tournament, held at Fordham University, Thoms and I confronted St. Brendan's in the final round. I listened as they presented their case and then made my arguments in response. When they tried to discredit the challenge by laying claim to the common law, I quoted almost joyfully what *Black's Law Dictionary* actually said. Regis brought home the first-place trophy.

But aside from that moment of triumph, the demands of the Hearn were making me an emotional wreck. Mr. Labonte, our head coach, was a major reason why. Previous coaches certainly wanted us to do well, but if we lost, they validated our efforts and worked to ratchet up our performance. By contrast, Labonte was fiercely competitive. His goal was to win, period. At tournaments, tension spilled out of him. He paced the hallways, waiting to hear the results. When Regis didn't win, the frustration showed on his face.

I took all this onto myself. It was my responsibility to win, and the pressure extracted a price. I can vividly recall the state championship in Albany. Winning it brought a berth in the national tournament in June. Thoms and I were slated for the final round. It was held in a meeting hall larger than any in which I had yet participated. We sat on a stage. When it was my turn to speak, I walked to the podium, carrying a set of index cards with the quotations I planned to use. My legs were shaking uncontrollably and my knees almost knocking into each other. As I began to speak and reached for an index card, my hand trembled to such a degree that I couldn't hold the card up as I read from it. Thoms and I won the championship, but the joy was dampened by the fear that had washed through me.

. . . . . . . . . . . . .

Add to this the uncertain future looming ahead. College was on the horizon, with all the decision-making that the application process entailed. The claim most often repeated about Regis was that every graduate went to college. This was what made Mom decide that her boys were going there. As Mom put it, "Your Dad graduated from high school and did better than Small Grandpa. If you graduate from college, you'll do better than Dad." I took it to be true, but at the same time had no clear picture of what going to college meant. Most of the Scamporlinos or D'Emilios hadn't finished high school. There was no guidance at home about college.

The help that Regis provided was locked within narrow boundaries. The school assumed that its graduates would attend Catholic colleges. Regis seniors chose mostly from among a few institutions: Jesuit schools in the Northeast; a few others with strong reputations, like Notre Dame; and local schools, like St. John's University. Regis did not even begin to send transcripts to non-Catholic colleges until my freshman year, after the lawyer father of a graduating senior threatened to sue the school. Regis yielded, and the floodgates opened. Seniors near the top of the class began applying to Ivy League schools.

The college application process became one more collective activity I shared with classmates. Our mornings in the cafeteria became discussions about the catalogs we received in the mail. It surprised me how many classmates knew what they wanted to do. Those in the science and math track talked about medical school, research science, and engineering. Some spoke of "Wall Street," a shorthand expression for a career in finance. I was clueless. My success in debate led my friends to declare me a lawyer-in-training. But I couldn't imagine arguing a new case for each client and filling my life forever with the tension that debate provoked in me. The only career Mom and Dad talked about was accounting, since that was what a college degree allowed bookkeepers like themselves to become. I knew that was not for me.

Of everything I studied, Latin and Greek gave the most satisfaction, so that shaped my choices. I applied to Fordham, which Mom insisted on because going there meant I would live at home, and no Italian boy ever left home before marriage. I also applied to Georgetown, filled with good memories from debate camp, and to Columbia, Princeton, and the University of Virginia, all of which had distinguished classics departments. I didn't know where studying classics would take me, but I anticipated the joys of several more years of reading the great works of Greek and Latin.

By December, applications were in the mail, and my classmates and I waited for the results. But as we waited and wondered where our futures would unfold, I was considering a different future, one that I told almost no one about.

............

Religion was built into the life of Regis. Besides four years of theology class, every Friday students and teachers walked across Eighty-Fourth Street to the Church of St. Ignatius for a late morning Mass. On Wednesdays before class started, I faithfully attended a "Guard of Honor" Mass in the school chapel. The priests and scholastics who taught us were a constant reminder of God's presence and the calling to serve Him. The guidance offered by our school counselors was framed in theological terms.

Besides the ways religion wove itself into daily experience, students attended a yearly spiritual retreat each fall. Usually it was a one-day experience. But for seniors, soon to leave the shelter and security that Regis provided, the retreat stretched over three days at a seminary upstate. Freed from the distractions of the city and the pressure of homework, our time was divided between religious services, silent meditation, and homilies from our retreat master. Father Burke, our retreat leader, was a white-haired Jesuit who looked to be almost the age of Big Grandpa. He projected a kindly demeanor and urged us gently but insistently to think about how to serve Christ in the next stage of our lives. Where might college take us? What might it lead us to do with our remaining years? They were questions that the process of applying to college was already provoking in me but for which I had no answers.

The figure of Father Burke, the monastery setting, the prayer and meditation: together they made the character of Alyosha almost a living presence. I reached for him, wanting to grasp his goodness and make it my own. For the first time in my life, I found myself thinking of the priesthood. Perhaps I had what was described as "a calling." I deeply admired the priests and scholastics who devoted themselves to me and my schoolmates. Could I become one of them? Though I didn't have the self-knowledge to admit this, I think I also hoped that a religious life might save me from myself. Living in a religious community would build a wall between me and the bodies of those men on the subways and streets.

I asked if I might meet with Father Burke during one of the meditation sessions. Sitting in his office, I told him that the retreat was making me think that the life of a priest, a Jesuit priest in particular, might be my vocation.

"It pleases me to hear that, son," he said. "Tell me why you think this might be true."

"I'm not sure, Father. I've always been attracted to the lives of the saints. Mom had a book about the saints, and I went through the stories again and again. I especially loved Saint Anthony. He spent his whole life serving people who needed help. I took Anthony as my confirmation name."

"Do your parents know you feel this way? Have you thought about this for a long time?"

"No, Father. There are no priests in my family. I've never considered it before," I told him. "But I love the Jesuits who teach me. I love how committed they are to helping us. They are trying to guide me to the best possible life. Maybe I could do that too."

We kept talking in this way, with Father Burke probing my motivations and me answering as best I could. He explained the process of applying. Everything he said, the way he looked at me, was so kind and loving that, unexpectedly, I found myself revealing my secret.

"Father, there's something else I need to talk about," I began. Then I hesitated. Except for the phrase "impure actions with another man," told in the darkness of the confessional, I had never spoken a word about my sexual desires. The terror must have shown on my face, because Father Burke reached over and took my hand. "Son, you are safe with me. I will never repeat what you tell me."

And so, I told him. I recounted the times on the subway, the sexual arousal it provoked, the men who responded. I described the experience with John in the summer. I spoke about my efforts never to do it again and my failure to live up to my promise. No shock appeared on Father Burke's face, no disgust at this boy describing two years of shameful sin. He continued to project the kindness I had seen during the retreat. Finally, after I had run out of sinful occasions to relate, he looked at me earnestly and said, "Let me ask you a question. Do you love children?"

"Oh, yes, Father, I love children," I said with conviction. "My younger brother, Jimmy—from the time he was little, I played with him every chance I had. I do love children, Father."

"Well, son," he replied, "if you love children, you couldn't be a homosexual. If you were, you would hate children. You would see them as the product of the love of a man and woman. You would resent them as something you will never have." He then told me that many young men, as their bodies matured, felt sexual desires they couldn't control. With time, he assured me, this would pass. I was so desperate, and Father Burke spoke with such conviction, that I grasped hold of his words. I needed to hear that I wasn't destined to struggle with this forever.

I came home from the retreat feeling a hopefulness that I hadn't experienced in a long time. Father Burke had instructed me to talk with Father McGuire about the call that I felt I had and about the sexual experiences with men and my desire to stop. When I met with Father McGuire, it wasn't as hard to tell him about my sexual desires as it had been just a few days before. Like Father Burke, he also didn't betray any condemnatory sentiments. We talked about this sense that I might have a calling, and Father McGuire seemed pleased. He explained at greater length the process. If I was accepted, and Father McGuire expressed confidence that I would be, he would then arrange a session with a Jesuit psychologist to explore more deeply whether my desires posed a barrier. He also told me to continue the college application process, since it was impossible to predict what I might decide after six months of reflection. He encouraged me to meet with him for spiritual counseling as often as I needed.

The talks with Father Burke and Father McGuire launched a period of roller-coaster emotions. I prayed with an intensity I had never experienced. For several weeks, I stopped sitting on my daily subway rides to avoid any physical contact with guys. It worked in the sense that I didn't have sex for a long stretch of time, but I was acutely aware that I still noticed men. And every time I did, it drove me into myself. I stood hanging on to the strap with my eyes closed as I prayed for help in controlling these impulses that seemed stronger than I was.

I had mentioned to both Father Burke and Father McGuire that I had never talked with my parents about the priesthood, and Father McGuire advised me to have that conversation. And so one evening that fall, I brought it up after dinner, when Jimmy had already gone to bed. I was sure they would be pleased. After all, the Scamporlino sisters were deeply religious. But as we sat at the table and I told them about the retreat and that I might be meant for the priesthood, the look on both their faces brought me up short. Mom's jaw had tightened, and Dad was looking at her with an expression of worry on his face. They were not expecting this. Since the summer, we had been having conversations about colleges. Now, suddenly, I was telling them I wanted to be a Jesuit. They peppered me with questions. Was I sure? Did I realize this meant no children or grandchildren? Could it just be a feeling that came up at the retreat? At one point, Mom burst out in a tone of exasperation, "But you have never talked about this before!"

I don't know how I pulled it off, but their upset didn't provoke me. I imagined Alyosha, projecting calm and offering assurance. I realized from the way they reacted, especially Mom, that this was not their vision of what an Italian boy does. Family comes before everything. Yes, pray to God and respect His will, but at the end of the day God is there to bless the family, and the family needs every member to pull together. That's what those Sunday gatherings at Big Grandma's house were saying: "Here we are, where we all belong." In as steady a voice as I could muster, I told them how much this meant to me, how it had come almost like a revelation. Yes, I will keep praying about it. But I needed to go ahead with the application because I believed it was God's will.

. . . . . . . . . . . . .

While Mom and Dad were less than happy, the decision was producing in me an excitement that, at least for a while, seemed to keep at bay the tensions provoked by schoolwork and the Hearn. At my lunch table of four, Jim Kuntz and Bob VerEecke had long decided that they had a call to be priests, and each planned to enter the Jesuits. Now I was claiming this as my future too. These precious friendships would become lifelong associations. We would become more than friends. We would be family.

I was too scared to tell them about my intentions. Partly I still couldn't believe I was embarking on this path. I also didn't want it to circulate among all my classmates. If it didn't work out, having everyone know that I had tried but failed would be humiliating. But I was also eager for Jim and Bob to know, and I anticipated the surprise my presence would cause when the applicants for admission gathered for the exam. As it turned out, they were surprised, and I loved the happy laughter that erupted. But my presence wasn't the only surprise. Vinny was there too! Apparently, he had been thinking about this for a long time but also wasn't prepared for everyone at school to know. Now, here we were, a table's worth of lunch buddies, taking the first step on a lifelong journey. It was a very special moment.

............

Wonderful as the day was, I knew I was going through a process that I assumed Vinny, Bob, and Jim weren't. I still faced an appointment with a psychologist. I had no idea what psychologists did. The idea of self-destructive patterns of behavior caused by early experiences whose effects lingered had no place in the mental world of my family. If you did something wrong, you got scolded and punished, went to confession, and had your sin forgiven. The Scamporlinos and D'Emilios did not live by the precepts of Freud.

The office was in Brooklyn Heights, and I was excused from class that Friday in order to go through the interview and tests. Like Father Burke and Father McGuire, the psychologist displayed compassion. He asked questions; he brought me back to my earliest years. I wanted to be honest with him, but part of me was in protective mode. I needed to make a good impression. I needed him to see the sincerity of my desire to leave these sexual yearnings behind. Most of all, I needed to convince myself that I was not one of those homosexuals that James Baldwin wrote about. And so I described my time with Arlene in elementary school, the dances I had gone to, the sexual arousal that girls provoked. I talked about crushes on girls at debate tournaments. To all of this he listened, occasionally taking notes.

Everything seemed to be going well, when he told me he would now administer a psychological test. He would show me a series of images, and I should tell him the first thing I saw as he displayed each one. He began, and I was horrified. It seemed that buried within every image was an erect penis. Even without knowing anything about what I later learned was a Rorschach test, I instinctively knew I could never admit to that. So I improvised. This one, I said, contained an image of the Florida peninsula. This one was a rocket launched into space. This was the Empire State Building.

The test over, he said he needed time to evaluate my responses. He suggested I take a break for lunch and walk along the Promenade, with its view of Manhattan's skyline. I took him up on the suggestion. The view was spectacular. But as

I walked to one end and back, I noticed the large number of men also strolling the Promenade or just standing and watching others. Though I didn't yet have the term for it, I had stumbled upon a popular "cruising" area for gay men. It completely rattled me. Here I had spent the morning trying to convince someone—and myself—that I was not a homosexual, and now I was surrounded by men looking for men. Feeling desires well up in me, I left as quickly as I could.

Needless to say, I did not mention this to my interviewer. When I got back to his office, he essentially delivered the same message as Father Burke. It was not uncommon for adolescent boys to experience such feelings. The fact that I was making a serious effort to resist them and also had feelings for girls were good signs. And, he added, it was significant that I only found myself attracted to strangers. It was a sign that I did not want this to be part of my life. He reminded me that all priests have sexual feelings and that part of what the priesthood involved was learning to contain them. In taking a vow of celibacy, I would join all my fellow Jesuits in a commitment to channel sexual desire into a love that expressed itself in service to others. In his assessment, I could pursue my calling.

As I headed home to the Bronx, I knew deep inside that I was not yet prepared for such a commitment. Try as I might to hold my desires at bay, they were never far away. I was deluding myself if I believed seminary would miraculously resolve these struggles. When the acceptance letter arrived several weeks later, I told my parents that I had decided I wasn't ready for such a commitment. I could see their relief. To my closest friends at school, especially to Kuntz, who was my best buddy, it was a disappointment. We had already begun imagining our years in the seminary. To Father McGuire I explained that I needed to test my faith in the world, outside the protected boundaries of a place like Regis, before making this lifetime decision.

. . . . . . . . . . . . .

Even as I pursued admission to the Jesuits, I also completed college applications. It was almost like having a double life, as I talked about the Jesuits with one small group of friends and discussed colleges with everyone else. Letters of acceptance—or rejection—were arriving at the same time as I received word from the Jesuits, and for a couple of weeks it seemed to be the only topic of conversation at school.

Princeton had been my first choice because of its reputation for classics. But Princeton put me on its waiting list, and I had to choose from among the other schools. Mom was adamant that I go to Fordham. Its location in the Bronx made it seem safe and familiar. If I went there, I would live at home. Its cost was modest compared with the Ivy League and it had offered a generous scholarship. But Columbia was what I wanted. I could live on campus yet still come home for a dinner or Sunday gatherings. The idea of Manhattan being there for the taking was very exciting. Columbia's core curriculum revolved around the Greek and Latin classics that I loved. And as I had told Father Mc-Guire, my internal struggles around entering the Jesuits had become framed as a question of whether I had proved myself worthy of being a priest. Attending Columbia meant thrusting myself into an environment where Catholicism was not the norm.

To my astonishment, Dad resolved the struggle between me and Mom by declaring that I could go to Columbia. Dad rarely disagreed with her. He let her make the basic decisions affecting how we lived. But every once in a long while he asserted his authority as "head of the house" and said, in effect, "No, we're doing this." Whenever he did that, and it happened rarely, Mom relented.

Dad's approval of Columbia also surprised me because the school had not offered any financial assistance. Dad's salary was modest, and we didn't have much beyond necessities; we certainly had nothing resembling luxury. We had taken only one vacation in all my childhood. We didn't own a car. We lived in a two-bedroom rental. Why wouldn't Columbia offer me a funding package? Where would the money for my Ivy League education come from? What made my ever-frugal father, who always deferred to Sophie, support me? Dad calculated that, with tuition, dormitory, meal plan, and books, he could pay for my four years of college with a $10,000 loan along with some dipping into family savings. But he also told me that I needed to find a job for what he described as "pocket money." With that, the decision was made.

There were still, however, a couple more months of school. By March, the demands of classes, the Hearn, and the stress of the choices that loomed were taking their toll. I began to beg Mom to call Regis and say that I was sick so I could stay home to catch up on schoolwork. Ordinarily, Mom would have dismissed a request like that. "You do what you have to and don't give me any baloney" was her approach to the stresses of life. But she must have seen what the year was taking out of me because she did make the calls.

The moment that best captures how hard the last year at Regis was came in Miami that May, at the National Catholic Forensic League Tournament. This was the culmination of four years of hard work. With the stakes so high, the tension was inescapable, and it showed in all of us, Mr. LaBonte especially. But Regis performed well, and I won the boys' extemp championship.

After the awards dinner on Saturday, a group of us went strolling on the beach. I was walking with Mary Ann, a dramatics speaker from Cardinal Spellman

High. Mary Ann was, frankly, beautiful. She had an air of sophistication that suffused her oratorical skills. That night, maybe because of the setting, maybe because of the confidence I was feeling after winning a national championship, I found myself holding her hand as we walked on the sand. We listened to the waves and looked up at the twinkling stars that were barely visible in the Bronx. Soon we were kissing. I felt a surge of romantic feeling that I had never experienced. In the midst of this, Vinny came running down the beach toward us. "LaBonte is looking for you," he shouted in the direction of the Regis team members. "He said it's too late to be out and you need to be in your rooms." The urgency in Vinny's manner was impossible to ignore, so several of us rushed back to the hotel.

The next morning, with the lobby full of debaters and coaches checking out of the hotel, Mr. LaBonte approached me and the rest of the team who were gathered together. He'd barely reached us when he launched into a harsh criticism of our irresponsibility in being out so late without telling him where we were going. Suddenly, before I could stop myself, I began screaming at him. "All we were doing was walking on the beach," I yelled. "The tournament was over. I won a championship. I wasn't doing anything wrong!" This was so out of character that Mr. LaBonte just stared at me without responding. I noticed everyone else nearby looking at us, and I walked away. At least for a moment, the boy had stopped being good.

. . . . . . . . . . . . .

Graduation was two weeks later. Parents and teachers gathered in the auditorium as all of us in the senior class marched onstage to receive our diplomas. It was hard to believe my time at Regis was ending. For all the struggle and all the stress, those four years had opened up whole new worlds of people and ideas and places. It had become home and family to me, and I wanted it to last forever.

# 13

...........

## Working in the City

The week after graduation, I started my first job. The issue of my working had been a sore spot between me and Dad for years. The first time it came up I was ten. A couple of friends had paper routes. Nothing could be simpler than a paper route in Parkchester. Large, adjacent buildings with elevators made it easy on delivery boys. Rain, snow, cold: you went up and down elevators, dropping off a couple of dozen papers, and then lugged a second pile a few yards to the next building. It was like free money. One day in the schoolyard, a kid with a route brought his savings passbook to show around. He had over $300. To me, this was riches. That night, I brought it up.

"I want to get a paper route. Billy got one over the summer. Konrad's been doing it for a year now, and he's got all this money."

I saw Mom glance quickly at Dad. Without taking a breath to reflect, he said, "Absolutely not. No son of mine is going out at six in the morning to haul papers through the streets."

"What streets?" I asked. "This is Parkchester. There are no streets. Anyway, it's good money."

"What do you need money for? You get an allowance. What do you need that you're not getting?"

"That's not the point," I responded.

"Don't 'point' me. I've said what I'm saying. It's out of the question."

The next day, I pleaded my case with Mom. This was a hopeless cause, I knew, since they almost never disagreed on anything. But I wasn't going to drop it.

"I don't understand why I can't have a paper route," I said to her while she prepared dinner.

"I'm sorry, but your father has made up his mind."

"But why? It makes no sense. I get up early anyway. Think of the money I could make."

"There are more important things than money."

"What's that mean?" I said.

"Look," she explained, "it's a matter of pride. Your father had it very hard as a child. He had to work from the time he was a young boy. It's important for him to know that he can support his family. If you go out delivering papers, he's worried that people will talk. I'm telling you to drop it."

Though I didn't press the issue again, Mom had piqued my curiosity. Unlike her, who launched into a story about the old days with the slightest encouragement, Dad hardly ever talked about growing up. One day, not long after the paper route debacle, I asked him what the Depression had been like since, as a topic, it was still very alive among adults in the 1950s. He didn't say much, but he did tell me about his first job, at the age of nine. In those days, movie theaters handed out programs. After school and on Saturdays, the local theater owner had him fold them and hand them to patrons. In exchange, he got to watch the movie and eat all the popcorn he wanted. Dad didn't say it, but the implication was obvious. It was popcorn or hunger. He was working to eat.

Later, in high school, I tried again. As guys turned sixteen and were able to get working papers in New York, some friends had summer jobs, mostly as baggers in supermarkets. Dad was no more agreeable to this than he had been to the paper route. But now, after high school, work was OK. In his eyes, you were supposed to work after high school. Besides, Columbia was going to cost a pretty penny. It was only right that I should be working now.

.............

Dad had spent most of his adult life working for Mr. Berkey. He started soon after the war, when Berkey owned a small camera shop, Peerless, near the Chrysler Building in Manhattan. Dad was the bookkeeper, and the business was small enough that everyone knew each other. From selling cameras, Mr. Berkey started acting as middleman for his customers, taking their rolls of film to be developed, which were passed on to Kodak for processing. But this was now the fifties. Business was good. Families were buying cameras, taking lots of pictures, and needing to have the film developed. Mr. Berkey didn't see why he couldn't challenge a corporation like Kodak and do his own film processing. And so Berkey Photo was born. The operation relocated to a big building on Broadway, in a low-rent district below Union Square. Offices were on the top floor, and the processing plant below. By the mid-1960s there was no question that "Berkey," as everyone who worked there called the company, was prospering.

Even as the business grew, Mr. Berkey was still very much a presence in its day-to-day life. He knew and kept track of the people who worked for him. In some ways, it was still like a family business. In summer, when the business was shorthanded because employees took their vacations just as the supply of film to process skyrocketed, the slack was taken up by sons and daughters of employees who needed temporary jobs.

Almost all of these summer workers were put in the plant. But maybe because of Dad's talking about my speech and debate victories or because a kid going to Columbia was by definition brainy, I got assigned to the offices on the eighth floor. I was handed over to Evelyn, a short, rotund woman well into middle age who was in charge of the payroll department. *Department* was perhaps too fancy a word. Payroll consisted of Evelyn and one assistant who, I soon learned, turned over with great regularity.

Evelyn wasn't easy. She had a crusty exterior and was a stickler for accuracy. She would stand behind her assistant, who was hunched over the adding machine and a time card, watching as the poor clerk added the hours and minutes of each employee. No mistake escaped Evelyn. The summer I was there, her assistant was a young woman in the advance guard of what everyone would soon be calling hippies. Dora had long, straight hair that reached far down her back; she wore loose clothes and a shawl that obscured the shape of her body. Dora could be fun. She lived in the neighborhood and told me about clubs she had gone to and music she had heard in the East Village. But to Evelyn she was a slacker. When, toward the end of the summer, Dora made the mistake of snapping back after being dressed down for an error, Evelyn sent her packing.

Yet, amazingly, Evelyn and I got along famously. She was the first adult who wasn't either family or a teacher with whom I had sustained contact. She offered a glimpse into a world that was foreign to me then but would become more familiar in the coming decades. She was a lefty Jew. Of course, coming from a family as conservative as mine, who had no connection to anyone to the left of a moderate Democrat, I thought of her as simply "liberal." But the world she grew up in on the Lower East Side was a place where the political spectrum started with New Dealers and moved left. She swore by FDR, adored Bobby Kennedy, and already hated the Vietnam War. Unlike in the matter of how to do the payroll, where she brooked no opposition, Evelyn loved discussing politics. Employees dropped into her office often. It took no effort to jump from whether a request for vacation had been approved to the demonstrations that Martin Luther King Jr. was leading in Chicago or to Ronald Reagan's gubernatorial campaign in California. I loved the joking and camaraderie, the way folks could argue but not have it linger.

Evelyn put me on a special project. She had decided to create order out of the personnel records. Each employee had a folder stuffed with every document about his or her time with the company. There were scraps of paper with scribblings like "Melvin, $5 raise, 6/1/65" or "Put Juan on night shift—10% increase." This passed muster when Berkey employed fifty and knew everyone, but now the workforce exceeded eight hundred, and the files were approaching chaos.

Evelyn, who loved poring through office supply catalogs, had found a company that made expandable manila folders. The front face had a very neat grid of boxes, similar to what an Excel spreadsheet looks like, on which could be entered in chronological order every event in an employee's work history. Evelyn set me up at an empty table in the corner of her office, and that was it. From Acanfora to Zuckerman, I was to spend my summer making my way through every folder and creating order.

Anyone else might have been driven stark raving mad by the job. Painstakingly precise, it required going through the same process over and over as I moved from one employee's file to the next. But I loved it. The job appealed to some ingrained Catholic desire for a universe of perfect order. Each file was like a mystery needing a solution. I was decoding the work history of each company employee. If someone had told me that this is what historians do for a living, I would have signed up on the spot. I was becoming privy to a thousand whispered secrets I was never meant to overhear.

Most of all, the world of salaries and wages, of what the reward for leaving home each morning amounted to, opened up before me. The unskilled batch workers in the factory earned sixty-five dollars a week, the starting wage in 1966. The office workers took home more, though their pay stubs were still modest. Then there was the small number of executives, who seemed rich to me. I'd be lying if I claimed these disparities offended me back then. Why shouldn't someone wearing a tie earn more than someone in overalls? That's why I was getting an education. That's why Dad was doing better than my uncles who worked with their hands.

Except for when Dad taught me how to budget my allowance, we *never* spoke about money at home. Mom, of course, was filled with adages that she spouted with regularity. Money doesn't grow on trees. A penny saved is a penny earned. They all meant the same thing: we don't have much. I had no idea how much Dad or anyone in the family earned, or how much an apartment in Park-chester rented for. I remember how, on Friday nights, Dad always came home with a small wad of bills, and after dinner, as I watched television, he and Mom sat at the table, a few envelopes and a sheet of paper spread before them, and a pencil in Dad's hand for calculation. How much was needed for the rent enve-lope? The clothing envelope? The Sunday church-contribution envelope? The Christmas-and-birthday-gifts envelope? Once he had apportioned the neces-sary expenses, the remainder got divided: allowances for each of them and money that Mom deposited into their savings account for the rainy day that was sure to arrive. Their bent-over backs were testimony to the gravity of the task.

Now, going through the files at Berkey, I suddenly knew every detail of my family's economic history. When Mr. Berkey rehired Dad in 1959, after a two-year hiatus during which Dad had tried, without much success, to work on Wall Street, Dad was making $125 a week. Seven years later, he was earning over $14,000 a year. There was enough so that Mom, who had taken driving lessons and received her license a few years earlier, was able to buy a used car that summer and pay cash for it. And there was enough so that I understood why Columbia hadn't offered me a scholarship. Even though Dad was doing better, he and Mom retained their old instincts. We had no debt. As far as the financial aid officers with their scientific formulas could tell, here was a man who could bear the weight of a college loan. He and Mom were being punished for their virtue.

I learned more about Dad that summer than the record of his earnings. In some of my most vivid memories of childhood, I am lying in my crib in the morn-ing. Dad is in the bathroom, and I can hear him retching. Mom is pacing around the room, tense from the sound. It didn't take much insight to figure out it made him sick to his stomach to contemplate heading to the office each morning.

Years later these impressions lingered, but I was seeing someone different in the office. At Peerless, Dad had been the bookkeeper. He didn't have a college education, and his efforts at taking night courses had never led to the fabled "CPA" after his name. When Berkey took the business public, he hired an ac-counting firm to balance the books. Dad became a jack-of-all-trades number cruncher, but most of all, he spent his day approving and signing checks. Years of experience made it obvious to Berkey that Vincent was utterly trustworthy. If checks needed his authorization, there was no chance anyone would make off with the company cash. Mr. Berkey's respect had made its way into Dad's psyche. As I watched him each day, I noticed a confidence I didn't see at home. He moved around the offices with assurance. Coworkers stopped by his desk with problems for him to resolve. They seemed to like him too. He was playful, told jokes, and had a mischievous sense of humor. He winked when he had put something over on you.

A couple of times each week that summer, we spent lunch hour together. We walked around the neighborhood, doing the circuit of Union Square, watching the characters standing on wooden crates hold forth about politics, the hordes of workers on lunch hour streaming in and out of Klein's department store with its bargain basement. Sometimes we headed down Broadway. He showed me the Strand, a bigger used bookstore than I ever imagined existed. He took me to the streets that were about to become the East Village but that Dad still knew as the Lower East Side, where he had lived until he was ten. It made his life seem real, the boy in the movie theater who ate popcorn for dinner because that's all there was. Dad seemed almost happy on these lunch hour tours, or at least livelier than he was at home.

The intimacy of these walks encouraged me to float questions about his family, and particularly about his father. Small Grandpa had died when I was an infant. He appears in a couple of photographs, a short man dressed in a suit, his head stiff on his neck and the eyes showing intense discomfort. In the movies of Mom and Dad's wedding, he's there enjoying the high spirits that weddings brought. During the few times each year when we visited Dad's sisters, they rarely mentioned "Papa." Now I learned why. Yes, the family had been poor, the way many Italian immigrant families were, and the Depression had made things more precarious. But Grandpa, as Dad now told it, could be scary. He drank. He went on binges, disappearing for days, and when he returned he'd be without a job. Sometimes he erupted in violent rages. Aunt Tessie would hide my Dad, the youngest, under the bed or behind a dresser, to escape Grandpa's wrath.

These stories dribbled out in response to my questions. Dad offered little commentary and no adornment. They were things that happened a long time ago. There wasn't much emotional nuance in my family's world, no psychological probing or commentary. I didn't draw many conclusions from what I learned, other than a feeling of sadness at how hard it must have been. But I realized, more clearly than ever, why he let himself be drawn so fully into Mom's family. And I understood as well why he supported my choice of Columbia. Having a son at an Ivy League college proved that he was a success at supporting his family and bettering the lives of his children.

. . . . . . . . . . . . .

Berkey was a unionized company. Except for a few employees, Dad among them, everyone had a time card. Each afternoon, when the clock hit five, there was a mass exodus from the office.

Despite working thirty-five hours a week, at that magic hour of five I became a kid without responsibilities for the first time since I had started high school. I was still living at home and of course had to make some accounting of my activities. If I stayed downtown past dinner, Mom wanted to know what I did and with whom. I also dutifully signed over my paycheck each week and, in exchange, received a somewhat enhanced allowance. But all things considered, I had more freedom that summer than ever before in my life. I had no summer reading, no Latin passages to translate, no debate cases to research. And on Friday afternoons, no preparations for weekend tournaments that tied my stomach into knots.

My Regis friends were in the same situation. We were biding time until we left for college or, in the case of Vinny, Bob, and Jim, entered seminary. A couple of times a week, we congregated somewhere in Manhattan after work. We went to the Delacorte Theater to see Shakespeare or to other free performances in Central Park. We attended Mostly Mozart Festival concerts at Lincoln Center. We congregated at Luigino's on West Forty-Seventh Street and lingered over spaghetti and meatballs; then we headed to Broadway to look at the blazing marquees announcing hit plays. Or we met at Mama Bertolotti's on West Fourth Street in the Village and after dinner wandered through Washington Square Park. Sometimes, if I had no plans, I'd go to the Strand after work and page through worlds I could barely dream about. I headed to Washington Square Park on my own, watching men strum their guitars and knowing I'd never be cool like that.

Some of this time I spent doing what I came to call "looking." Most of the sexual experiences during my Regis years felt like accidents. Who could predict if some husband on the way home to his family would lock eyes with me on the subway? Now, on days when I spent my lunch hour alone or roamed Union Square and the East Village at the end of the day before heading to Parkchester, I was more aware of men on the street whose eyes wandered like mine, whose look lingered too long, and who locked glances with me in a way that spoke desire.

Several decades and many worlds later, when I found myself teaching college courses on the history of sexuality, I labeled these years in which I came of age "the worst time to be queer." I displayed PowerPoint images of the cheap lesbian pulp novels that circulated widely in the 1950s and 1960s. My students would comment on the tacky vocabulary. Strange, twisted, tortured: words like these saturated the jacket copy. Today, that language seems so overwrought that it can't help but provoke laughter. It reads like the content of a comedy skit.

But in 1966, as I walked through Manhattan and those glances made desire rise inside me, each one was like an electric jolt that, yes, tortured me. I looked and I wanted, yet I also looked away from my wants in almost the same instant. I looked *all* the time—"desperately" as the pulp paperback copy said—yet I almost fled from any man who looked back. But then, "desperate" for more, I returned the next day to the block where some guy had checked me out in the hope that he would walk by again. Could I convince myself, a good Catholic boy who promised not to sin again, that I wasn't intending for something to happen? Conveniently for me, nothing could happen, because I had to return to the office before lunch hour was up, or meet Regis friends at a movie theater, or arrive home for Mom's dinner. If I took a walk in which I engaged in too much looking, instinct had me repeating indulgences as I hurried back to Berkey's offices. How many times did I have to whisper "Mother of Mercy, pray for us" to erase a lunch hour's worth of looks?

The subways posed a different kind of threat. At Regis, by the time I boarded the subway, the crowds had started to thin as downtown workers exited at each of the uptown stops. Now, I was getting on the train at Union Square at the height of rush hour. Scanning faces on the platform below as I descended the stairs, I was drawn toward the good-looking men clustered near the center of the station. Before too many days had gone by, I discovered that, on the trains arriving on either side of five fifteen, men looking for men congregated at the last door of the fifth car and the first door of the sixth car of the Lexington Avenue express. That's how carefully mapped the geography of gay desire was. At Grand Central another infusion of office workers rushed in, and for the next few minutes we were packed around the pole, several men deep. There were no women here. All eyes looked straight ahead. Hands wandered beneath the field of vision, while butts pressed back against the hardened bulge of another commuter. Once inside this tangle of bodies, there was no leaving. Though I couldn't bring myself to grope a man or press with intention my body against anyone, neither did I push away the hands that touched my crotch. I took in a bit of breath, and except for an involuntary shudder, I moved as little as I could. On days when the train was running fast, it would get to Eighty-Sixth Street before an "accident" might occur. As a mass of passengers flowed out, I hoped that my erection would subside fast. But at least a few times that summer, the train was slow and my sexual yearnings overwrought. My jaw tightened, and I gripped the pole as I ejaculated, praying that the semen didn't soak through and leave stains for the world to see.

More than physical touch distinguished these subway rides from my lunchtime walks or my subway rides as a Regis student. The same men got off work at the same hour and took the same train home every day. After a while I recognized them, just as they recognized me. We were all maneuvering into the train with intention, a community of familiar faces squeezing into a few feet of space and creating a temporary safe zone for sex play. Some of them, especially those exiting in Manhattan, were looking for more than just a four-minute grope.

I noticed one man especially who kept staring in my direction and trying with an ever-so-slight shift in expression to suggest that he was interested. One afternoon, when he exited at Eighty-Sixth Street, I followed. He stopped at the corner of Lexington, across from the pizza shop where I had spent so many afternoons, and told me he lived a few blocks north. "Do you want to come home with me?" he asked. His name was Ted and he worked for an ad agency. He asked me this and that, and I tried to come up with plausible answers that wouldn't allow him to somehow find and contact me. Our conversation remained awkward. While he talked, I was calculating how much time I had before I would be late for dinner. I needn't have worried. Once we got to his place, the sex was hurried and uncomplicated. Ted was probably doing his own calculations, figuring there wasn't much promise of a repeat performance. And in fact, I never could have gone back. How could I and still be sincere in my promise never to sin again?

............

As the summer wore on, the social routine with my Regis friends grew more intense. My evenings at home included phone calls to Vinny and Jim, calls that stretched until Mom's trips into the kitchen, where the phone hung from the wall, grew so frequent that I knew I had to hang up. A series of Saturday excursions got planned. One weekend a bunch of us took the Long Island Railroad to Floral Park, where Bob VerEecke and John Fox lived, and we spent the day grilling burgers and hot dogs over a barbecue as we laughed and horsed around together. Another Saturday took some of us to Connecticut, where Gerry Hackett's family had a summer home. Perhaps the best excursion was to Far Rockaway, where Tommy Gaye's family had a bungalow. We all hooked up in Manhattan and made our way to this beach community that I'd heard about but had never visited. Several of us brought dates. I took Mary Ann. Our romantic walk along the beach in Florida had left me infatuated, and we had already gone on a few dates that summer. To me she remained as sophisticated and beautiful as any girl I had ever met. We were outside, on or near the beach, most of the day. Every radio, it seemed, was playing the same song: "Hot town, summer in the city / Back of my neck getting dirty and gritty / Cool town, evening in the city / Dressing so fine and looking so pretty." The urgency of the rhythm created an energy that flowed through us as we ran along the beach and got our feet wet in the surf. Later, we watched the setting sun turn the clouds over the ocean pink and orange. We lingered as long as we could, each couple making out until it was time to begin our long treks home.

Despite the freedom of that summer, doom hovered around the edges of my consciousness as the weeks passed. I knew college was supposed to be a great opportunity, but I was dreading it. Not so much the going to college, since I didn't have a clear sense of what that would be like or what it would mean to live somewhere other than the apartment with Mom, Dad, and Jimmy. Yes, I'd have to study a lot, and I'd be thrown in with a group of guys I didn't know. But I'd done that once before when I came to Regis, and it had worked out pretty well.

No, I was dreading the impending loss of a world where I had made a place for myself. "Blood is thicker than water," Mom had intoned throughout my childhood. When I wanted to join my Parkchester friends on a summer day, the bonds of family *always* trumped these ties. Regis had kept these demands in check. Mom couldn't argue that a day at Grandma's house was more important than the state championship tournament, and she wasn't going to stop me from staying home on a Sunday because I had so much schoolwork to do. Over those four years, I spent a lot more time with my Regis friends than with Mom and Dad.

Many were going away to college. Though we wouldn't see each other a lot, I knew that with letters and their trips home the circuits of communication would remain unbroken. But Vinny, Jim, and Bob were my inner circle, my lunch partners each day, the guys I goofed with, as we said back then. They were entering seminary. St. Andrew's was actually nearer than some of the colleges that other friends were going to, but it seemed an eternity away. They were leaving to do God's work. They were becoming part of a worldwide community—a family to which they would belong forever and to which I never would. Even though Jesuits prided themselves on being of the world, not apart from it, the three of them were about to relinquish a lot of personal freedom. There'd be no more telephone calls in the evenings, no moviegoing. Early in their novitiate year they would enter a monthlong period of silent meditation. Thirty days without even a word from Jim or Vinny? It was beyond imagining.

The three of them were reporting to seminary at the beginning of August. Late in July, a group of us planned a final dinner together. We congregated on Eighty-Sixth Street and Lexington, the scene of so much after-school hanging out, and then headed east to the Rainbow Lounge. One of the pictures taken by Vinny shows Bob, Tim O'Connor, and me at a table, each in our white short-sleeve shirts with our ties removed, as glum as three teenage boys have ever looked. The camera catches each of us staring, disconnected from one another, lost in thought. We might as well have been attending a funeral for all the joy that wasn't showing at that table.

When we finished eating, no one could bear to go home. We headed down Lexington Avenue, trying hard to make conversation and bring life to . . . what? Our Last Supper? In the East Seventies, we turned toward Fifth Avenue and the edge of Central Park. We walked until we reached the fountain outside the Plaza Hotel and the Paris Theater. We lingered a bit, but it was getting late and we each had to take our separate trains to Lower Manhattan, to Queens, to Long Island, and to the Bronx. Did we hug each other goodbye? I can't remember. I know there weren't any tears—teenage boys would never do that.

I rode home to Parkchester, more bereft than I had ever felt. Regis had given me a whole new life, a life of the mind that I treasured more than I could have imagined four years earlier. And I had found at Regis a whole crew of guys with whom I had shared this life. They were dearer to me than anything. They had become my family. What would I do without them?

Scamporlino family, early 1930s. My
mother, Sophie, is the youngest.

*This page*

Wedding photo,
Vincent and Sophie
D'Emilio, 1947.

.............

*Far page*

Big Grandma
holding me on my
first birthday, with
Small Grandma
watching, 1949.

Dressed for my first
Holy Communion,
with Mom and
Dad, 1956.

My brother Jimmy's first
birthday, with Big Grandma,
Big Grandpa, and cousins
Laura and Paul, 1958.

Playing with my
brother in Big
Grandma's backyard,
circa 1959.

*Far page*
Kissing Cardinal Spell-
man's hand at an award
ceremony for the Mooney
Essay Contest, 1962.

.............

*This page*
Graduation party with
my St. Raymond's friends,
Tavern on the Green in
Central Park, 1962. I am
seated, second from right.

With trophies won at a
high school speech and
debate tournament, 1964.

With coaches and members of the Regis Hearn Society, at an airport while traveling to a debate tournament, 1964.

Regis senior class retreat,
1965. I am kneeling behind
the sign.

Retreat at
Gonzaga
Oct. 28 1965

# COLUMBIA 🛇 SPECTATOR
## FOUNDED 1877

Vol. CXII, No. 102          NEW YORK, N.Y., THURSDAY, APRIL 25, 1968          FIVE CENTS

# Faculty Recommends Halt to Gym Construction; Campus Closed Down, SDS Holds Kirk's Office

## Protesters Occupy 2 New Buildings

By ROBERT STULBERG

The University administration yesterday called New York City police onto the campus and later sealed it off during a confused day of protests, in which defiant demonstrators occupied several administrative offices in Low Library and three University buildings.

During the course of the day, which was marked by several near-violent outbreaks, members of Students for a Democratic Society barricaded themselves inside the offices of President Grayson Kirk, while militant black students and community protesters remained in control of Hamilton Hall.

Late yesterday afternoon, School of Architecture students in Avery Hall refused to leave the building when the administration ordered all buildings closed. As of 2 a.m. today, students still had completely free access to Avery.

Early this morning, more than fifty students also moved into Fayerweather Hall and a number of

JUST WALK AWAY: Dean Coleman (r.) speaks to reporters a few minutes after he and Proctor Kahn (l.) were released by the black students barricading Hamilton Hall. He stated that he had been well treated but had not felt "free to leave."

## Outsiders Influence SDS Action

By MICHAEL STERN

Members of Columbia SDS led 450 demonstrators — almost all of

passed out of SDS's and their supporters' control.

Community protests against the

## Offers by Administration Are Directed To Blacks Barricading Hamilton Hall

The faculty of Columbia College yesterday recommended that the University arrange an "immediate suspension of on-site excavation of the gymnasium facility in Morningside Park."

The recommendation was one of several passed at an emergency faculty meeting held yesterday afternoon in response to a student takeover of Hamilton Hall which continued into its second day. Late last night several offers and demands had been exchanged between University officials and black students occupying Hamilton Hall and it appeared that informal negotiations were actually in progress.

Black students in Hamilton have apparently focused on but two of their six demands: stopping gym construction and granting amnesty for all those participating in the current demonstrations.

The faculty voted overwhelmingly in favor of an immediate suspension of gymnasium construction and recommended that the University be prepared to review the location and character of the gymnasium with a group of community spokesmen designated by the mayor of New York.

In a University statement prepared late last night, President Grayson Kirk indicated that he would ask the Trustees to consider the faculty's recommendations. It is understood that Dr. Kirk is attempting to arrange a special meeting of the Trustees for today.

The prepared statement also noted that yesterday evening the

strators sang or listened to various speakers, mostly SDS leaders.

Periodic announcements

*Columbia Spectator* front page, April 22, 1968, when protesters released the college dean from Hamilton Hall. I am the face in the upper left of the photo.

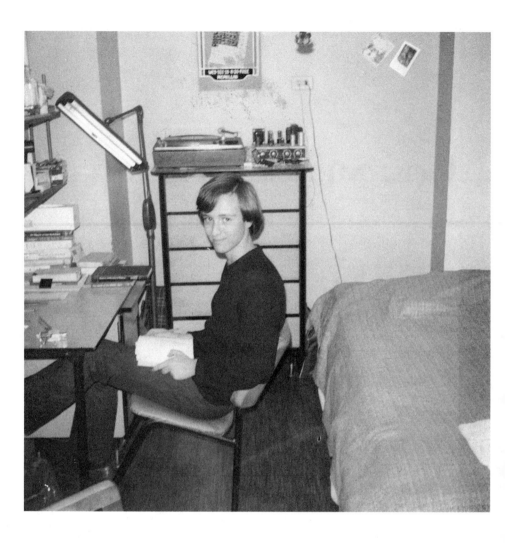

*This page*

At my desk in my small bedroom at 400 Riverside Drive, senior year.

*Far page*

Selective Service form declaring me unfit for military service, 1970.

In cap and gown, Columbia campus, 1970, with housemates. Jim Hazen, Kurt Meyers, me, and Jack Collins.

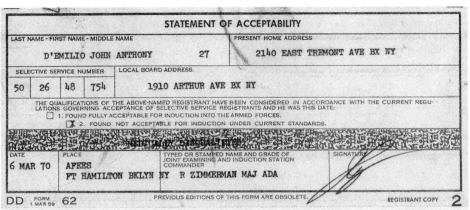

STATEMENT OF ACCEPTABILITY

| LAST NAME - FIRST NAME - MIDDLE NAME | | PRESENT HOME ADDRESS |
|---|---|---|
| D'EMILIO JOHN ANTHONY | 27 | 2140 EAST TREMONT AVE BX NY |

| SELECTIVE SERVICE NUMBER | | | | LOCAL BOARD ADDRESS |
|---|---|---|---|---|
| 50 | 26 | 48 | 754 | 1910 ARTHUR AVE BX NY |

THE QUALIFICATIONS OF THE ABOVE-NAMED REGISTRANT HAVE BEEN CONSIDERED IN ACCORDANCE WITH THE CURRENT REGULATIONS GOVERNING ACCEPTANCE OF SELECTIVE SERVICE REGISTRANTS AND HE WAS THIS DATE:

☐ 1. FOUND FULLY ACCEPTABLE FOR INDUCTION INTO THE ARMED FORCES.

☒ 2. FOUND NOT ACCEPTABLE FOR INDUCTION UNDER CURRENT STANDARDS.

MEDICAL DISQUALIFICATION

| DATE | PLACE | TYPED OR STAMPED NAME AND GRADE OF JOINT EXAMINING AND INDUCTION STATION COMMANDER | SIGNATURE |
|---|---|---|---|
| 6 MAR 70 | AFEES FT HAMILTON BKLYN NY | R ZIMMERMAN MAJ ADA | |

DD FORM 62
1 MAR 59

PREVIOUS EDITIONS OF THIS FORM ARE OBSOLETE.

REGISTRANT COPY 2

Any inquiry relative to personal status should be referred to your Local Board

# PART III

# Everything Changes

..............

# 14

.............

## God Is Dead

For decades, Mom had a ready explanation for the direction my life took. She blamed Regis for everything. Regis ruined me. The Jesuits taught me to think for myself; now I'm a lapsed Catholic and never set foot in a church unless it's old and in Europe. The Jesuits taught me useless languages like Greek and Latin; I became a blue-jeans-wearing professor with no common sense instead of a straight-as-an-arrow accountant wearing shirts with button-down collars. Regis sent me to debate tournaments across the country and gave me a taste of the world. But for that, I'd have always lived at most a bus ride away, eating her food every Sunday.

When I challenged her line of reasoning, she glared at me. She looked up from the stove, waved the utensil she was holding during one of these outbursts, and spit out: "Don't give me that. Look at your brother! He went to Regis, too. He doesn't go to church, he's a college professor, and he's another world traveler. It was Regis and the Jesuits, believe me!"

Mom was wrong about Regis. Yes, it was an extraordinary place. It took a far-flung group of brainy Catholic boys, brought us together in a rarefied academic environment, and honed our intellectual skills. But it didn't quite teach us to think for ourselves. Instead of reciting by memory the content of the Baltimore Catechism, I now could argue into the ground (or, with my debate training, fancied that I could) anyone who dared challenge my faith.

No, Mom. It wasn't Regis that ruined me.

In some ways going to college was thrilling. I was living on campus and away from home, not just for an overnight tournament but week after week. Even though I was still in New York, the distance between Parkchester and Morningside Heights might as well have been measured in light-years. I had no curfews, and I didn't have to account for where I'd been. Not a soul that my family knew was likely to spy me on Manhattan's Upper West Side.

Halfway into orientation week, on a night with no planned activities, several of us headed down Broadway to the Gold Rail, a few blocks south of campus. The drinking age in New York was eighteen, and I had turned legal a couple of days before. Most of the rest of us were not quite there yet, but I never remember anyone getting carded at the Rail. Unlike the West End bar, whose ties to figures like Allen Ginsberg gave it an aura of sophisticated cool, the Gold Rail was a drinking dive. Small, dark, and smoky, it boasted a nightly blue plate special that was so cheap it was practically free food. The intent was clear: "Come in, guys, and spend your money on booze!"

That first night, six of us stuffed ourselves into a booth along the back wall. Jack, a friend from Regis who was one of "the clique," was there, as was Jim Periconi (known to all as "Peri"), another Regis grad. They brought their roommates: Kurt, an intense kid from New Jersey with a wicked sense of humor, and Bill, a New England prep school graduate whose father was a New Orleans lawyer. I still didn't have a permanent place in the dorms and had been temporarily assigned to a double room with Jim Hazen. He was from Erie, Pennsylvania, and unlike anyone I'd ever met. A big guy whose movements suggested the word *lumbering*, he spoke slowly and casually, as if he, and we, had all the time in the world to listen to not much of anything. Accustomed to the rapid-fire speech of New York kids, I didn't know what to make of Hazen. But his goodness was apparent, and before long it became clear that anyone lulled by his speech patterns was in for a surprise. His intellect was razor-sharp, and in his small-town way, he could shred a flawed argument into tatters. None of us, I'm sure, would have predicted on this first off-campus outing that Jack, Kurt, Hazen, and I would become the best of friends over the next four years.

Our server was a hefty young woman with a booming voice, a prerequisite for working at the Rail, where the din was ear-splitting and ordinary conversation was conducted at a high decibel level. She could carry four pitchers, or six mugs, of beer without a spill. We immediately nicknamed her "Steina Light" after her most common call to the bartender. But that night, we were not into single steins. Pitchers arrived in rapid succession. At some point Jack suggested I try a screwdriver to celebrate my birthday. I'd never had hard liquor before—Mom and Dad didn't keep any in the apartment and only drank an occasional beer—so I couldn't quite fathom the perils floating in a small glass of orange juice with vodka. I was on my fourth in no time at all. A couple of hours later, we were lurching back to campus. I was drunk out of my mind, but where the others seemed to have a judicious respect for the effects of alcohol, I was enthralled by this new sensation. Mesmerized by the way the buildings on Broadway were moving, I found I could intensify the effect by twirling around as I walked. Hazen tried to shepherd me along, and Jack issued friendly warnings, but there was no talking sense into me. I kept spinning in circles all the way to the dorm, and then heaved my guts into a toilet for what seemed like hours.

.............

Alcohol was the least of what Columbia placed in front of me. My faith, my intellect, my sense of who I was in the world: all were in constant turmoil almost from the moment I set foot on campus.

I remember a conversation from the previous spring with Father McGuire, when I explained why I was deciding not to enter seminary. I couldn't admit how agitated I still was over my sexual desires. Instead, I told him what I was telling myself and what certainly had more than a trace of truth: like the saints I most admired, I needed to test my Catholicism among a world of nonbelievers.

At Columbia the tests came steadily. For orientation week, freshmen were divided into groups based on common interest. Led by an appropriate faculty member, they met throughout the week. In my application essay, I had written about my religious faith, and so I found myself in a group led by the Protestant campus minister. I sat there stunned as he informed us that "God is dead." He had us read and discuss *Life against Death* by Norman O. Brown, whose goal was to reinterpret Freud for the contemporary world. Mom would have scoffed at the notion of an unconscious mental life. Nor did the Catholicism I'd imbibed have much use for this way of thinking. But here I was being told that it was time to look deep inside and face my repressed desires. This was exactly what I was trying not to do!

These discussions were barely over when the incoming class assembled in the auditorium of Ferris Booth Hall, the new student center. There, a history professor, James Shenton, was introduced to us. Shenton, I learned later, was one of the most popular professors on campus. He had a reputation for delivering lectures that often led the class to applaud wildly when the session ended. This night, from where I was sitting, he seemed to be lecturing without a prepared text. He set up a debate between two opponents, one defending a war in the most chauvinistic nationalist rhetoric and the other criticizing the war with reasoning that drew on the loftiest American ideals. It seemed evident that Shenton was talking about Vietnam, a subject that, except for an occasional extemp speech, I had given little thought to, but that my patriotic, conservative parents supported unconditionally. The drama intensified as the two sides squared off, yet the actual language remained strangely vague. And then, as Shenton's booming voice reached a crescendo, the mystery unraveled as we learned that the antiwar orator was Abraham Lincoln, challenging on the floor of Congress the decision to go to war with Mexico. They're teaching me that God is dead and war is wrong, and I haven't even started classes yet!

. . . . . . . . . . . . .

I approached my fall courses with all the cockiness of a successful Regis double major who had been inducted into the Homeric Academy. What challenges could Columbia hold for me, beyond the excitement of learning more?

It didn't take long to discover. Columbia had a math and science requirement, not my talent, and my adviser encouraged me to take a course nicknamed "Poet's Math." It was designed for students for whom math was not their strength and who didn't need to learn any for career purposes. And it was true. We learned no math skills at all. Instead, the professor spent the semester lecturing on theoretical conundrums, such as squaring the circle. I couldn't make any sense of his lectures and had to beg the graduate teaching assistant for help. Then there was the language requirement, which I was sure, after my Regis experience, would be easy. I found myself in class with a teacher who, from the first meeting, spoke only French to us and expected us to understand and respond in kind, which most of my peers did. Finally, there were the horrors of Professor Landow's English class. My high school record allowed me to place out of freshman composition and register for a literature course designed for "advanced" students. Jack and I both signed on for a section where we spent the entire semester reading a single book, *Bleak House* by Charles Dickens. I could not understand why our professor had us go through each chapter at the same pace I might have translated Virgil's *Aeneid*. Apparently, few of my classmates grasped it either, and Landow's response to our difficulties was to throw harsh insults in our direction.

If I found any intellectual comfort that first semester, at least early on, it came through the required humanities and contemporary civilization courses. Columbia was famous for its core curriculum. It immersed students in a survey of the literature, philosophy, and culture of the West from the ancients to the early twentieth century. The two-semester humanities sequence was very familiar. I had already read Homer and Virgil in the original as well as the great

Greek tragedies in translation. Wallace Gray, the kind-faced professor who taught my section, always looked benevolently in my direction as it became apparent that I loved our readings and the issues they raised.

A companion course, Contemporary Civilization (or CC as we dubbed it), took us through the great thinkers from Plato to Nietzsche. At first, it no more challenged my intellectual cockiness than did the humanities course. Plato's sensibility seemed Catholic in everything but name. The Old Testament and the early Christian philosophers were old hat. When we read Augustine, I patiently explained to my classmates the difference between predestination and foreknowledge. Protestants believed in the former, I announced, and it stripped man of free will. But Catholics simultaneously recognized the omniscience of the Creator and the freedom He bestowed on us to choose between good and evil. In the midst of my disquisition, our instructor, Mr. Connor, thrust an arm outward, shook a finger in my direction, and proclaimed in mock horror: "Young man, you must have been educated by Jesuits!" I felt caught and exposed, but after class Connor explained that he, too, had gone to a Jesuit school. Only the Jesuits, he said, could train an adolescent boy's mind to argue like that.

The course continued along familiar paths for a while longer. Aquinas's proofs of God's existence comforted me immensely. I dismissed the dictum of Thomas Hobbes, that life was nasty, brutish, and short, as the rants of a crabby old man. But by spring semester, as I encountered Enlightenment philosophers, my moral foundation was shaken to its roots. After David Hume offered his five proofs that God did not exist, I became a confused Catholic soul. My inability to counter his arguments so agitated me that for the rest of the semester, as the class marched through Kant, Hegel, and Nietzsche, I wandered lost, unable to make sense of what they had written.

Jack and Periconi had enrolled in different sections of CC, and we were all reading the same pages each week. Late at night, after we had prepared for the next day's class, we gathered in a campus coffeehouse and earnestly debated the content of the course. Now and then on weekends, Regis friends who were attending supposedly safe Catholic schools like Georgetown or Boston College would meet us on Morningside Heights. They, too, were experiencing intellectual crises. Together we huddled, struggling over questions about God, the purpose of life, and the content of ethical living.

More often than not, no matter how lofty the subject of these conversations when we started, by the end it came around to sex. Ours was not, however, the banter of adolescent boys. We may have been horny, but as serious Catholics, we needed a moral justification to act on our yearnings for sex before marriage. Was love a good enough reason? How could one know that the feelings were love? Short of intercourse, what was permissible? All of us, even those attending Catholic schools, were tasting the freedom that leaving home had given us. We were dating with much less supervision than in high school, and we had stories to share about our moral struggles, whether of the flesh or of the intellect.

But the fact is I was out of my Catholic cocoon. Every one of those Saturday nights ended, my Regis buddies headed back to their new lives, and I was left in my single dorm room having to navigate a world I'd never experienced. At Regis, by senior year, we were all pretty cocky. Our Jesuit teachers stretched our minds every day and made us think we were young men of consequence who would do great things as soldiers for Christ. At Columbia I was no big deal. Forget about the upperclassmen, who seemed so mature and sophisticated. Even many freshmen were several notches up on me. We had students from forty states and a dozen countries, and their worlds seemed not only different, but also bigger, than mine. Take Sam and Eden. Both of them were private school kids. They were outgoing and easy to be with, and I enjoyed their company over meals. But they occupied a different mental universe. For one thing, they already identified in some sense as "radical." I wasn't sure I even grasped what that meant, but I knew it wasn't me. Then there was religion. I nearly fell off my chair the time Sam casually mentioned that he didn't believe in God.

"What do you mean you don't believe in God?" I asked.

"I don't believe in God, that's all. We never went to synagogue, and it's never been a big deal," he said.

"But how can you not believe in God? Where do you think we came from? How do you decide what's right and wrong?"

"Evolution," he responded. "And you still have to make ethical decisions whether you believe in God or not."

I was flabbergasted. The idea that someone not only didn't believe in God but also had grown up without God was something I couldn't take in. All I could think was, "Wow. Without God, he'd never have to worry about whether he was going to hell, whether he'd make it to confession in time, whether his Act of Contrition was sincere. He'd never even have to go to confession." It wasn't as if I began conjuring up a life of blissful dissolution. But the idea of even a day without the dread of damnation? I touched it for maybe an instant before it was sucked out of reach.

These guys talked about sex, too, but they weren't anguished about it and weren't engaged in passionate debate. Their relationships with girlfriends were matter-of-fact. I was having sex, too, of course—with men—but I knew it was wrong, I certainly wasn't going to talk about it at lunch, and I definitely was anguished.

Thankfully, I had a place where I shared at least some of the agony that those first months at Columbia aroused in me. Throughout freshman year, I kept up a correspondence that today, in an era of tweets and texts, I find staggering. To friends from Regis and to some of my former teachers, I sent multipage hand-written letters that, in the course of a semester, would have filled the pages of a book. Vinny, Jim, and Bob received the longest and most frequent letters. I missed them; and the possibility that I might lose them, in the way I had lost my Parkchester friends after I started Regis, was something I did not want to happen.

At first, I filled these letters with stories about life at college, to friends who were cloistered in a Jesuit seminary. I wrote about my dorm, John Jay Hall, a fourteen-story structure filled with single rooms stretching down a corridor that seemed at least the length of a football field. It was an odd experience to be in such close proximity to a group of strangers—shared showers, shared toilets, yet also living behind closed doors. But the rooms were so small that life spilled into the corridor. It felt at times like the animals in the zoo had been let out of our cages, and we were going to make the most of it. I also wrote about homework. The workload at Regis had been heavy, but I prided myself in my ability to succeed at it. At Columbia, three hours a night would have seemed like a vacation. I often found myself studying in the reading room of Butler Library until it closed at 11:00 p.m. When Christmas break came in December, I reported to Vinny that I had more than two thousand pages to read over the holidays.

But more and more, as weeks went by, letters became the place where I played out the troubling debates going on in my head. Why do we believe in an almighty Creator and an eternal afterlife? Isn't it just a way to calm our worries about the death that awaits us? Is hell just a vehicle to keep people in line by promising that sinners will burn forever? Why do we need to claim that Jesus was the Son of God? Why can't we simply acknowledge the beauty of his life and the wisdom of his words? What is the church but another institution controlling our lives? Can't we live a moral life without it?

These questions didn't get posed by someone who knew his mind, had resolved these profound issues, and was now moving on with his life. I was playing out my doubts on paper, testing with a captive audience whom I trusted ideas that I had never entertained. The emotional upheaval that these life-altering perspectives provoked in me must have come through because all of them—each in their own way—tried to offer me comfort, even as they expressed concern over my obvious anxiety and depression. At times, I clearly pushed the limits of what these priests-to-be could handle. After one of my letters questioned the divinity of Jesus, Bob wrote back expressing outrage. "How can you so spit in his face and blind yourself to everything he does and did for you?" he wrote, calling me "cold and heartless."

Fortunately, the back-and-forth of our letter writing was steady, and combined with several trips I made that year to visit them in seminary, we succeeded in calming whatever passions a particular letter unleashed. I was also writing to other friends who were engaging in the same kind of internal debates. Most of all, and to my surprise, I received the strongest validation from some of my teachers. Here they were, Jesuit scholastics and Christian Brothers, affirming my struggles. Mr. DeLuca wrote unambiguously, "What you're questioning needs to be questioned," and advised me to "follow your conscience." Brother August was completely supportive as well. "That you should be rethinking your faith from the roots is terrific," he declared in a letter. Coming from someone who was studying for an advanced degree in theology from Catholic University in DC, his encouragement was deeply comforting.

At some point that year, in one of those lunches with Sam and Eden, one of them suggested that I major in religion. The idea caught me up short. It hadn't occurred to me that a secular college like Columbia might offer religion as a field of study. But sure enough, it did, and as I looked at course descriptions in the catalog and visited the department for information, my enthusiasm grew. Suddenly my doubts and questioning were leading in a productive direction. I would plunge into the study of religion across history and cultures. I would read not only the holy texts but also the criticism and philosophical debates that believers and skeptics engaged in.

Soon after this, on a visit to the Bronx for dinner, I told Mom and Dad about my decision. I hadn't been expressing to them, of course, the misgivings about Catholicism that were enveloping me. But as I told them about my intention to major in religious studies, Mom exploded. "You are not majoring in religion! You have a religion already and it's the only true one. Why would you waste your time and our money studying things that are wrong?" Before I could even attempt to respond, she looked at Dad and said, "If he does this, we're transferring him out of Columbia. I am not using our savings to have him study a bunch of false religions." I looked at Dad, who had supported my decision to go to Columbia over Mom's preference for Fordham. But all Dad said was, "You heard your mother." Sophie the boss had made her intentions clear.

Mom didn't follow through with her threat to withdraw me from Columbia. Her vision of a son with a college degree was too important to her, and she wouldn't have known anything about how I might transfer to another college. But her explosion over my desire to major in religion was only the first out-burst of many during my time at Columbia. Over those four years, more were to come around issues that, in those early months, I couldn't even begin to imagine. Politics, sexuality, a future career: all would become arenas for change and upheaval.

# 15

...........

## War and Peace

Besides Catholicism, a conservative Republican politics was a key feature of the Scamporlino clan. Hatred of Franklin Roosevelt, a love of Senator Joe McCarthy, diatribes against Russia: they were all part of family gatherings at Big Grandma's. When Mom and Dad watched the television news each evening, they kept up a running commentary on those evil communists, though their banter made it hard to distinguish between a communist and a Democrat.

When I started at Columbia in the fall of 1966, the idea of protesting had never entered my consciousness. Yes, news of the civil rights movement was everywhere. Black Power was starting to make headlines. There had been uprisings in Harlem in the summer of 1964. When President Johnson authorized bombing North Vietnam and sent ground troops to Southeast Asia, demonstrations against the war began. As an extempore speaker at Regis, I had to know enough about these events to speak intelligently if I drew one as a topic. But it didn't register that any of it might have something to do with me. I had never participated in a protest march or rally, and it wasn't on my agenda when I moved to campus that autumn.

............

Almost from the moment I arrived at Columbia, the issue of the war was unavoidable. Professor Shenton had made it the subject of his impassioned speech during freshman orientation. *Spectator*, the campus newspaper, carried stories about how a war thousands of miles away intersected with the university and its students. The fall and winter saw a steady stream of rallies protesting the campus presence of CIA representatives who were recruiting prospective graduates to work for them. At noon, while most students rushed from building to building as they changed classes, protesters gathered by the hundreds at the center of campus, listening to speakers and shouting chants. Sometimes they marched across campus. At least once that year, they occupied the building where a CIA recruiter was interviewing job candidates. In a letter to Vinny that fall, I was harshly critical not of the CIA but of the protesters. "They talk about fairness for all," I wrote, "but how fair were they being?" I accused them of "hypocrisy" in denying students the opportunity to work for the CIA. But aside from an occasional comment like that, I mostly did little more than notice that this was happening on campus.

It was harder to ignore the debates about the issue of student deferments. The military draft touched every male aged eighteen to twenty-five. At age eighteen, each male had to register with his local Selective Service board, which then dispensed a status ranging from 1-A (eligible to be drafted) to 4-F (not eligible under any circumstances). In between were a series of temporary deferments. One of the most common classifications—2-S—provided students in college as well as in graduate or professional school with a deferment. Such widespread deferments worked when the United States was not actively engaged in war. But as the number of troops in Asia rose rapidly, Selective Service needed to increase the number of 1-A classifications.

During freshman year, the policy discussion centered around student deferments. With so many baby boomers in college, the percentage of males with 1-A status was declining. The first big step Selective Service took was to eliminate grad student deferments. But it also trained its eye on undergrads. It scheduled a test for November that all male undergraduates had to take. Those who scored in the top 50 percent on each campus retained their deferment; the bottom 50 percent would be reclassified 1-A. The proposal aroused so much criticism that Selective Service never acted on the results. Instead, it issued an order that, at the end of the school year, every college must submit class rankings to Selective Service. Again, the top half would retain deferments; the bottom half would lose them. Now, every exam in every class potentially contributed to whether students might find themselves fighting in Vietnam.

While class rank was a more reasonable approach than a one-test-decides-all policy, Selective Service's action effectively recruited many more students to the antiwar movement since, suddenly, the war affected them. Campus antiwar activists across the country staged protests to demand that their college not cooperate. At Columbia, the faculty voted to ask the administration not to submit rankings. A student referendum overwhelmingly voted against cooperating. *Spectator* editorialized not only against basing deferments on class rank but against the war itself. Students for a Democratic Society, or SDS, the most vocal activist group on campus, debated whether to call a student strike. Finally, the board of trustees, a group filled with wealthy corporate executives and lawyers, took a stand against the proposal. The outcry was so loud and consistent that Selective Service dropped the plan and, at least for the present, undergraduate deferments seemed secure.

The student deferment issue affected me directly in a way that CIA recruitment never would. Getting drafted was not something I had imagined happening to me. But now, policies were being debated that might throw me into the pool of eligible young men. I found myself going to campus rallies and listening to what speakers were saying. Yet I still remained detached. During those first months, the raging debates about the war did not arouse the kind of introspection and emotional upheaval that challenges to my religious beliefs had unleashed.

. . . . . . . . . . . . .

I might very well have stayed aloof from the growing protests were it not for Rey, a senior at Columbia. Rey had been a debater at Brooklyn Prep and knew of me through my involvement in forensics. Early in the fall he presented himself as a "big brother." We got together many times, mostly for conversation in the café in the basement of John Jay. Rey was a willing listener to the debates that were raging inside me and that spilled out in my letters to Vinny and others. But unlike my Regis friends, who were either in seminary or in Catholic colleges, Rey had been outside of a Catholic world for three years. He had worked through the challenges that Columbia threw at good Catholic boys. He commented from the perspective of someone who had experienced something similar. Religion, the challenges of the curriculum, the campus turmoil about the war: all were fodder for our talks. Rey offered relief from the storms swirling inside me. He gave me space for reflecting that felt safe and, at least momentarily, calming.

At some point that winter, Rey told me about a retreat he planned to attend. There would be a few students from other colleges, a couple of teachers and some nuns, and a priest who would lead it. It would convene in an apartment near campus. The main focus of the gathering was the war and what a moral response to it might be. The memory of senior retreat at Regis and its impact on me was still fresh, and I jumped at the chance to go.

Other than Rey, I never saw any of the participants again, and so most of the specific details of the day have blurred. But a few things remain vivid. For one, neither the priest nor the nuns wore clerical clothes. Except at recreational events, I had never experienced a member of a religious order without the garb that identified them as a servant of God. Now several were sitting in a circle behaving just as any ordinary soul might. They projected a warmth and friendliness that put me at ease.

More profound was the content. Yes, the war hovered around us. That is what brought us together. But rather than the rhetoric of student radicals, the priest and nuns framed their thoughts in the language of the Gospels. The message of Jesus was clear. We were never to approach another in anger. We must love our enemy. No one deserved our hatred. There was no place for violence in the life of someone trying to live the teachings of the Gospels. Woven into these discussions was commentary on the war. How could we reconcile what Jesus told us with the bombings that left masses of Vietnamese, including children, dead? Why were we doing this to a people who had never done us harm, but instead had experienced suffering as a colony of a Christian nation of Europe? What would it mean to say no to the war?

I said very little that day, but what I heard affected me deeply. For one, I found myself returning to Sunday Mass. I had stopped going about halfway through the fall term. Now I was attending regularly again. But the retreat impacted much more than how I spent an hour on Sunday. The Catholicism expressed at the retreat was not about the sins we commit and the road to hell that, as a young boy, kept me fearful. Instead, it was about being in the world, standing up for what is right, not remaining silent. It was the Gospels, which I knew practically by heart, in action. It was the Catholicism of Father Daley at Regis, now addressing itself to issues on a world stage and expecting all of us to act on these principles.

I began attending campus rallies about the war whenever I didn't have class scheduled. Not long after the retreat, I saw a notice for an open meeting of SDS and decided to go. It was held in one of the big lecture rooms in Fayerweather Hall, and the room was packed. As the meeting went on, I felt more and more alienated. I didn't understand much of the rhetoric and analysis. Calls for revolution were not where I was coming from. But more than anything, the angry, fist-waving, emotional tone was foreign to me. It was not what moved me about the retreat, and though I kept going to rallies, I never went to another SDS meeting.

Jack, my Regis buddy at Columbia, had a job at Earl Hall, the interdenominational campus religious center. He mentioned that a speaker named Igal Roodenko was scheduled to talk there. Roodenko worked for the War Resisters

League, a pacifist organization in New York with a history going back almost to the First World War. He had spent much of World War II in prison for refusing military service and had participated in some of the first demonstrations in the South against racial segregation on buses. I would not learn these things about him until many years later. That day, the talk was about Vietnam. Yes, he discussed Cold War politics and the legacy of colonialism. But as I had experienced at the retreat, I found myself listening to someone who spoke from the heart. Something deep inside made Roodenko devote his life to the cause of world peace. A goodness flowed from him, a sincerity that made me want to listen to his every word. This was not a debater pounding his audience with evidence and demolishing his opposition. Roodenko was showing us his soul. Kindness encircled him. In his quiet way, he was drawing me and others inside that circle.

After the talk and discussion were over, several people in the room lingered to ask him more questions. I wanted to approach him but had no idea what to ask. He must have noticed my hesitation because he smiled and asked what had brought me to the event. I described the retreat and how it had given me a different sense of what Catholicism required. I told him that I was attending campus rallies, wanted to do more, and had gone to an SDS meeting, but it didn't seem right for me. Roodenko listened, the gentle smile always on his face, and asked if I knew of the Catholic Peace Fellowship. The name itself intrigued me. I had no idea such a group existed. It shared offices with the War Resisters League downtown. He gave me its address on the Lower East Side and encouraged me to visit.

I was still working part-time at Berkey on Saturday mornings, and the Peace Fellowship offices were nearby, so I walked there one afternoon after my shift ended. It was an old building, with a narrow flight of stairs taking me up to a set of offices. Several people were sitting at desks, some on the phone and the rest stuffing envelopes. I explained that I had heard about the Peace Fellowship from Igal. A woman somewhat older than my mother invited me over to where she was and began describing the group's work. They published a newsletter that they sent to members around the country. They had participated in actions against testing nuclear weapons in the 1950s but now were almost entirely focused on Vietnam. A lot of their work centered on Cardinal Spellman, a big figure in the Catholic Church and a strong supporter of the war. She gave me a copy of the most recent newsletter and a membership form and encouraged me to return. "As you can see," she said, pointing around the office, "there is always work to do."

I did join the Peace Fellowship. Since it was close to the end of the school year and I would be living at home during the summer, I provided my Parkchester address on the membership form. It didn't take long for mail to start arriving. When I came home for dinner that spring and, later, when I got home from work during the summer, Mom always handed me the mail. Her classic look of disapproval reliably appeared on her face, but the fact that the word *Catholic* was on the envelope at least saved me from one of her outbursts. If it was Catholic, she couldn't question it, even if she didn't like it.

That summer, I worked in Lower Manhattan at the Bureau of Customs, in a civil service job that the federal government made available to college students. It was easy to go to the Peace Fellowship offices after work, and I did go back a few times to help with mailings and other tasks. Once I joined a small group that stood across from St. Patrick's Cathedral and distributed flyers about the war. But even though I found the Peace Fellowship more compatible than what I experienced at my one SDS meeting, I found it hard to get involved. Almost everyone who worked with it was older, the age of my oldest aunts and uncles. They had been doing this for decades. They all seemed so much wiser, so much more experienced, that I hardly knew what to say to them.

Instead, my involvement in the antiwar and peace movements was as a face in the crowd, one among many at protests and rallies. Mostly it was campus based, but occasionally I learned about off-campus events. In April of freshman year, just as I was considering pacifism seriously, a major march was scheduled for a Saturday. Crowds were to assemble in Central Park, march to Forty-Second Street, and then continue to UN Plaza for a large rally where Dr. Martin Luther King Jr. was to be the main speaker. That Saturday, I rushed up to Forty-Second Street immediately after I finished at Berkey. The march was already nearing its end, and I joined in at the back. When we turned to head north to the UN, the crowd was so large that I was too far away to hear or see the speakers. But even so, there was something empowering about it. So many people had gathered together. The spirit was warm and friendly, as if a community, a new nation almost, was being created on the spot.

Not all demonstrations shared that aura. The following fall, SDS publicized a protest against the upcoming appearance in New York of Dean Rusk, the secretary of state and someone closely associated with the government's war policies. Rusk was to give a speech to an association of foreign policy experts who were meeting at a Midtown hotel. It promised to be a large protest, designed to make antiwar sentiment visible not only to those at the hotel but also to ordinary New Yorkers finishing up work on a weekday.

The protest began simply enough. Police kept the crowd on the other side of Sixth Avenue from the hotel, just north of Radio City Music Hall. But the crowd kept growing, and soon people were spilling into the street. The police responded by pushing us back onto the sidewalk. Through all this, SDS leaders led chants through their megaphones, and the noise kept getting louder. Then, unexpectedly to me but perhaps planned by the organizers, they called on us to get into the streets. "We will shut the city down," one of the leaders shouted, "until Rusk and his associates listen to us and stop the war." Suddenly, as the crowd surged forward, I was in the middle of Sixth Avenue. The police responded instantly and soon were beating demonstrators with their clubs and handcuffing some. When one of the SDS leaders yelled, "This way," many of us quickly filled a side street as we headed toward Fifth Avenue, New York's luxury shopping street.

The decision must have caught the police by surprise, because we made it there without being stopped. Once we arrived, we stayed in the street and marched south, blocking traffic and shocking many pedestrians. I'm sure I was not the only one who had never disrupted traffic in the heart of Manhattan as part of an angry crowd. The excitement of breaking all the rules to stop a war that was killing thousands was exhilarating. At some point I found myself next to a young female student from Queens College. We held hands as our march accelerated to a trot. But exuberance rapidly morphed into fear when cops on horses started converging on us. Soon, our hand-holding tightened into a grip, as we found ourselves, along with many others, racing down Forty-Seventh Street. Horses galloped into the crowd, and cops swung their nightsticks at anyone within reach. Some demonstrators scattered up and down Sixth Avenue, while others of us kept running until we reached Broadway and disappeared underground into a subway station.

When I got back to the dorm, I described to Kurt, my roommate that year, everything that had happened. It was exciting, to be sure, but the demonstration also left me shaken. The good boy who was raised in a respectable white ethnic neighborhood, where police mainly filled the role of helping old folks cross the street and lost boys find their mothers, had suddenly seen the cops in an entirely different light. Dodging charging horses and wooden clubs was not something Parkchester had prepared me for. It would be many years before I could look at a police officer again and not feel threatened by his presence.

............

I did keep attending campus rallies and other protest events, but for a while at least, I also kept a distance between myself and actions that promised to turn into chaos. The retreat with Rey, Igal Roodenko's talk, and my slight involvement with the Peace Fellowship had all pushed me to reflect on the values I was trying to live by. Yes, I was slowly detaching myself from the institutionalized, often dogmatic, Catholicism of my youth. But I was also trying to retain the spirit of it, especially the call to live in a way that improved the world around me and recognized the worth of everyone. The problem wasn't just a "bad" war in Southeast Asia; the problem was violence itself.

Through the Peace Fellowship, I was learning more about conscientious objectors, a term that Selective Service used to describe individuals whose religious beliefs and moral outlook did not allow them to engage in violence. For COs, serving in the military in any capacity would violate their deepest values. As I read its materials, this seemed right to me. Only once in my years in Parkchester had I gotten into a fight with another boy. I found the experience so viscerally upsetting that I made it a point to stay as far away from physical conflict as possible.

Folks at the Peace Fellowship encouraged me to seek counseling from the Society of Friends—the Quakers—who had a centuries-long history of refusal to engage in violence. They had a meeting in the Gramercy Park neighborhood of Manhattan, easy to walk to from my Saturday job at Berkey. They provided a great deal of information about what would be expected of me to prove the legitimacy of my CO convictions. It could be a challenge, the man who counseled me explained, for those raised Roman Catholic to persuade their draft board that the application was rooted in their religious training. Pacifism was not central to Catholicism, and Cardinal Spellman was an outspoken supporter of the war. But there was also a history of saints who resisted violence, and the Gospels certainly provided support for the position, even if the church did not.

By the start of sophomore year, I had decided that I wanted to follow this path. I was prepared to give up my student deferment and spend two years in a community service job, which was expected of COs. The advice I received emphasized that it was vital to get letters of support from adults who could testify to my sincerity. I had written to Brother August, my eighth-grade teacher, and to Mr. Ridley, a Jesuit scholastic from Regis, about what I was thinking of doing. Both wrote back that they would be happy to submit letters. But as I prepared to move forward, I knew I needed to raise the issue with my parents. The Quaker counselor and the folks at the Peace Fellowship emphasized that letters from parents were critical. If parents didn't write, it cast doubt on the truthfulness of the applicant.

I had not been discussing with Mom and Dad my attendance at antiwar protests and rallies because I knew it would upset them. To them, the war was a fight against communism. As Mom saw it, communists were not only anti-American but also atheists. Nothing could be worse. Even so, I felt pretty sure that if I framed my pacifism in terms of Catholic teaching, it would open a door for discussion and let them support me.

That fall, on a visit home for dinner, I was ready to talk about my plans. I brought a draft of the statement I was working on to submit to my draft board. After dinner was over and they had washed the dishes, we were sitting at the table again, and I opened the conversation.

"Mom, Dad, there's something I need to talk to you about. With all the stuff going on about the war, I've been thinking about the draft and what I would do if I got drafted."

"Why do you need to think about that?" Mom asked. "You have a student deferment."

"Well, yes, I do. But I've been praying about it and talking with people and—"

"What people!" Mom exclaimed.

"Religious people, Mom. Please," I said. "I've decided that I can't participate in war and violence, and that I'm going to apply for conscientious objector status. I'll need—"

Before I could even ask them for letters of support, Dad had jumped up from his chair and begun screaming. "You will not do that and call yourself my son. Get out! Get out!" he shouted. "Do you hear me? Get out!" He was thrusting out his arm, his index finger pointing toward the bedroom. "Pack all your stuff right now and get out of here! You are not part of this family anymore."

His behavior and words stunned me. Dad was not the screamer in the family. Yelling was Mom's way of displaying upset. Dad usually just retreated into silence. But here he was, standing and screaming. I had no idea how to respond. Before I could even open my mouth, Mom had stood up, too. With a look of pure panic on her face, she stretched one arm toward Dad and one toward me, trying to reach each of us and pat us both on the arm.

"No, no, don't listen to him," she said, her voice shaking. "He doesn't mean it. You'll always be our son, always. You don't have to leave, you don't have to leave."

Dad settled down, though he didn't retract what he had said. We sat there awkwardly for a few seconds until Jimmy came out of the bedroom and asked what was going on. Mom waved his query away, simply saying we were arguing about the war. I had said nothing during this outburst, and I didn't say anything more about the topic that evening. But when I left to return to campus, I knew that, much as I wanted to apply for CO status, I wasn't prepared for the feelings it brought up at home. This decision would have to wait.

.............

While I put aside a decision about a CO application, protesting the war remained part of my life. The period 1967–68 saw such an intensification of protest that it made my freshman year seem like barely more than a staged reading for the full production still to come. Student protesters targeted anything that suggested Columbia's support for the American defense establishment. They organized actions against campus recruiters for the CIA and the Dow Corporation, who produced the chemicals that were ravaging Vietnam. When word spread that an institute on campus did work for the Defense Department, it became a focus of student rage. Demonstrators also descended on the Whitehall Street Induction Center near the south tip of Manhattan. Besides extending protests off-campus so that workers in the financial district would get a taste of the anger the war was generating, activists were also strategizing how to stop "the war machine." If induction centers could be shut down, they reasoned, maybe the US military would be unable to continue the fight in Southeast Asia.

I went to one of the Whitehall rallies. But the demonstration against Dean Rusk had happened just a few weeks before, and its effects still lingered. The memory of police charging on horses and wielding clubs as I ran for what seemed like my life remained vivid. After I came out of the subway at South Ferry and began walking toward Whitehall, the police presence was overwhelming. There looked to be more cops than demonstrators. I stayed for a while, but the risk of being arrested or, worse, beaten scared me too much, and I went back to Morningside Heights, feeling more than a little ashamed at my cowardice.

Campus protests seemed safer, though even there the police occasionally made an appearance. In the spring, SDS called for a one-day boycott of classes, and many professors cooperated by canceling class. There was a sit-in at Low Library, the campus administration building, to protest Columbia's ties to the Institute for Defense Analysis, even though the university had banned demonstrations inside campus buildings. A sign of the escalation of protest tactics came at an event that I was able to attend. Earl Hall, the religious center where Jack worked, had opened a draft counseling office that year to help students navigate the system. In its commitment to open dialogue, Earl Hall had naively invited a Selective Service official to speak about what students would face upon graduation. But SDS members were among those who packed the meeting space, and at a certain point they started chanting from the back of the room, grabbing the attention of all of us to see what was happening. A few seconds later, the speaker had a cream pie covering his face and dripping onto his clothes. That was the end of his talk, and the last time Earl Hall pursued that course of action.

By winter, actions against the construction of a new university gym were added to the antiwar protests. Columbia had won city approval to build a gym on land that was part of a park in Harlem. Local activists immediately took up the cause against an elite Ivy League school that was stealing a community resource. Stokely Carmichael and H. Rap Brown, two high-profile Black Power advocates, appeared on campus to attack Columbia's actions. Brown spoke in a theater in the basement of Butler Library, where I did much of my studying. By the time I got there after my class finished, the hall was filled to overflowing and I couldn't even get into the building. After it was over, Sam, a student who had been in CC class with me, told me with great excitement that Brown had called for the overthrow of the government.

Meanwhile, events beyond Morningside Heights seemed to be spinning out of control. In Vietnam the Tet Offensive, a major military push by the opponents we supposedly were defeating, called into question everything the Johnson administration was claiming about the war. Eugene McCarthy, an antiwar senator, was challenging President Johnson in the Democratic primaries, and some Columbia students worked on his campaign in New Hampshire. Robert Kennedy, New York's senator, declared that he, too, would run against Johnson, and then Johnson announced that he would not run for election. A few days later came the horrifying news that Dr. Martin Luther King Jr. had been assassinated in Memphis. Columbia's administration suspended classes for a day in commemoration of Dr. King. The political shifting was so dramatic that even Columbia's chancellor, Grayson Kirk, whom many student activists saw as our local enemy, gave a speech calling for an end to the war.

And then, while the passions aroused by Dr. King's assassination were still fresh, the Black student group on campus seized control of Hamilton Hall, the main undergraduate classroom building, and kept Henry Coleman, the college dean, hostage. To support the Black students, SDS invaded several other campus buildings, including Low Library, the main administration building at the center of the campus. Columbia shut down. Classes were canceled, and campus life became thoroughly focused on the protests and the issues they were raising. Columbia was in the news, nationally and locally. The campus turmoil was in every city newspaper, and local TV reporting was covering it as well. It was a strange experience to see myself in the middle of events that were so newsworthy and that were making history.

Even though I was not a member of SDS, it was hard to remain just a face in a crowd. I found myself on the picket line outside Hamilton Hall, where Dean Coleman was still being held, as we carried signs supporting the occupation and opposing the new gym. It led to my one moment of notoriety. When the Black student union released the dean, I was there next to him as the bulb flashed on the camera, and my picture appeared the next day on the front of *Spectator*. A couple of days into the protests, a group of conservative students—frat boys and jocks, as we dubbed them—formed a Majority Coalition in opposition to the building occupations. Surrounding Low Library, they blocked supporters from delivering food and other supplies to those inside. I joined the crew who threw packages of food over their heads to the occupiers who were standing on the building's ledge. I may not have been very good at softball in Parkchester, but I did throw my packages accurately enough that they were caught.

The campus shutdown lasted a full week before Columbia responded. The administration authorized New York's police to come onto campus in massive numbers and forcibly end the occupation. By the time the night was over, police had arrested about seven hundred students and, again, Columbia was in the headlines. Classes resumed, but the campus could hardly be described as returning to normal. Faculty voted to give undergraduates a pass-fail option that semester, and the administration announced it would not confer class rankings that year. For reasons other than politics, the decision was a relief to me. I was barely above the failing mark in the chemistry course I was taking to fulfill Columbia's science requirement, and a "pass" looked much better than the D I was earning.

I had deliberately avoided going home to dinner during the most intense stretch of campus protests, but the media coverage made it easy for Mom to keep abreast of events. She was writing letters to me throughout these weeks, telling me to behave myself and stay out of trouble. When I did resume my trips home, it was impossible not to argue about what had happened. I wish I could say that I exercised restraint. But my voice was often as loud as Mom's as we fought over the actions of student radicals and the war that was provoking them.

Soon after Columbia announced it was not giving academic rankings that year, Mom sent perhaps the angriest letter I ever received from her. Referring to the SDS leader whose name became synonymous with the campus protests, she wrote that "Mark Rudd has accomplished his feat . . . he has completely destroyed a university." She then dropped her bombshell: "Your father and I have definitely made up our minds to transfer you out of Columbia. Make up your mind which university you would like to go to. Our decision—it's a final one."

As with the threat that erupted when I revealed my desire to major in religion, Mom and Dad never acted on it. But it did highlight again the gaping divide that was developing between the outlook and values of my family and the person I was becoming at Columbia.

# 16

.............

## This Is Me

As it happened, I was not on campus when the massive police bust occurred. I was spending that night in Greenwich Village, in the apartment of Billy, my boyfriend—or *lover*, the word then most commonly used among gay men. The turmoil of those first two years at Columbia had not extended just to God and nation. There was also the matter of my sexual desires. At Columbia, I was able to rethink my understanding of sex as a sin on the road to hell. By the time student radicals were shutting down the campus in the spring of 1968, I had managed to achieve a certain peace within myself. But the journey was not an easy one.

.............

At Columbia, I could explore my sexual attractions in ways that simply were not possible during my Regis years. For the first time, I was living without the supervision of my parents. I no longer moved about each day in a setting where priests were ever-present and all my peers shared a religious upbringing. Instead, I was surrounded—in class, the library, the student center, and especially the dorms—with masses of young men enjoying a new level of freedom. Yes, Columbia imposed constraints. Girls were not allowed to visit in our rooms except for a few hours and with our doors left ajar. But by 1966, baby boomers were in the first stages of provoking a "sexual revolution," and protests were beginning to challenge such restrictions.

One sign of the male sexual energy that always seemed ready to explode came just a few weeks into my first semester. On Halloween night, word spread quickly through the dorms that we were to gather on Broadway by the Barnard campus for a panty raid. There we were, hundreds of Columbia undergrads packed together on the street, shouting up to the windows of a dormitory, as residents teased the crowd by waving panties at us. Occasionally a Barnard student flung an undergarment out of a window, and dozens of guys competed for possession of it. At some point, campus security shooed us away, and the crowd dissolved amid raucous laughter and off-color remarks. But the message of the event was clear: sex is what this bunch of horny guys want.

Panty raids, of course, were exceptional. More common were the mixers that brought Columbia and Barnard students together. The first one, for new students only, was held during orientation week. Periconi and I went together and experienced the awkwardness that we knew well from Regis dances with nearby Catholic girls' schools—the girls on one side of the room, the boys on the other. But in the midst of this, we saw two Barnard students approaching us, one of whom was waving at me. It was Eileen, a girl I had known from the Catholic speech tournament circuit. With her was Patsy, a first-year student from St. Louis. Soon the four of us were chatting it up, and by the end of the evening, I had asked Eileen for her phone number.

It didn't take us long to begin dating regularly. We met on campus for lunch and coffee. Sometimes we double-dated with Periconi and Patsy. Eileen's smile and the warmth of her personality made it easy to feel relaxed in her presence. We held hands when we walked down the street and enjoyed long kisses at the end of dates. I wrote about Eileen in letters to Regis friends, effusively describing how much fun we had and how much I felt drawn to her. We shared a Catholic school background, and some of the challenges Barnard was throwing at her were not very different from what I encountered in Columbia's classrooms.

Yet, when Eileen and I were not together, my thoughts didn't turn in her direction. Instead, the pull toward men asserted itself, and I had to wonder whom I was trying to fool by dating her. In one sense, the answer was everyone. Eileen provided a protective cover for feelings I still couldn't share. But more than anything, dating a girl whose company I enjoyed kept alive the illusion that my desires for men did not define who I really was.

Even as I dated Eileen, I pursued those sexual feelings. The summer of working at Berkey had given me a sense of walking the streets as a way of looking for men, even if I didn't yet know places, other than Times Square, that I was likely to find men searching for men. And so, on nights when I finished studying early and didn't have plans to meet Jack or Kurt or any of my other new buddies,

I went walking. I walked down Broadway to the West Nineties and Eighties, looking. I strolled up and down West End Avenue, a residential street without any retail businesses, looking. Almost without exception, the looking led to nothing.

Riverside Drive proved different. Especially on the park side of the drive, there was little reason to be walking after dark. Most of the men strolling alone on the edge of the park were there for the same reason I was. They were "cruising," as one of them described it to me, and the drive was filled with entrances to Riverside Park, where pairs of men disappeared into the bushes. There, they—or, I should say, we—engaged in a rapid sexual exchange. These experiences felt safer than subway restroom sex. There was less likelihood of discovery and exposure. But in other ways it was the same—quickly over, little conversation, and men then going their separate ways. In the several times that year that these explorations led to sex, at the end of each encounter I was just where I was when I started—alone with my desires.

Besides the street cruising, I also found myself looking on campus. Studying in the reading room of Butler Library, I often noticed when a man entered and I wondered whether our eyes would meet. Later in the evening, I might take myself to the coffee shop in the basement of my dorm, again wondering if a pair of eyes would lock with mine. On a few occasions, it did happen. The pattern was predictable. I seemed to focus on men who were older rather than fellow undergraduates. Whether in the coffee shop or the reading room, we had a period of returning looks that lasted for several minutes until he got up and walked out slowly, while noticeably staring at me. Some nights, I felt too scared to follow. But other times, I did. I wasn't prepared to bring someone to my room for sex. A few times, guys I met lived nearby and invited me to their place, where we stripped naked and had sex in bed. But even when they offered me their phone number, I knew I wasn't coming back. In my struggles during those months with my Catholicism, I was no longer going to Mass and confession each week, but I still believed that this was wrong, and I could never admit that I was going to do it again.

The sense of religious conflict came through very clearly in one of those experiences that year. José, a man I met in the Butler Library reading room, lived a couple of blocks away. He was a student in General Studies, a division of Columbia meant for adults pursuing a bachelor's degree; he had been raised in Cuba and came to the United States after the revolution. We kissed and touched and slowly undressed. As we got into his bed, and he was lowering his body on top of mine, I noticed that he was wearing a religious cross around his neck. Shock in my eyes, I blurted out, "How can you wear that while we're doing this?" He paused for a few seconds, looked at me in puzzlement, and then, in the kindest voice imaginable, said, "But why wouldn't I wear it? Jesus loves me too." The idea was inconceivable to me.

. . . . . . . . . . . . .

By winter, the power of these urges made it impossible to continue deluding myself by dating Eileen. I made excuses. Schoolwork was too demanding for me to date anyone seriously. My struggles over religion were making it hard to focus on our relationship. Thankfully, Eileen took it well. "You've given me a lot of happiness these past few months," she wrote in a letter. "I could never hate you. I understand your reasons. It's been a wonderful five months."

Even though I initiated it, the breakup pushed my emotional anguish to higher levels. That February, with Jack and a few other campus friends, I saw the French movie *A Man and a Woman*. A lyrical love story, it made finding one's true love seem a joyfully exuberant experience. The soundtrack had my heart beating fast, and the group of us left the theater almost floating in the air, having absorbed the ecstasy of romantic longings fulfilled. But the ecstasy didn't last. Back in my dorm room, I felt closed within myself. I needed someone, anyone, to open my heart to. Writing to Vinny a few days later, I told him that I was "craving love," that "I need someone, something, so terribly that the want causes agony."

Through the winter and into spring, I sought places of help and solace. Glen, one of my new Columbia friends, mentioned that he was seeing one of the psychologists that Columbia provided for students who needed counseling. I wasn't aware that such help was available. With the information from Glen, I made an appointment to see a counselor.

The psychologist assigned to me was friendly and outgoing. He gave me a great deal of freedom to talk, but when embarrassment or shame slowed me down, he peppered me with questions to keep me going. I was honest about the contradiction at the heart of my situation. On one hand, I kept promising myself to stop pursuing sex with men. But on the other, I regularly broke the promise and searched for encounters. Unlike the Jesuit psychologist who had been clear about the sinfulness of homosexual acts, the Columbia counselor maintained a neutral stance. His goal, he told me, was to help me work through the emotional conflicts my sexual desires were causing until I finally knew the path I wanted to follow. The sessions brought some relief. The simple opportunity to not keep everything trapped inside made those weeks a bit easier. I found myself cruising less than before.

After several of these sessions, my counselor told me with great excitement that Columbia's team of psychologists had discussed "my case," as he described it, and agreed that I should be transferred to long-term therapy. The way he communicated the decision made it seem like a positive commentary on me rather than an indication of desperate need on my part, and so I thanked him for the opportunity. But my new psychologist had quite a different style. For most of the hour, he simply sat there, communicating through hand gestures and nods that I should keep talking. There was little interaction, little commentary from him. His whole affect suggested concern about what I was coming to see as my "condition." I soon found myself saying what I thought he wanted to hear. I came in with positive stories about resisting the pull to have sex with men and feeling less agitated.

The winter also saw me return to Sunday Mass. Something about the retreat that Rey had brought me to and the contact with the Catholic Peace Fellowship pushed me back to attending Mass, which I had stopped doing in the fall. After several weeks of attendance, along with the pause in sexual experience that the counseling was producing, I decided to return to confession. I had no idea how to calculate the number of times I had masturbated in those months, but I was quite clear about the number of sexual experiences with men since my last confession early in the fall. That Saturday, at the parish church just north of campus, I sat near the confessional until no one else was waiting. Then I entered, and when the priest slid the other panel closed, I began.

"Bless me, Father, for I have sinned. It has been five months since my last confession. I accuse myself of." In as quiet a whisper as I could manage, I went through my list. "I was disrespectful toward my parents eight times. I missed Mass eighteen times. I had impure actions with myself many times." I finished with "I had sex with men eleven times" and waited for the formulaic response. Instead, I heard him say, "Where did you meet this man?"

I thought the embarrassment of having to explain my acts might kill me. After a brief pause, I responded. "It wasn't the same man each time, Father."

"I see. Well, then, where have you met them?"

"I meet them in different places, Father. Sometimes in the park at night. Sometimes walking on the street. A couple of times on campus. I try not to, Father. But I can't seem to help myself and I keep doing it."

I waited for his response, wanting something, anything, that might offer a path out of this misery. Then, I heard him say in a kind and solicitous voice, "Have you thought about coming to our church socials and meeting someone there?"

His question shocked me, until I realized: the darkness of the confessional box, the quiet whisper in which I had spoken, had made him assume that, of course, I must be a young woman.

"You don't understand, Father. I am a man."

He must have been as shocked by his mistake as I was by his question, because in short order I heard him forgiving my sins and giving me a modest penance of prayers to be said.

That was my last confession. Something clicked. I grasped that I would not find help that was useful to me at the confessional or at Mass. The next week, I told my psychologist that I didn't need any more sessions. I didn't have it in me to reveal that I was no longer going to run from my desires. Instead, I made up some story about the sessions giving me a confidence to pull back from them that I hadn't felt before. Who knows what he thought? He probably saw right through me.

It would be fanciful to claim that I was suddenly able to embrace happily my homosexuality. I had no picture at all of the life I might build for myself. I didn't even know if I could build a life. The fear of what might happen if others learned about this remained deep within me. But even so, I felt some relief. I had stopped trying to say no, stopped promising myself—and God—that I would never do this again. The struggle to control these desires, to pretend to myself that it wasn't me, was finally over.

. . . . . . . . . . . . .

That summer, I had a job at the Federal Bureau of Customs, whose offices were in Lower Manhattan near Battery Park. The job was available through a federal Great Society program designed to provide work experience for college students. In my case, the job was a farce. Assigned to the personnel division, I was pointed by my supervisor to a long row of filing cabinets containing the personnel folders of every bureau employee and was told to put them "in order." He didn't provide any substance for the phrase, and so I began arranging the files alphabetically and putting the materials in each file in chronological order. Soon, I was taking longer and longer lunch hours, and no one seemed to notice. I used those midday breaks to explore a part of Manhattan that was unfamiliar to me—the streets of the financial district, the waterfront at Manhattan's southern tip, the huge construction site from which the World Trade Center would soon rise. And as I walked, I looked. Nothing ever emerged from that cruising, since all of us were on lunch hour and could not retreat anywhere for a sexual encounter. But it did confirm in my head that this was the path I was on.

After nine months in a dormitory, living at home that summer was not easy. I couldn't talk to Mom and Dad about anything that mattered to me. Politics, religion, and, of course, sex: none of it was safe ground. The dinner conversation about family happenings that had so engrossed me as a child no longer held my interest. More and more, I found myself staying in Manhattan after work and not getting home until it was almost bedtime. Mom and Dad expected me to account for my whereabouts if I didn't come home for dinner. There were many evenings for which I did have a story to tell. I often hung out with Regis friends who were back from college for the summer. But more than a few times I had to invent something, since I had stayed in Manhattan to wander the streets looking, and sometimes finding. Besides the Times Square area, I had noticed on one of my movie nights at a theater in the East Fifties that Third Avenue was, perhaps, an even heavier cruising area than Times Square, so it, too, became a hunting ground.

One evening, walking on Third Avenue, my eyes locked with someone. His name was Luis, and, as with José, he was a Cuban who had fled the revolution and now worked at the UN. He lived nearby and took me to his apartment, where we had sex. But instead of my leaving immediately afterward, which had always been the case with the few experiences that did not involve public sex, Luis invited me to stay for dinner. Maybe because I had now turned a corner and was seeing myself as homosexual, I began talking to Luis about my life. I told him that I was a student at Columbia, that I was hoping to major in religion, that I had always lived in New York. Luis made me comfortable enough that I felt the freedom to share the struggles I was having. He listened patiently, talked about the hard times he had gone through earlier in life, and assured me that things would change. I so wanted to believe him. He gave me his phone number and encouraged me to call; as I was about to leave, he signaled to me to wait. He walked to a bookcase in his living room and pulled out a thin volume.

"You should read this," he said as he placed it in my hands. "A friend gave it to me a few years ago. It offered a comfort that I badly needed as I was struggling with my love for a man. Maybe it will help you too."

The book was *De Profundis*, by Oscar Wilde. I knew a little about Wilde. His play *The Importance of Being Earnest* was a standard work on literature reading lists. He was the only historical figure I was aware of who was identified as homosexual, and I knew that the scandal surrounding this had resulted in a prison sentence. I thanked Luis, we kissed goodbye, and I took the subway home to the Bronx.

That night, I couldn't sleep. The conversation with Luis had left me awash in feelings. Finally, I got up and tiptoed quietly to the living room, closed the door to the hallway so that I wouldn't wake anyone, and turned on a light. I opened *De Profundis*, began reading, and finished it in a single sitting. Fifty years later, I still place it among the most profound pieces of writing I have ever encountered. Nothing else that I have read changed my life to the extent that it did. Yes, James Baldwin made me realize that there were men who desired men. David Hume made me question whether God existed. But Oscar Wilde's words allowed me to see my sexual desires in an entirely new light and to imagine a life with integrity.

Written while he was still in prison and composed as a letter to Lord Alfred Douglas, *De Profundis* detailed the story of Wilde's love for Douglas and how it led ultimately to his trial and imprisonment. Wilde is unsparing in his criticism of Douglas. And yet, even though his passion for Douglas brought complete ruin, *De Profundis* is very much a paean to love and, surprisingly, one that Wilde grounded in the story of Jesus. To Jesus, according to Wilde, "love was the first secret of the world." His power resided in the way that he projected love wherever he went. The lessons Wilde drew from the moral vision of Jesus spoke to me directly. "The real fool," he wrote, "is he who does not know himself." Wilde's peroration, repeated many times in the course of the text— "whatever is realized is right"—was like a clarion call. I read it as a command to recognize the rightness of my deepest feelings. Reading those pages, I considered for the first time that loving men might be morally good. It is barely an exaggeration to say that *De Profundis* saved my life.

At one point in the text, Wilde declared that "to speak the truth is a painful thing. To be forced to tell lies is much worse." Anyone aspiring to a Christlike life "must be entirely and absolutely himself." His frequent invocation of Jesus allowed me to embrace my sexual desires and still retain a sense of myself as an ethical being. It was possible both to be gay and to live out the values that I had so deeply internalized in my Catholic upbringing, even if the church as an institution no longer had a place in my life.

One sign of the indisputable power of Wilde's words over me is that, a few days later, I "came out" for the first time, though I didn't yet have those words to describe what I was doing. In a letter that I addressed to both Bob and Vinny in seminary, I wrote that I was now approaching life and religion "from a path previously unseen." I described my reading of *De Profundis* and how it had wrenched my soul. But the melody of Wilde's message, and especially his presentation of Jesus as love personified, also was like a revelation. As I explained to them, it was allowing me to recognize that the attractions I had long felt for men, but had never revealed except to priests and a psychologist, were natural to me. Acknowledging some of the encounters that I'd had in the last two months, I brashly declared, "I don't feel guilty anymore." But although I was opening up to them, I asked them not to reveal it to anyone else. "Of course, it's still a secret thing," I wrote in closing. "It has to be."

# 17

............

## I Come Out, Sort Of

In many ways, it made sense that my first coming-out was to Vinny and Bob. They had been part of my inner circle at Regis. They were making a lifetime commitment to embody the lessons of Christ, and so much of my emotional conflict over my sexual desires was framed in religious terms. For almost a year I had been writing them passionate letters about the upheaval in my religious beliefs. The fact that I was communicating by letter, rather than face-to-face, created the safety of distance.

An indicator of the transforming power of Wilde's essay is that it did lead me, soon after the letter to Vinny and Bob, to tell someone, in person, that I was homosexual. Peter was among my extended circle of Regis friends. He had a reputation for an outlandish, irreverent sense of humor. He provoked uncontainable laughter when he played one of the female roles in a Regis production of *Arsenic and Old Lace.* Peter was attending Catholic University in DC. I had seen him there in the fall, on a trip during which I had also visited Brother August and Mary Ann, whom I had been hoping, without success, to continue dating.

That summer, Peter was working in Manhattan, and we spent more time together than we ever had. He had a willingness to push beyond what was normative that I found liberating. For instance, Peter knew all about Andy Warhol, the avant-garde cultural figure whose name barely registered for me. He had learned where Warhol's "Factory" was located on the East Side. We spent more than one evening across the street from it, trying to be unobtrusive while Peter eagerly explained who each of the folks arriving and departing was. Peter had also formed a connection with an older man named Bruce Millholland, who'd had a life in the theater. Bruce was something of a mystic, claiming that flowers talked to him and that he could see through the back of his head. The first evening I spent with him and Peter, walking through Central Park, I wondered if he was crazy. But Peter's almost awestruck interest in Bruce—Peter flooded him with questions and seemed to hang on his every word—fascinated me, and I loved listening to Peter later as he processed the seemingly fantastical things Bruce had told us.

Peter was also seriously dating Connie, his high school girlfriend. In our wanderings in Manhattan, he talked freely about the euphoria that being with her induced in him and the contrasting dejection he felt when they were apart or when conflict arose. I think the easiness with which he spoke about the relationship created a safety that allowed me to reveal my struggles. Not long after writing to Vinny and Bob, I came out to Peter on one of our evening jaunts through Midtown Manhattan.

Peter responded in characteristic fashion: he was intensely curious and wanted to know more. So I began describing my sexual history, not the details of what I did with men sexually, but how I met men who wanted sex with men. This was 1967. It might have been the "summer of love" for hippies and other young rebels of the sexual revolution, but homosexual life was still hidden from anyone not a part of it. Peter was intrigued by my description of cruising. He insisted that I demonstrate for him. So one evening after work, I walked along Third Avenue in the East Fifties, with Peter a few dozen steps behind. Every time I made eye contact with a guy walking in the opposite direction, I turned around to look back at him after a few paces. Inevitably, he did the same. But because this was for demonstration purposes only, I kept walking rather than stop and talk. Peter was enthralled by it, and it made me feel as if I was the possessor of a precious secret knowledge rather than engaged in shameful behavior.

. . . . . . . . . . . . .

I suspect that these steps toward self-acceptance explain another event that summer: my first crush on a man. One evening in August, when I was supposed to meet a Regis friend after work, I was exiting the subway at Fifty-First and Lexington and passed a stunningly handsome guy who was heading down the stairs. Our eyes locked, we each turned to look, and in that instant I abandoned my plans for the evening. I went back into the station, and we introduced ourselves. His name was Ron. He lived a few stops north in the East Eighties, and he invited me home with him.

I can't claim that the sex was special. Almost all of my sexual encounters to this point were so completely shaped by the secrecy, fear, and shame that surrounded my desires that I could hardly give myself to the experience and certainly had little in the way of lovemaking skill to display. But in the case of Ron, none of it mattered. His body took my breath away. A few inches taller than me, he had a beautifully defined swimmer's physique, the suggestion of muscles on his arms, chest, and legs, and light-brown hair scattered across his skin. I found myself wanting to hold him close forever, to snuggle in his arms and feel him stroke my body tenderly. He seemed to embody some vision I had internalized of an ideal masculinity. He carried himself confidently; he spoke with assurance; and he took charge of our time together.

I stayed long enough to learn some things about him. Twenty-nine years old, he had grown up in a rural community in Missouri, enlisted in the army as his way out, and now worked as a travel agent. He sang in the choir of St. Bartholomew's Episcopal Church on Park Avenue and frequently attended opera performances at the Met. Ron suggested that we might go to a concert together, and I eagerly agreed, even though I knew nothing about classical music and had never been to an orchestral performance. He gave me his phone number and said I should call.

And call him I did. Sounding happy to hear from me, Ron said he had two tickets for a concert the following week and invited me to go. I was thrilled: for the first time, an actual date with a man. He said we should meet for dinner beforehand, and I suggested Luigino's, the restaurant I had gone to so many times with Regis friends. The next evening, when I met up with Peter, I told him with an almost uncontainable glee that I was in love! On impulse, I invited Peter to join us for dinner. The only friend with whom I was sharing the mysteries of my new life had to meet this guy with whom I was already infatuated.

Ron was surprised, I'm sure, when I showed up with Peter at the restaurant. But I was in no position to judge his reaction, as the novelty of the occasion had me vibrating from head to toe. Later, sitting next to Ron in the concert hall, I thought of those subway rides when I had pressed my leg against the man next to me, hoping yet also terrified that it might generate a response. But now, here, our legs did press together, and I felt as if I understood what it meant. This was my man, letting me know that he wanted me as much as I wanted him.

I couldn't go to Ron's place after the concert, since I needed to get to the Bronx at an hour acceptable to my parents. But I promised to call, and after a few days, I reached him, and we made a date to meet at his place after work later in the week. Again, it was rapturous. To have him run his hands up and down my body as we lay in bed after orgasm: to this eighteen-year-old, it was the stuff of dreams.

Summer was now ending, and a week or so later I was back on campus, still living in John Jay but this time sharing a room with Kurt. Classes and studying were again filling my days and nights, but that didn't lessen my obsession with Ron. I called often from the pay phones in the basement of John Jay but never reached him. This was before voice mail or telephone answering machines were commonplace, and so unless Ron picked up the phone when it rang, there was no way for him to know I had called. With each day, and then week, that I didn't talk to him, I began to doubt my certainty that we were meant to be a couple. But whatever he might be imagining, *my* feelings for him did not abate.

It was obvious from our limited time together that music meant the world to Ron. The Metropolitan Opera had just moved to Lincoln Center the year before. Ron had mentioned in passing that on Sundays at noon, the Met sold a week's worth of standing-room tickets at a mere $2.50 each. Opera lovers who couldn't afford season tickets or seats began lining up outside the Met late on Saturday night. So that fall, once I was back on campus, I headed to Lincoln Center shortly before midnight on Saturdays, course books in hand to read while I waited. Beyond the overture to *Carmen*, opera was completely unfamiliar to me. As I soon learned, I was plunging into a time of great sopranos. That season had me listening to Renata Tebaldi, Montserrat Caballé, Leontyne Price, and Mirella Freni. Knowing this was something Ron loved allowed me to be swept along with the beauty of it.

My time at the Met did more than introduce me to a world of high culture. To my amazement, the crowd waiting for standing-room tickets in the wee hours of Saturday night and Sunday morning contained a huge proportion of men whom I was now hearing described for the first time as "gay." All of them opera fanatics, they spent these hours engaged in dialogue that moved between the passionate and the hilarious. Each had a favorite soprano whom he praised to the heavens while casting aspersions on rival singers. Despite the harsh tone, none of it appeared personal. At any moment, an exchange of insults might suddenly provoke laughter that spread among the crowd, and the insult seemed immediately forgotten. These Saturday nights and Sunday mornings were my first experience of gay men interacting with each other for reasons other than a sexual encounter.

Those hours on the standing-room line intensified my yearnings for Ron. A couple of times on a Saturday, after I finished at Berkey, I took the subway to his neighborhood and walked the streets, hoping I might see him. Sometimes

I stood across from his building and stared up at what I imagined to be his window. After weeks of no contact, I did manage to reach him by telephone and told him how much I missed him. I don't know if he heard something in my voice that revealed my longing, but he invited me to come over that Saturday afternoon. We did, of course, have sex, and afterward, as we were lying in bed, I confessed my love. Ron was so sweet. He gently stroked my body, telling me that he understood how special it was to feel that way. But he also suggested, in a tone that was very caring, that a relationship between us was unlikely. I was young, he explained, and needed to have more experience before someone became my lover. And then, unexpectedly to me, since he seemed to be saying no to my love, he invited me to the service the next day at St. Bartholomew's, where he sang. Several friends were coming, and I could join them afterward for brunch.

This began a new routine that stretched into the winter. Instead of waiting in line for opera tickets, I went instead to the morning service at St. Bart's and joined Ron and his friends as we walked down Park Avenue to Forty-Second Street, where we ate, fortunately for me, at a modestly priced diner. These Sundays were even better than the hours among the crowd of opera lovers. Here was a group of friends who were gay. Some had met through a sexual encounter. Some had met at gay bars. But most exhilarating about the time I spent with them was the openness they shared. They weren't needing to hide their homosexual desires. They could exchange stories about sexual encounters, gossip about men they knew in common, and laugh about the escapades that animated this hidden social world. I tried to take in as much as I could, almost as if this was a college class in how to be gay. Most of the men were of Ron's age, in their late twenties and early thirties. Like Ron, they had made their way to New York because it promised the possibility of meeting others like themselves and being free of the constraints that family imposed.

The one exception was Jack, a native New Yorker. He was older, probably about fifty, and he seemed to play the role of benevolent uncle. One Sunday, he invited me and Ron to his place after brunch. At one point, when Ron had gone off to the bathroom, Jack looked at me and asked, "You like him, don't you?" The question made me catch my breath. I teared up a bit and could only nod yes. Jack took hold of my hand and, in the kindest voice, said, "Don't be upset. This will pass. You'll get over it, and you will meet someone else."

I wanted to believe that Jack was right, that I would move beyond my feelings for Ron. But it wasn't happening. Even though I knew there was no possibility of a romance, I still wanted to be with Ron, even if only for a couple of hours a week. And so, after the break for the holidays, when Sundays remained a Scamporlino family affair, I returned to the Sunday outings.

One of the occasional attendees was Bob. He was a huge man, perhaps the heaviest person I had ever encountered. The rolling fat across his body when he laughed reminded me of Big Grandma. Bob was an editor for a science publisher. Maybe because he worked in the field of publishing, he seemed to harbor interest in my education at Columbia. He asked about the courses I was taking and expressed curiosity about Regis. As we left the restaurant one Sunday, he invited me to his place in Brooklyn Heights for dinner on Friday.

The only time I had been to Brooklyn Heights was for my interview with the Jesuit psychologist. Getting off the subway at Borough Hall and walking toward the Promenade brought a flood of memories. Just two years earlier, I was working to suppress my desires for men and hoping to become a Jesuit. It was hard to believe how much had changed. I was still a teenager, but between the revolution in my stance toward religion and the discovery of a world of antiwar activism, nothing seemed like it did on that morning in the fall of 1965. Now I was walking to the apartment of a new gay friend who was making dinner for me.

When I got to Bob's apartment, I had barely taken off my coat when he pulled me close and began kissing me with a passionate intensity. "You're beautiful, you're beautiful," I could hear him whisper between kisses. Soon he was stripping me and himself of clothing. The deep kisses, the way he squeezed my body, the oral sex he performed: all of it bespoke something more than the sex I was accustomed to having with strangers. With Bob that evening, I was experiencing what I had hoped to receive from Ron. All I can remember about the meal is that he kept reaching for my hand and squeezing it. By the time dinner was over, we both seemed ready for another round of sex, and this time it came with confessions of love on his part.

Bob proposed that we see each other again the next Saturday. He had tickets to *The Fantasticks*, a musical that had been running for years off-Broadway. I couldn't imagine refusing this man whose every look in my direction expressed longing. On Saturday, we met in the Village and he treated me to dinner, another first in my life, before we headed to the theater. As the musical unfolded, I sat enthralled. A story of two young lovers, it followed the ups and downs of their romance as their fathers plot to make sure their love survives and they marry. For a while, the romance seems to fall apart. But of course, by the play's end the two rediscover their love, and their happiness seems limitless. As I watched them express, in song, their eternal commitment, I thought of Bob next to me and realized, yes, this is the kind of love I want, but no, I will never feel this for him. Afterward, we went back to his place, and his lovemaking was as intense as the first time. But I didn't feel present. Even though I was responding physically—how can a nineteen-year-old male's hormones not respond?—I was not giving him my heart. When we had finished, I told him that I needed to return to campus because I had a lot to do the next day.

On the train back from Brooklyn in the late hours of the night, I didn't know how I would explain to Bob that I didn't love him the way he loved me. As phone messages accumulated, I felt awful. I wondered if Ron had felt this way in response to my expressions of love. But Ron had treated me with compassion. I didn't know how to offer that to Bob. I understood too little about this world of love and romance, beyond that I wanted it. And so I never returned his calls. I also never went back to Ron's Sunday gatherings. What if Bob was there? And how could I face the man I had been claiming to love from the bottom of my soul after having sex with one of his friends? I felt completely humiliated by the impulsiveness of my desires. This period, consisting of months of desperate longing, ended as abruptly as it began. I never saw Ron again.

.............

While the relationship with Ron didn't materialize, the effects of falling for him continued in ways that were good. It was one thing to keep silent when my sexual experiences seemed shameful. But how could I keep secret the fact that I was sure I had met the love of my life?

That fall, one by one, I told my three closest friends at Columbia that I was homosexual. Over a period of several days, I told Kurt, Hazen, and Jack. Kurt and I had begun rooming together in a dorm, and I raised it one evening just after dinner, as we returned to our room to study. From the time I met Kurt during orientation week, he had shown an intense curiosity about everything and, like Jack and me, had moved in the direction of an antiestablishment politics. I hoped that this bent toward nonconformity would make him accepting of my announcement, and I was right. He asked questions about how I knew and how I found others, and I explained, without including the more lurid details. And of course, he wanted to know about Ron. Kurt took in everything I was saying about this mysterious and unknown world without displaying any shock or disapproval.

Hazen received my announcement in the way he did with almost everything he learned—nodding slowly and seemingly reflecting upon this new bit of knowledge. But it was Jack who provoked the most surprise. We shared several years of friendship and common experience, including the Catholic education that was so condemning of most sexual expression. Like me, he had left Catholicism behind in our time at Columbia. Still, might this push him too far? Jack had moved off campus that year, and I broached the subject one evening as we sat in his room. I had barely gotten the words out when I saw him smile broadly and say, "Me too!" I couldn't believe it. Whereas I had struggled to have dates while at Regis, Jack had been a constant dater in high school and now at Columbia. But here he was telling me that, yes, he was attracted to girls, but he also liked men. Neither of us had the word *bisexual* to attach to what Jack was describing. I was beside myself. The guy who was becoming my best friend since we started at Columbia was telling me that he shared the longings that seemed to express the deepest part of me. At this point, I had far more experience than Jack. He was curious about everything, about how and where I met men, and where were the best places to look. And he encouraged me to tell him about Ron.

These coming-outs were revolutionary for me. Vinny and Bob were miles away in seminary. Peter was attending college in DC. But Jack, Kurt, and Hazen were here on Morningside Heights, taking similar courses, going to the same demonstrations, sharing meals, and enjoying outings to the movies. Until I revealed this news about myself, I hadn't fully grasped how much, since starting at Columbia, my sexual secret was creating distance between me and everyone around me, even those with whom I felt a real kinship. I might be sitting with a group of dorm buddies talking excitedly about the latest demonstration, or engaged in a lively classroom discussion with my fellow students, but I felt as if I had a wall around me, designed to protect myself. Now, at least with these three, I had a sense of the safety I once had among family at Big Grandma's, a place where I was accepted, pure and simple.

Meanwhile, through this year, both in my yearning-for-Ron phase and afterward, I was adding to my knowledge of this hidden gay world. On one of my weekend standing-room lines, a guy started to talk with me. Jim was in his midtwenties and seemed at ease among the gay men in the crowd. He quickly picked up that I was a newcomer, not only to opera but to being gay, and he took on the role of instructor. One Sunday, after we got our tickets, he invited me to come to the Village. He steered us toward the Hudson River, and we strolled along the piers where men in large numbers were hanging out, not to enjoy the view but to cruise for sex. Another time, after a performance, he brought me to the Village again and took me to my first gay bar, Julius. The idea that there were such places was a revelation.

I had other tutors besides Jim. Sal and I found ourselves standing together at a performance, and it didn't take long before subtle body contact began. It turned out that he, like José, was a student in Columbia's General Studies Division working toward his bachelor's degree. He was also the first man that I met who was from an Italian family, and that in itself seemed to stoke attraction. Sal lived in the large YMCA on West Thirty-Fourth Street, and he took me to his room after the performance for what was very passionate sex. These were in the weeks when I was failing to reach Ron by phone. I opened up to Sal about my feelings for Ron. He was good enough to express understanding. We did see each other a couple more times. I learned from Sal that the Y had a reputation as a wild cruising ground. He also walked me one Saturday afternoon through Central Park to reveal yet another space for cruising.

Then there was Angel, who worked in Butler Library. We caught each other's eye one afternoon as I checked out books, and I turned back to look at him as I entered the reading room. Later, when his shift ended, he walked into the reading room, looked in my direction, and indicated by gesture that I should follow him out. Angel lived a few subway stops from campus, and I went to his place for sex. At this point, my seeing Ron had ended. As we shared stories about cruising and sexual experiences, Angel asked if I had ever been tested.

"I get tested all the time," I responded. Angel laughed and began to explain about venereal diseases and how, because I'd had sex with a lot of partners and had never seen them again, there was no way of knowing whether I was infected.

"But I could never tell our family doctor that I needed to be tested for sexual diseases," I said. The thought was unimaginable.

"No, you don't have to. The city has an office where they test you for free, and they won't tell anyone. You can take the train from Columbia to Twenty-Eighth Street and get there easily."

And so, a few days later, I made my way there. As a reflection of my nervousness about this new world of sexual diseases, and no doubt displaying my mother's injunction to always make a good impression, I dressed in a suit and tie. But as I discovered the moment I walked in, I needn't have. The clinic served the poor of New York, and my clothes marked me as the outsider I already felt myself to be.

The test results were all negative. The anonymous sex I had been having hadn't yet infected me with anything but a desperate need for love. And, yes, I was still craving this thing I called love. I had written Peter that winter about the sudden ending of my connection to Ron that my foolish behavior had provoked. He responded immediately with a letter filled with sympathy but also reflecting back to me the intensity of emotion that a need for love aroused in both of us. "Love is the most destructive thing we can ever possibly know," he wrote. "We are left naked by love. It cuts out and away everything within us. Your heart cries to touch and be touched." Melodramatic as Peter's words sound to me several decades later, they capture how notions of love and romance had made their way deep into my teenage psyche.

One afternoon, again in the library reading room, I saw a man eyeing me. He had a thick swath of brown hair that reached down his neck and covered his ears, in the hippie style that was spreading fast by 1968. When he gathered his books, walked slowly out of the room, and signaled by his glance for me to follow, I complied. I saw him head into the men's room, and by the time I got there he was standing at a urinal and obviously playing with himself. No one else was there, but any chance of being discovered was too unnerving to risk, and so I whispered that I'd meet him in the lobby. We made our way to Ferris Booth Hall, where we had coffee and talked.

Billy was a graduate student in history, researching a dissertation on medieval Europe. Like Ron, he was ten years older than me and also a migrant to New York. His grandparents had come to the United States from Croatia and settled in a Colorado mining town. His parents met and married there. When a fellowship for graduate study at Columbia gave Billy the opportunity to come to New York and make a gay life for himself, he seized it. Though still working on his dissertation, he had been teaching history for two years at Brooklyn College and came to campus only when he needed to do research.

This was the first time I was meeting a guy where I felt I was hearing echoes of my own life—his immigrant grandparents, his intellectual/academic leanings, and his commitment to historical studies, which was something that I was starting to become excited about. As we talked in the student center over coffee, I almost forgot that our encounter began as two men cruising for sex. Billy told me that he had a place in the Village and invited me to his apartment. We rode to the Christopher Street stop and walked the few blocks to the corner of Greenwich Avenue and West Tenth Street, where he lived.

Billy had a studio apartment with barely the hint of a kitchen. As we stripped off our clothes, I couldn't help but notice how much his body reminded me of Ron's—chest, arms, legs, and stomach covered by brown hair; well-built and toned; muscular but not excessively so. The sex felt a bit awkward, but it didn't seem to matter, because it had barely ended when our conversation picked up again. We shared more about our family backgrounds; we talked about Columbia. I listened to stories of gay life in New York, which Billy naturally knew a great deal more about than I did.

That afternoon in March initiated an accelerating intimacy that, over the next three months, saw us together at Billy's place for much of every weekend and often for a night during the week as well. We were becoming lovers rather than tricks, a progression I had never experienced before. The fact that our bond seemed to be less about an uncontrollable sexual passion and more about enjoying our time together also made the relationship with Billy a new turn in my developing gay life.

A good part of the excitement, I realize in retrospect, came from the fact that Billy was taking me on almost as a project. He was serving as an instructor and tour guide of sorts, introducing me to a gay world that, even after those Sunday brunches with Ron and his friends, I didn't know existed. Jim from the opera standing-room line had taken me one evening to a gay bar in the Village, but I never returned. We had walked to the piers along the Hudson, which simply added one more site to my list of cruising areas. But these were isolated excursions. They never brought me back to the Village. Now, dating Billy, I was spending two nights and parts of three days there every week.

As the season turned to spring, more of our time was spent outside. One of Billy's favorite activities on weekend afternoons was simply to exit his building, stroll over to one of the parked cars on Greenwich Avenue, lean back against it, and watch the parade of pedestrians. I soon discovered that the sidewalk was filled with gay men passing by. Some were actively cruising, and it quickly became a game between us to guess which efforts at cruising would succeed and which would fail.

But it was a surprise to realize that much of the sidewalk traffic wasn't about sex. These guys were walking the streets of their neighborhood, engaged in the tasks of daily life. Many stopped to talk because they knew each other already. Billy himself had ties to quite a few. Guys waved and said hello, engaged in conversation, and often suggested getting together for a drink. After they moved on, Billy filled me in on who they were and how he had come to know them. Most often, it had been through a sexual encounter.

Besides the people-watching and the gossiping that went with it, Billy introduced me to many places in the neighborhood where gay men congregated. His favorite was Tor's, a small coffee shop and restaurant on his corner, where we often had breakfast. When I had joined Ron and his friends for Sunday brunch, I was very aware that we were the only group of gay men in the restaurant. But at Tor's we were often in the majority. On any given day, there were men at different tables who knew each other, and the easy familiarity was not unlike sitting in a campus coffeehouse and casually waving and acknowledging someone I knew from class. I loved it. As the weeks went by and I came to recognize some of these men from previous visits, they would nod at me. I felt I was being initiated into a gay club.

There were other places as well. Billy wasn't what he described as "a regular" at the bars, but occasionally he took me to one as part of his guided tour of gay life in the Village. We went back to the bar that Jim had brought me to. Billy told me that the bar, which was named Julius, had been the source of a legal case that had stopped the police from raiding bars just because they were gay. Seeing so many men packed together at close range and watching the cruising that never seemed to stop brought up every feeling of insecurity I harbored about whether I looked good enough to attract attention. The fact that I was with my boyfriend and so had no need to meet anyone didn't make it any easier. By contrast, when he took me to a bar on Christopher Street, the Stonewall Inn, I didn't give the cruising a second thought. My attention was completely captured by the sight of young men standing atop the bar, dressed in nothing but a thin G-string and dancing erotically to the music that was blaring. I couldn't believe that a place like this existed. Here was a world full of energy and laughter that anyone could enter. Sure, no one would know from the outside that this was a gay dance bar, but it was there to be found and, once found, to be enjoyed.

On another Saturday afternoon, Billy took me out of the neighborhood to the other side of Washington Square Park. There, amid the old run-down warehouses, was a small bookstore with a nondescript storefront that one could easily pass without noticing. To my surprise, the store's name was Oscar Wilde. Its makeshift shelves were filled with books about homosexuality, mostly novels, some biographies, a few "studies" of the homosexual. The number of books hardly compared with what one encountered in most New York bookstores. But it was a revelation. I would never have expected on that afternoon in 1968 that the Oscar Wilde Memorial Bookshop and its founder, Craig Rodwell, would become iconic elements of a new gay world that was closer to being born than I—or anyone—knew. Nor could I imagine that, someday, I would write books that would be found on its shelves.

# 18

..............

## Her Name Is Margaret Mead

Through the four years of college, I had two part-time jobs that did more than provide the spending money I needed. In different ways, each served as a refuge. I found myself around adults who were not horrified by my abandonment of Catholicism. Nor were they outraged by my opposition to the war and my turn toward pacifism. Rather than finding it a source of stress, as jobs can often be, I eagerly anticipated the hours I spent at work each week.

..............

Money wasn't treated casually in my family. Early on I was taught how to budget and save. Sometime soon after I had learned to add and subtract, Dad announced that it was time I began receiving an allowance. He sat me down for my first lesson in careful spending.

"You'll get twenty-five cents a week, and we'll give it to you on Sunday night," he told me. "You want to get to the next Sunday with some money left over."

"How do I do that?"

"You make a budget, that's how. Think about some things you'll want to buy for yourself." We went through the list—Bazooka gum, Hershey candy bars, Good Humor pops.

"So let's see what they cost. Bazooka is a penny. A Hershey bar is a nickel. A Good Humor Creamsicle costs twelve cents. If you buy one Bazooka on Monday,

Tuesday, Wednesday, and Thursday, that's four cents. If you have a Hershey bar on Friday, that's another five. And then on Saturday, you can treat yourself to a Creamsicle. What have we got?" He grabbed the pencil resting on his ear and wrote out each of the items, as if he were balancing the books at Berkey Photo.

"Look," he said. "It adds up to twenty-one cents. That leaves you with four cents at the end of the week."

"But what about Sunday? What if I want something on Sunday?"

"No," Dad said. "We go to Big Grandma's house on Sunday. There are always cakes and cookies. Why waste your own money on Sunday when you know you'll get things at Grandma's? No, it's more important that you save. We'll give you a piggy bank, and you can put the extra in there. When it gets full, we'll put some of it in a savings account that we'll open for you, and some can go for something special, like a toy or a game that Santa didn't bring."

So began a life of budgets, calculations, and savings. When report card time came and my parents gave me a reward for my grades, I kept a little for a treat and the rest went into Piggy. Now and then I would lift Piggy and shake him. When he got especially heavy, we opened him up, counted the coins, and mostly put it into a savings account. It seemed very grown up, and I was proud of myself.

. . . . . . . . . . . . .

The allowance grew incrementally as I progressed through St. Raymond's and Regis, but now that I was at Columbia, it was officially over. Dad had determined that, with the loan and dipping into savings, he and Mom would cover the cost of tuition, room, a meal plan, and books for classes. But once I left campus, I was on my own. Dad pointed out that my friend Jack, the oldest in a family of eight kids, was expected to work on campus as part of his financial aid from Columbia. Dad was the source of my financial aid. Like Jack, I too had to carry my weight and find a part-time job. But how was I going to find one? My summer job was the only one I'd ever had. Dad showed me ads in the *Daily News*, but these were full-time positions.

A couple of weeks before freshman orientation, just before my summer job ended, Evelyn came to my rescue. She asked if I was, by any chance, interested in staying at Berkey part-time. She had to come in every Saturday morning to do the weekly payroll, she explained, and now that she had let Dora go, she needed someone to help her. It would mean getting there no later than eight in the morning. She could guarantee five to six hours a week, and there might be extra work during holiday season, when the photo processing plant was especially busy and the payroll temporarily expanded.

I stayed at Berkey the whole time I was at Columbia. Evelyn became like a benevolent favorite aunt. She peppered me with questions about protests on campus. Unlike with Mom and Dad, however, her questions weren't antagonistic but instead expressed an eagerness to know more. Evelyn didn't approve of the war. She remembered fondly the many protests of the 1930s, when she was coming of age. She loved the idea of students holding rallies, giving impassioned speeches, and marching across campus. My time with her each week was more than hours spent at a job. It was a chance to defuse, to display excitement at the new world I was discovering and the views I was taking in, to get validated for my developing opposition to the war rather than be castigated for it. She was generous toward me as well. Because the union contract gave workers time and a half for Saturday hours, Evelyn paid me at that rate. I was earning $2.75 an hour to start, and she paid me off the books, which meant that I walked away each Saturday with about fifteen bucks. Each year, when the pay scale went up, she gave me a raise, too.

Still, this was cutting it close. If I budgeted carefully, and Dad had certainly taught me to budget, I could make it through the week with my Saturday earnings. But there was no room for extravagance of any sort. A movie now and then, a simple dinner off campus once in a while, a couple of beers at the Gold Rail, some midnight snacks bought at the deli on Broadway: even that would stretch the available cash. There was my savings account in the Bronx, accumulated from the coins dropped into Piggy. But that was my "nest egg," as Dad called it, money for an undefined point in the future when something really important came up. I was not going to win a battle with them to withdraw money to spend on a Saturday night. No, I knew I needed a second job.

. . . . . . . . . . . . .

One evening during the fall of freshman year, Jack and I were hanging out at the Lion's Den in Ferris Booth Hall when he mentioned Julia Crane. She was a friend of his mother, had gone back to school later in life, and was now finishing her PhD in anthropology. Miss Crane, as Jack referred to her, needed to hire a student for a few weeks to help proofread her dissertation. She had called him to see if he was interested, but Jack was already working as many hours as he could handle.

"Aren't you looking for another job?" he asked.

"Well, I am, as a matter of fact. But, Jack, don't laugh. I don't know what a PhD is, or a dissertation, or proofreading."

I have no idea how Jack knew all this, but he proceeded to explain: A PhD is the final degree if you keep going to school after college. It allows you to become a college professor. A dissertation is what you write to get the degree. It can be several hundred pages long. And proofreading? Jack wasn't sure how it was done, but it was the way writers corrected mistakes.

I called Miss Crane, who lived near campus, and she invited me to her apartment. She seemed about Mom's age, in her early forties, with a quiet but warm personality. She asked me questions about myself and school, told me about knowing Jack's family, and then got down to business.

"We'll do this together. I have the original typed manuscript and a carbon, which you'll work from. I need to make sure everything is correct. The spelling, the punctuation, the grammar. You'll read aloud to me from the carbon copy. Every time you see a word that's capitalized, you need to say "cap." Every time you come across any punctuation, you need to say it—comma, period, semicolon. I'll be reading along with you silently. Hearing you will keep my attention focused on the page and allow me to see any errors. If there's anything I'm not sure of, I'll interrupt your reading."

So we began. It didn't require creativity, just precision. The time with Miss Crane was my first clue as to what a scholar, or academic, did. Until then, most of my reading had been novels and plays, the "great works" of literature. The first year at Columbia added a new set of great works, this time by philosophers who sat contemplating until they had a profound idea. Miss Crane's work was different. She had spent a long time in the Caribbean, living on an island colonized by the Dutch. She had talked with people about their lives, observed their routines, and now was writing about them. Miss Crane was describing a whole world. She was interpreting and analyzing. Her conclusions were bigger than "this happened."

One evening, when we were near the end of her manuscript, Miss Crane asked if I was interested in another job somewhat like this. The professor who was supervising her dissertation needed someone to proofread another manuscript and to check the accuracy of the footnotes. The professor's name was Margaret Mead, and her office was at the American Museum of Natural History.

The museum had been one of my favorite places as a child. Once or twice a year, Mom and I, along with Paul and Aunt Lucy, took the Tremont bus to West Farms and then rode the subway to the West Side of Manhattan. The museum covered a huge chunk of ground, stretching for several blocks along the edge of Central Park. Entering at Seventy-Seventh Street, we immediately faced a massive canoe populated with life-size figures of Native American fishermen. But the heart of the museum to my boyhood eyes had always been the halls filled with dinosaurs: the big and luggish brontosaurus, with a head so small that it held only a pea-sized brain, according to Mom, and the monstrously scary *Tyrannosaurus rex*.

The idea of going there every week as an employee was beyond anything I had imagined. I jumped at the opportunity. I thanked Miss Crane and told her that I definitely wanted to do it. That evening, I visited Jack in his dorm room and told him the news. He nearly fell off his chair. "You're going to work for Margaret Mead!" he exclaimed, his eyes nearly popping out of his head. I had had no idea who she was.

. . . . . . . . . . . . .

I called the number that Miss Crane had given me. The woman who answered spoke with a pleasant lilt. Every sentence seemed to start at one pitch and end at another. Her name was Miss Gordan, heavy accent on the second syllable. Was she French, I wondered? We set a time for me to come to the office. Nothing specific was said about the job.

When the afternoon came, I put on my very best clothes and took the Broadway bus to the museum. Miss Gordan had told me to make my way past the canoe to the large elevator and to tell the operator that I was going to Dr. Mead's office. The elevator operator, a jovial Irishman named Steve, with white hair and a contagious friendliness, took me to the fifth floor, which was above the areas of the museum open to the public. "Walk to the end of the hallway," he told me, "and you'll see a staircase. Take it to the top and you'll be there." The corridor he pointed me down was almost the length of a city block. There were no offices along it, just floor-to-ceiling cabinets against the walls. As I learned over the next three years of working in the museum, they were filled with bones, fossils, and artifacts from across the globe, accumulated by curators who had built the museum's collections over many decades.

As I approached the end of the hall, sure enough, there was a staircase. It actually seemed more like a fire escape, all metallic, and circling around a metal pole at its center. It took me into a small section of the museum called "The Tower," an isolated place that Mead had occupied for decades. No one accidentally entered those offices. The area was so hidden that it guaranteed Mead's privacy. I found myself in a cramped space with a tiny window in one corner, two desks, and more floor-to-ceiling cabinets and bookcases. It was a strange-looking room; I had never seen an office like it.

Seated at the desk by the window was Miss Gordan. As I soon found out, she was a native French speaker, but from Belgium. She had escaped to England just before the Nazi invasion, and from there made her way to New York. Miss Gordan was an artist and teacher, but she only had occasional part-time positions at private schools in Manhattan. Her dependable paying job was as Mead's bibliographer. The core of her work consisted of compiling bibliographies and perfecting footnote citations for the stream of writing that Mead produced. But it also involved tracking down the titles and publication information for works that Mead wanted her graduate students to consult. When they turned in their papers, Mead would read them and jot in the margin "see ___" or "check ___," and Miss Gordan had to figure out what book or article Mead was referring to so the reference could be passed on to the student.

Miss Gordan explained what my job involved. Edith Cobb, a friend of Dr. Mead, had been working for many years on a book manuscript, and Dr. Mead had promised to read it when a draft was done and help prepare it for publication. Miss Gordan pointed to a thick stack of paper at the corner of her desk. "Here it is," she said. "You need to read it paragraph by paragraph, as you did for Miss Crane, and every time you see an error of any sort, note it in the margin. But also, as you read, you'll see that she quotes from many writers. Your job is to identify where the quotations come from and provide a precise citation— the author, the book or the article, the page number, everything. When you're done, the manuscript will have a complete set of footnotes and the bibliography to go with it. Are you interested?" Apparently, I was already hired in the minds of Miss Gordan and Dr. Mead. As with Miss Crane, the pay was two dollars an hour. We arranged that I would come to the office every Friday afternoon and put in additional hours as needed at the Columbia library as I searched for references.

After little more than a semester at Columbia, I was still learning the art of compiling footnotes and bibliographies, which extended the research skills that my debate experience had taught me. The job certainly appealed to the love of precision that I had absorbed from my bookkeeper parents. And I was already captivated by the environment. The hallway, the staircase, the hidden protected world in a tower that almost no one entered: I imagined myself describing everything to Mom. With all the conflicts that were erupting at home over my questioning the truths I was raised with, this at least might provide some conversation that pleased her. But the prospect of working there was also more than a bit intimidating. Jack had described Mead as "world famous." She traveled to Washington and testified before congressional committees. She spoke at conferences around the globe. Her books had been read by millions. Would I be up to her standards?

The job certainly challenged me. The manuscript was much longer than Miss Crane's dissertation. Cobb had read endless literature, both fiction and nonfiction, about the experience of childhood across many centuries, and she was putting it together in a grand interpretation. But unlike proofreading, where I simply read what was on the page, now I had to go in search of exactly where each quotation came from. And as Miss Gordan put it, Cobb wasn't as helpful as one might wish. The manuscript was filled with phrases like "as William Wordsworth wrote in *The Prelude*." It was then up to me to skim the eight thousand lines of Wordsworth's prose poem until I could confirm that the quote was accurate.

It took a whole semester to work through the manuscript. As I was close to finishing, Miss Gordan asked if I would like to stay on staff long-term. There was always more work of this nature to do, and she and Dr. Mead, whom I had spoken to only once through this endeavor, were pleased with my performance. Mead also had a project that Miss Gordan believed I would do well. Mead's office, which was just a few steps away from where I had been working, was filled with shelves where books were randomly piled, as well as a wall of floor-to-ceiling pull-out drawers in which reprints of articles from colleagues and former students had been stuffed for years. It was almost impossible to find anything. My job, Miss Gordan informed me, was to create order. The books could be arranged alphabetically by author. The scholarly articles had to be arranged first by geographic region and then by author; those articles not defined by geography had to be shelved separately. In a way, the work was not unlike what I had done for Evelyn in my summer job. Creating order out of chaos was becoming my trade.

And so a routine began that, with the five or six hours I spent on it each week of the school year, took several semesters to complete. Reshelving the books proved easy. But there were thousands of articles. I must have sorted through the work of every anthropologist who had ever lived. I wish I could claim that I learned about our planet's varied cultures. But I never took an anthropology course at Columbia, and all I retained were the names of a few anthropologists who kept surfacing in the mass of books and articles.

Looking back on my time at the museum, I can only describe the work I did as tedious. Decades later, when reading a biography of Mead, I learned that she had a policy of helping pretty much anyone who came within her sphere. She needed someone to work on the Cobb manuscript so she could meet her promise to help a friend. But once I was moving along the edges of her circle and had proved through my work and what Miss Gordan was learning about me that I was reliable and also needed financial help, Mead invented a job to keep me on the payroll and support me through college.

But the satisfaction of the job didn't come from the work I did. It was the environment of the museum, the sense of being in a special space, and, most of all, the interactions I had with the rest of Dr. Mead's staff. Except for Valerie, who, like me, was an undergraduate needing work to support herself through college, the staff were all young adults making their way in the world. Karen had graduated from Carleton College, Laurie from Reed. With the limited information that Regis had offered about non-Catholic schools, I had never heard of these small liberal arts colleges that had the quality of a self-contained community. Jeanne had dropped out of college but was now attending the New School, which mostly served adult students. Although only four or five years older than me, these women seemed to exude worldly wisdom. They were living on their own, away from family. In working for Margaret Mead, they had all landed a job that impressed everyone they told. As I sorted and shelved, I found myself listening in on their conversations, privileged to hear how they had spent their evenings in the big city, free of work or school responsibilities. Karen had expectations of going to graduate school at some point. Jeanne, who came from a left-wing family, was very political. At one point, she started sharing stories about a women's "consciousness-raising" group and the actions it was planning. None of us had ever heard of such a thing before. Laurie, too, was an activist and participated in antiwar protests. And they were all eager to hear about what was happening at Columbia. The freedom to talk about it to an interested audience, away from the intensity of the actual events, brought so much pleasure. I could show my excitement, while leaving behind the nervousness that was never far away when I was at a rally or demonstration.

Soon after Thanksgiving each year, my normal responsibilities and those of the other staff were put on hold as Dr. Mead presented us with a holiday season task with a definite deadline. The ultimate networker, she maintained a list of addresses so long that it seemed to contain the name of everyone she had ever met. Each December, she had a special holiday card made, perhaps a photo with her daughter or of herself in the field. Mead's holiday cards were never to arrive with impersonal typed mailing labels or addresses. Instead, the job of all of us was to address by hand every envelope, put a signed card in each one, lick a stamp, and then seal the envelope. While this, too, might seem like just another tedious task, addressing an envelope to people whom we read about in the newspaper or who had written several of the books I had shelved often brought gasps and sometimes hilarious exchanges.

As a reward for our special labor, after all the cards were mailed, Dr. Mead invited us to her apartment at Eighty-First Street and Central Park West. She shared it with another anthropologist, Dr. Rhoda Metraux, who had a work space in the most remote corner of the museum tower and whom staff were all instructed never to bother. There, in her home, Dr. Mead entertained us for the better part of three hours with an almost continuous flow of stories from her years of fieldwork and her engagement with public policy. Dr. Metraux hovered in the background, rarely speaking.

It wasn't until two decades later, long after Mead had died and when I read a biography of her, that I learned that Dr. Metraux had been her intimate life partner for many years. Would knowing this have helped me come to terms with the gay self and gay world that I was slowly discovering? It is not a question I will ever be able to answer.

# 19

.............

## And Then I Studied

Off-campus jobs. Coming to grips with my gay self. A new world of activism. The upheaval in my religious beliefs. Conflict and tension with my parents. All this, and still I was a student, with the demands of an Ivy League college and the need to figure out what I wanted to study and where this education would take me.

.............

When I started at Columbia, I planned to major in classics, as the study of Greek and Latin was then called. The language skills I had developed allowed me to place into an advanced course in Greek, which is what I most loved. But that fall, the department was offering a course on the Greek comedies. To my overly self-assured mind the comedies couldn't hold a candle to the grand tragedies of Sophocles, Aeschylus, and Euripides. So I enrolled instead in a French course to fulfill my language requirement. As the year unfolded, with my intellectual and moral grounding in turmoil, the idea of classics faded. I never read a page of Greek or Latin again.

Instead, I found myself driven toward religious studies. I imagined that delving into the variety of religious systems would provide more solid grounding—a justification, in effect—for my decision to leave the Catholic Church. I trusted that Mom would not pursue her explosive threat to pull me out of Columbia if I majored in religion. A college education was too central to my parents' hopes for my future. So when it came time to register for sophomore year courses, I scoured the offerings.

Measured by intellectual stimulation, the year was a success. A class on Asian civilizations was filled with readings on the religions of East and South Asia. I took a course in moral philosophy. Best of all was a class at Barnard on comparative religions. I loved engaging with the varied approaches to the divine and how one determined what was moral. But the excitement I experienced as I read the materials did not impress my professors. My grades were lower than what I was accustomed to getting. I seemed unable to deliver whatever professors in these fields demanded.

The exception to this academic mediocrity was a course in early modern European history that I took in the spring. Taught by Orest Ranum, it covered the Reformation and the Enlightenment. I saw it as an opportunity to explore the various theologies and philosophies that emerged in those centuries. By the time student demonstrators were shutting the campus down, Ranum's teaching had won me over. He wasn't offering the universal truths of theologians or philosophers. Instead, history seemed to be storytelling—stories about human beings struggling to create the lives they wanted and stories of nations and the conflicts between them. How these events were understood might vary, but the variation depended on mobilizing evidence to support an interpretation—the very skills I had developed as a debater. History papers brought me back to the practice of research. I seemed to have a talent for it, at least based on how Professor Ranum responded.

..............

Ranum's course could not have been better timed, because I was planning to travel across Europe that summer. Within weeks of starting at Columbia, I began hearing about classmates who intended to spend the summer in Europe. Given that my family had taken only one vacation, this seemed unimaginable to me. A whole summer traveling across a continent to the famed cities of Western civilization? The students doing it after freshman year tended to come from privileged backgrounds, with fathers who worked in the professions and had the surplus money to cover the cost. But impossible as the idea sounded, I decided that, one way or another, I would go the following summer.

Much to my surprise, Mom supported the idea. One of her cherished childhood memories was a trip to Sicily at age five with Big Grandma, to bring Big Grandpa's mother back to Sortino since she was unhappy in the Bronx. Mom delighted in describing her rides on a mule, eating olives she picked herself, and walking through a village in which Big Grandma knew everyone. The idea that her son might have memories of his own was so attractive that it overrode the frugality that governed my family's life. Mom reminded me of something I had forgotten. After I had broken my arm, she and Dad had sued the owners of Parkchester for negligence and won a settlement. After legal fees, almost $1,700 remained. Columbia organized charter flights, and the fare was reasonable. A Eurail Pass would allow unlimited train travel through Western Europe. The most popular travel guide of that era, *Europe on 5 Dollars a Day*, provided lists of cheap accommodations and eateries from one end of the continent to the other. Dad's calculations determined that the broken-arm fund would more than pay for my summer travel.

And so, in sophomore year, I began planning. I bought a seat on a flight that would take me to London in mid-June and return from Paris in early September. In between, I imagined hitting the big cities as well as using my Eurail Pass for day trips to smaller towns with historic churches. Brother August was studying at a university in Tübingen, Germany, and he invited me to visit. And the big surprise: soon after Billy and I started dating, I learned that he, too, was taking one of the flights to Europe. As a graduate student in medieval history, he would bring a knowledge of history, art, and architecture to his travels that I didn't have.

Billy's flight departed a couple of days after mine, so I arrived in London on my own. That first evening I took a walk and found myself on the edge of Hyde Park, where—lo and behold—men were cruising in abundance. I met a fellow who took me to his pad, as he described it. It was like a jump back in time, to the working-class men I had met on subways and with whom there would be no second time. But there was comfort in realizing that the gay world I had discovered in New York had a counterpart across the Atlantic.

Wandering around London the next day, I was overwhelmed by the abundance of possibilities. But once Billy arrived, he became my tour guide, as he had been in the Village—although this time on a much grander scale. As we walked across the city, he pointed to notable buildings that he instantly labeled "baroque" or "Victorian" as I tried to grasp what made a building one style or another. Most memorable in our eight days of sightseeing was a side trip to Ely by train to see its cathedral. As we reached the large, open green field that led to the cathedral's entrance, I was stunned by the awesome power of the structure. A massive gray tower rose magnificently from the ground; layer upon layer of arched windows reached toward the sky. In barely an instant I was a convert, ready to travel the continent to see every cathedral that was still standing.

At the end of our stay in London, we headed in separate directions. He was going to Florence, his base for a good chunk of the summer and where he planned to stay with Lawrence and Robin, a married couple who were good friends. Traveling alone for three weeks put me on edge more than I realized it would. I had never been on my own before, separated from anyone I knew, and now I was doing it in countries where English was not the language. Finding places to eat, taking meals on my own, figuring out how to communicate: everything was a challenge. But each day brought pleasurable discoveries, and I was swept along by the excitement of the experience.

By the time I reached Florence, I was thrilled to be reunited with Billy. I had a place of my own to stay, since Billy had never talked to Robin and Lawrence about being gay. He would present me as an undergraduate history major whom he had met at Columbia. In Florence, as in London, Billy was my tour guide. Florence was so rich in architecture and art that it made previous stops seem like preparation for the real thing.

Evenings were spent with Lawrence and Robin, often eating in their apartment, where Lawrence took great pride in cooking Italian-style meals. He was easygoing and loved recounting tales from his earlier time in Italy. Robin was another story. With each meal together, I sensed a growing impatience with my presence. I imagined her saying to Lawrence when Billy wasn't there, "Why does he have this kid around?" But whatever she might have felt, she didn't prevent my coming along on day trips to explore the hill towns of Tuscany, where medieval towers rose majestically above us.

One of these trips, to Perugia, was the setting for my summer's disaster. As we headed to the train station to return to Florence, I couldn't find my Eurail Pass. Following the advice of the travel guide, I kept my wallet, passport, and train pass each in a separate pocket, and I suppose I should have been thankful that the pocket that was picked didn't contain either of the other two. But the Eurail Pass was my ticket for unlimited travel. At that point, my plan was to go farther south in Italy, then head north to Switzerland, Austria, Germany, and Denmark, and end the summer in Paris. Now I would have to pay for every train ride I took.

I had been sending postcards and letters every day to the Bronx. A trip like this was so outside the family routine that my letters describing what I had seen, and especially the postcards illustrating the sights, provoked many letters in return. When the theft happened, I wrote home immediately, and letters of concern came rushing back. Mom wrote that Dad was wiring $500 to an office that Berkey had in Rome. I was to make sure that I still took the trip to Tübingen to see Brother August. "We want you to go," she concluded. But even with the money Dad sent, the theft forced me to curtail sharply my travels for the remaining seven weeks. I resolved to stay in Rome for most of my time, then head to Tübingen for a few days, and finally to Paris for the last week before returning home.

.............

Arriving in Rome, I had the address of a hostel and simply needed directions to get there. But before I could locate an information booth in the train station, a woman began tugging at my sleeve and speaking in Italian, with bits of broken English. She pointed at my suitcase and made gestures with her hand and head that suggested sleep. I didn't know how to escape her without making a scene, and so I found myself practically pulled by her onto the streets until we reached a modest-looking building several blocks away. The woman, whose name was Magdalena, took me up the stairs to a large apartment where most of the rooms had multiple beds. She wrote out a price, which was affordable, and delivered my suitcase to one of the rooms.

By now it was dinnertime, and Magdalena led me to a window and pointed to a trattoria down the street. "Bene, bene," she kept repeating. The next morning, she served me espresso and a small pastry. As I was leaving the table, she gestured at me and said, "Carta?" I paused for a moment and then realized she was asking if I had a map. I showed her the map that was inside my travel guide. Shaking her head no and replying with phrases I didn't understand, she left for a minute and returned with a much larger map. Spreading it on the table, she proceeded to show me where we were and then pointed to places she clearly considered priorities for my first day in Rome.

Over the next days, I walked from one end of Rome to the other, which was no small achievement. Two thousand years of history rose from the ground, from the ruins of the Coliseum through the baroque statues of Bernini. Every day brought something new that made me gasp. I may have been a lapsed Catholic, but it was impossible not to stand awed inside St. Peter's in Vatican City, its ceiling seemingly as high as the sky. Any street might lead suddenly to a large piazza with another church to visit, with paintings by yet another great artist, or an outdoor sculpture that demanded that I stare forever. At the end of every day, Magdalena seemed to be waiting for me to show her on the map what I had seen and then to make new suggestions. I quickly felt so at home that I wrote to Billy that he had to stay here. When he arrived the next week, I met him at the train station and led him to her place. For the next few days, I reversed the role that Billy had played earlier in the summer, as I guided him to the sites that had most impressed me.

I ended up spending five weeks in Rome. Partly it was financial necessity. But something more was keeping me there. The people I encountered in my daily wanderings seemed delighted with themselves and each other; they seemed pleased with the world they had inherited by being Italian. After only a few days in Rome, I felt that I had come home, that I had unearthed an essential piece of myself that had remained buried for a long time. The gestures, the facial expressions, the pitch of the voices of people on the street, the sound of phrases that I didn't understand but that seemed familiar: all of it restored to life those times at Big Grandma's house when a birthday or anniversary brought the older relatives together to celebrate, and their conversation in the language of the home country filled the room. No, the dialect of Sicily did not duplicate the Italian of Rome. But it didn't matter. I felt at home. It was a striking contrast to the alienation that Columbia often provoked in me, the feeling that for whatever reason—the Catholicism that shaped me, the working-class immigrant background, the gayness that I had to manage so carefully—I didn't quite belong.

But there was something more specific to the sense of homecoming I was experiencing, something that stretched across my childhood and teenage years. I found myself thinking about the many times I had confronted the view that Italians were inferior. Some of these occasions were routine and mundane, the stuff of life in New York. There was the annual commemoration of Saint Patrick's Day that the archdiocese promoted. The pride of the Irish at St. Raymond's shone brightly in the days leading up to it, and with it came taunts aimed at all of us, mostly Italians, who were not Irish. Other moments were more directly pointed at me. Once, in eighth grade, Brother Bernard was lecturing about church history. In the middle of it he shifted to describing a trip he had taken to Italy. Suddenly I heard him tell the class that everything in Italy was dirty—the streets, the restaurants, the people. I was so furious that, when he looked in my direction, I instinctively stuck my tongue out. He began screaming that I had to go to the principal's office. I headed toward the door, but just before reaching it, something struck me in the head. Brother Bernard had thrown his shoe at me and now was shouting at me to get back to my desk. Or there was the time at Regis when I happened upon the principal, Father McCusker, in a hallway. He stopped me, stared for a moment at my head, and then, with a smirk on his face, said, "I've never seen a blond Guinea before."

Now, seeing before me the culture of the ancient world and the Renaissance, seeing millennia of history in which Italians had created so much to admire, I felt the kind of enthusiasm that classical studies had produced in me at Regis. Suddenly I knew that I wanted to learn the history and absorb the culture of Italy with all its glories and challenges. I had no idea what career paths it might open, but I didn't care. I simply felt this was meant to be.

I stayed in Rome until mid-August. I took a train to Munich and then to Tübingen, where I spent a few days with Brother August. As always, he was completely supportive. He was studying for a doctoral degree in theology, and the intellectual in him encouraged my newfound desire to study Italian history and culture. While I was there, Russia invaded Czechoslovakia, and Brother August translated the huge headlines that splashed across the pages of every newspaper. I then made my way to Paris, where Billy and I reconnected. By the time I boarded the plane to return home, I felt more than ready for the year ahead.

............

When I reflect on my time at Columbia, junior year stands out as the most satisfying and least stressful. Partly the calm can be explained by the resolution of my religious conflicts and the new grounding I had in a gay world. Partly it was the lower level of political turmoil on campus for most of the year. My being away for the summer had also calmed the waters at home. Mom and Dad were happy to have me safely back, and issues like the draft were thankfully still on hold.

I immediately threw myself into the task of learning more about what I was describing to myself as my heritage. I searched the course listings for anything that allowed me to study things Italian. European history courses topped the list. All of my history professors that year and the next praised my work. I researched papers on Italian unification and Italy's emergence as a nation in the nineteenth century and on the resistance to fascism in the 1920s. I became familiar with a set of heroic figures, such as Garibaldi and his role in Italian unification, and the socialist Giuseppe Mazzini, who was assassinated for opposing Mussolini. And naturally, I took introductory Italian language courses. The instructor, Mr. Santorini, was a gem of a teacher, Italian by birth. Listening to him as he moved energetically around the classroom, gesturing spontaneously with almost every phrase, made it seem as if I was still in Rome. Maybe because the language was embedded in me from all the times I heard Big Grandma and her daughters speaking, I found myself picking it up faster than I had with French. As the year went on, trips to the Bronx became opportunities to drop Italian phrases into the dinner conversation. It always brought a smile to Mom's face.

............

My coursework also became the stuff of conversation with Billy. The culture of the Middle Ages and the Renaissance was the heart of what he was studying, and he fed my enthusiasm. We were still very much lovers that year, though the setting for our relationship had changed. The apartment on Greenwich Avenue was overstretching his budget, and after coming back from Europe, he moved in with a friend of his, Michael, who lived in a small basement apartment in the West Village. Billy and I no longer had privacy. I couldn't stay over on Friday or Saturday nights. Sex between us happened only when Billy knew that Michael would be out. But even so, the year continued to add to my sense of a gay world. We still roamed the streets of the Village. Michael, Billy's roommate, was also something of a shocker. He merited the description of gorgeous blond. His flirting on the street or in a restaurant was uncontainable. One evening, Michael casually mentioned that he was sure he had passed the thousand mark in terms of tricks. The disbelief must have shown on my face because he then began to explain. "Well, I came to New York when I was twenty-one. That was six years ago. If I figure two hundred men a year—oh, I'm sure I've reached a thousand!" It made my mere forty-something set of sex partners, which had once left this Catholic boy racked with guilt, seem like a model of virtue.

Even with less sex between me and Billy, I didn't feel a pull to cruise when I was back on campus, certainly not the way I did during my first two years at Columbia. The relationship with Billy provided stability. I was also developing a gay social life of my own. Jack, Hazen, and Kurt were all living off campus that year. Mom and Dad wouldn't hear of my living "unsupervised," as they put it, so I was back in a single-occupancy room in John Jay. A few doors away was a sophomore whom I almost immediately recognized as one of my tribe. Gerritt had aspirations to become a poet. He seemed to know the name of every literary figure in New York and often went to public readings. One of Gerritt's good friends was Richard, who also lived in John Jay. Richard displayed an edge of flamboyance, and he deployed it in the dorm as a way of daring anyone to bother him. Active in the city's gay scene, he entertained us by describing his adventures in Manhattan's gay bars. There was also Todd, who embodied the studious nerd. He had no gay tales to share, but he frequently joined the three of us in Gerritt's room and absorbed the stories we were telling.

Jack and Hazen lived three blocks from campus on Riverside Drive and 112th Street, in what New Yorkers called a "railroad flat." I visited often and also saw Jack on campus, since he still worked at Earl Hall, a center of antiwar activism. Though he was dating girls and developing a steady relationship with Judy, a Barnard student, he was open with her about his attraction to men. From the time I came out to him the previous year, Jack was curious about every detail I could provide about the gay world I was discovering. Once I began dating Billy, he wanted to know all about the Village scene, and I regularly gave him updates on new cruising places and gay-friendly restaurants to which Billy was introducing me.

The fact that my three best friends from freshman year were all living off campus opened the door to another piece of the times. I had not even heard the word *marijuana* before starting at Columbia, but once there, it popped up frequently in conversation. The summer after freshman year, when hippies seemed to take possession of San Francisco, hallucinogens entered the picture as well. Billy didn't use marijuana, but intellectual that he was, he had recently read a book by Aldous Huxley, the acclaimed author of *Brave New World*, in which Huxley described his experience with mescaline. Billy gave me *The Doors of Perception / Heaven and Hell* to read. I was enthralled. Still drawn to the mystical and the divine even as I let go of Catholicism, I was taken by Huxley's description of his experience with mescaline. Words like *transcendence* and *the infinite* appeared again and again. He described a connection to the universe that seemed holy, and he presented it as a powerful contradiction to the isolation—what he called "a society of island universes"—that often seemed to envelop me at Columbia.

Billy wasn't able to find a source of mescaline, but when he proposed that we take LSD, I agreed. We dropped acid in his apartment on a Saturday afternoon. At first, nothing happened. But then, suddenly, the physical environment came alive. The wall that we were facing retreated into the distance. A glass on the table glowed and vibrated. My sense of time unraveled, and eternity no longer seemed abstract. At some point, Billy proposed that we go out to eat. Walking along Christopher Street, I felt as if everyone was floating through the air. But this sense of lightness soon ended. We entered a diner near Sheridan Square. We sat at the corner of a two-sided counter, and as the waiter reached to give us menus, his arm stretched and grew and then grew more until a giant hand was about to encase me. I looked at Billy, my eyes bulging in terror. He was simply staring into the distance and grinning broadly. The moment passed, but it left a dark cloud that seemed to obscure the previous hours of blissful hallucination.

There were no more acid trips with Billy. But Jack and Hazen's move off campus had made marijuana an occasional part of their evening at home. The first time they introduced me to it, they demonstrated how to inhale from one of the joints they had made. I copied their intake of breath. I noticed that Jack and Hazen kept looking at each other and laughing, even though no one had said anything funny. Between bouts of laughter, they would sink into the couch and sigh. I was determined to be part of the scene, and so I laughed with them. But I kept wondering, What is all the fuss about? This pattern repeated itself on two or three occasions. Then, one night, after several rounds of inhaling, I seemed to begin floating toward the ceiling. My eyes widened. I started giggling, and they began laughing as well. After that, I was always ready to share a joint. I was on board for the trip, wherever it might take me.

............

While the return from Europe unleashed an energy that I was pouring into my studies, I also wondered what the year would bring in terms of campus activism and antiwar organizing. The demonstrations and police violence at the Democratic National Convention in Chicago were the hot topic of discussion, and we were in the middle of a presidential election in which no candidate reflected the antiwar views of student radicals. Despite this, the campus was relatively quiet that fall. Eldridge Cleaver gave a talk that made headlines, and there were a few demonstrations, but it was nothing like the previous two years when rallies and marches were the stuff of daily life. It wasn't clear why. Nixon's victory in November seemed like a symptom of the decline of America into cynicism and despair, but he was also claiming that he was going to bring the troops home. Were SDSers and other antiwar leaders waiting to see if he would deliver? I wasn't close enough to the center of action to know the explanation.

But my pacifist convictions still asserted themselves. A draft counseling center at Earl Hall was working steadily, even if quietly, to provide assistance to guys who did not want to be drafted after graduation. Its work at Columbia was one small part of a strategy to make it impossible to continue the war by reducing the number of eligible draftees. Jack's job at Earl Hall kept him up-to-date about the activities going on there, and through conversations with him, I decided to volunteer. The spark behind the counseling work was a senior named Jeff. Tall, thin, with a long blond ponytail, Jeff lacked the drama of SDS leaders who spoke at campus rallies. But he made the counseling center a place that delivered what it promised: information and resources to make someone unsuitable for the military.

After receiving my training, I made time each week to provide advice to the guys, mostly Columbia students but occasionally others, who sought help. All of us who counseled potential draftees had to become experts in Selective Service regulations. I learned what conditions protected someone from being classified I-A. The draft counseling center maintained a list of doctors and psychiatrists willing to meet with potential draftees, examine the young men, and write letters supporting a deferment. One of the hidden pieces of the antiwar movement was the large number of professionals who used their privilege to keep young men from being drafted.

As winter turned to spring and it was more comfortable to be outdoors, SDS asserted itself again. Nixon was not delivering on his promises, and so antiwar activity, especially directed against the ways Columbia cooperated with "the system," reappeared. There were calls to shut down the campus, and some attempts to occupy buildings, but nothing like the previous spring when events at Columbia were the stuff of newspaper headlines.

.............

Truth be told, my mind was elsewhere, for I was planning a second summer in Europe, this time entirely in Italy, where I hoped to become fluent in the language. The sense that I was meant to reclaim my Italian heritage and immerse myself in its history and culture remained vibrant all year. Mr. Santorini's class was especially a delight. At one point, he told me about a summer language program in Perugia, the scene of my disaster a few months earlier. He provided me with information about it, and almost immediately I was won over.

The biggest question was where I would get the money. I hadn't fully depleted my broken-arm fund, but it wouldn't cover a second summer's expenses, even if I stayed in one place much of the time. I spoke to Evelyn, and she promised extra hours of work during the holiday season. I also mentioned my need to earn more to Miss Gordan at the museum, and Dr. Mead granted me a small stipend to help me along. But that still left a gap, and I tried to accumulate the remaining funds by eating the simplest diet possible. Mom and Dad's concession to my desire to live off campus had been to take me off the meal plan at school and instead give me the funds to manage my own food budget. It would be training, they told me, for living within my means. And so, that year, I seemed to live on peanut butter and jelly sandwiches and Campbell's tomato soup. Always thin, as spring arrived I was weighing only in the mid-120s. Still, when it came time to purchase my charter flight ticket, it remained unclear whether I had enough money to last the summer.

That's when Billy intervened. As the time approached to pay for the plane, he made a proposal. What if, this year, we actually had a summer together in Europe? He would rent a car in Paris and pay for it, so the cost of train fare would vanish. We would stop at a few places in France, but most of our time would be spent in Italy. We could sleep in the car and at campsites outside the small towns we visited, and that would save money as well. He laughed as he told me that the trip would still allow me to improve my language skills since, in exchange for his driving, I would do all the talking with the Italians we encountered. Suddenly, the money problem was disappearing, and it would be amazing to visit an array of villages off the main itinerary of most summer tourists.

As with all the Columbia flights, we flew to London and stayed for a handful of days. A London theater was featuring a production of *The Boys in the*

*Band*, a gay play that had opened in New York the previous year and that every one of Billy's Village acquaintances was talking about. As we sat waiting for the performance to begin, I thought of how the theater district in New York had been my first cruising area, and how James Baldwin opened *Another Country* with a desperate Rufus in a Times Square theater getting picked up by a trick. *The Boys in the Band* was another world. These New York gay friends were full of sharp wit and caustic banter. Yes, they experienced internal conflict about being gay. But their homosexuality was a fact of life. I had seen or read nothing like this before.

In Paris, Billy picked up the car. Growing up in the Bronx without a car and dependent on the availability of uncles and aunts for rides to anywhere, I had no experience of a long drive that stretched over more than ten weeks of travel. Now, each day brought discoveries, and every drive provoked wonder. The first day, Billy drove to the Loire Valley, with castles from centuries in which royalty ruled the country. We then made our way along smaller roads into the hills and valleys of central France. I especially remember the village of Conques, buried deep in the forest and containing a Romanesque church of breathtaking beauty. How, I wondered, did a community so small and remote come to construct a place of worship of such quality that it has lasted for almost a thousand years?

But Italy was our destination, and I was happy to have weeks of traveling through the Italian Peninsula. We stopped in towns that, from the early centuries of Christianity through the Middle Ages and the Renaissance, had seen the flowering of art in all its splendor—not just the architecture of churches but mosaics and paintings that filled the walls of these houses of worship. Each hill town invariably exceeded my expectations. Approaching Orvieto and seeing its walls rise up from the green fields and hill below, I could imagine the need of these villagers long ago to protect themselves from the attacks of invading troops. The cathedral was a place of both architectural splendor and spiritual calm.

Most of our stops were for just one or two nights, but we did spend a week in Rome, and Magdalena welcomed us with a kiss on the cheek. I wasn't, naturally, able to engage in fluent conversation. But my year of language class and the three weeks of walking through towns where I heard Italian all around me had made it possible to do more than speak a word or phrase. Magdalena smiled at my effort, and she helped me along by pointing at things she was talking about to improve my vocabulary.

As we traveled toward Sicily, I anticipated arriving in the territory of my family. Palermo was a lovely city, very walkable, with views of the Mediterranean that brought peace and calm. But most spectacular were the sites of ruins from the Roman era. Walking amid the stone pillars of Agrigento, I felt the content of my Latin classes at Regis spring to life. The remains of ancient theaters in Siracusa and Taormina had me visualizing men in togas and events that brought whole towns together.

Billy, naturally, enjoyed the trip every bit as much as I did, and while I brought a good bit of knowledge to our travels, he added a depth and detail that I didn't have. And since I didn't know how to drive, he was responsible for every mile of the trip. I couldn't have had an experience like this without him. Yet the trip exacted a toll. I had never spent so much continuous time with anyone before, and certainly not with a lover. As the summer wore on, I felt myself wanting to be free of him, to be on my own without his guidance. But at the same time, I was completely dependent. I didn't know how to assert myself, how to say something as simple as "Let's explore on our own today and meet for dinner tonight."

............

We spent the last few days in Paris. Walking the streets of the Left Bank one afternoon, we passed a newsstand and noticed the *Village Voice*. It seemed a sign that, yes, our summer was ending. Billy bought a copy, and we sat with it at a café near the river. The front page described a police raid of the Stonewall Inn on Christopher Street, not far from where Billy used to live. We had gone to the Stonewall in the first months of our relationship. The dancing go-go boys wearing nothing but a thin strap to cover their genitals were not easily forgotten. Reading about the street riots the raid had provoked was fascinating; neither of us had ever heard of such a thing happening. What were we coming back to? we wondered.

# 20

.............

## Now What Do I Do?

The fascination of the news report in the *Village Voice* notwithstanding, I knew what I was coming back to: senior year. The last time I faced senior year, at Regis, it felt like I was preparing to leave the safe and familiar and venture into the unknown. But at least the unknown had a name—college. Now I was facing decisions about the rest of my life at a time when everything was uncertain. The campus, the city, the nation: all seemed ready to explode. Even a gay bar in Greenwich Village.

.............

The weeks of driving through Italy had confirmed the feelings of the previous summer. Walking along streets lined by buildings many centuries old, staring at murals and mosaics depicting religious figures and stories that moved my soul, listening to the rhythm of the language as it was spoken on the streets and watching people gesture as they talked: these experiences gave me a sense of home, of a connection that made me think of the warmth and goodness of Big Grandma. By the end of the summer, I understood more and more in my encounters with Italians, and though I responded slowly and haltingly, they understood me, too. The previous spring, Mr. Santorini had encouraged me to think about skipping second-year Italian and enrolling in his literature course. I now felt the confidence to do it.

Some of my history professors were encouraging me to apply to graduate school, and I did apply to the University of Michigan and the University of Minnesota, since each had well-respected specialists in Italian history. But Mr. Santorini, who was aware of my opposition to the war and my pacifist convictions, told me about a master's program at the Johns Hopkins University School of Advanced International Studies in DC. The first year was spent in Bologna. "We call it the People's Republic of Bologna," he told me laughingly as we talked after class. Billy and I had spent three days there. It was a city of beautiful street colonnades, where one could stroll casually for hours. The idea of returning was very appealing. I also suspected that the possibility of a year in Italy would please Mom, something I had not accomplished often since starting college. Of course, I knew not to mention the "People's Republic."

. . . . . . . . . . . . .

Even as I completed applications, graduate school seemed abstract and unreal. If anything felt concrete and immediate, it was the war. Nixon's actions were breathing new life into the antiwar movement. An organization calling itself the Moratorium announced coordinated demonstrations for both October and November. Its leaders called on activists to plan protests in their home communities for October 15. Then, in November, all were to descend on Washington for a massive antiwar march. That fall, when I returned to Dr. Mead's office, I discovered that two of her staffers, Laurie and Jeanne, had already begun organizing moratorium events at the museum. I immediately volunteered to help. We distributed a flyer to all staff inviting them to the events we had planned. We reserved an assembly room in the museum for a staff "speak-out" against the war.

On Moratorium Day we set up large posters at the museum's entrance listing the number of casualties in Vietnam: American service members, Vietnamese civilians, and Vietnamese fighters. On the steps facing Central Park, staff held up a banner calling for immediate withdrawal of US troops. We circulated petitions asking for an end to American involvement. We collected fourteen hundred signatures and sent copies to President Nixon and our senators. We distributed thousands of flyers outlining reasons for opposing the war and urging people to write members of Congress. The staff speak-out was so exhilarating that we began meeting weekly over lunch to share stories about what we were doing—not only against the war, but other forms of activism, too. Jeanne was participating in one of the radical feminist consciousness-raising groups springing up in New York, and she shared with us the powerful insights about sexism, a new word for the rest of us, that emerged from those sessions.

Meanwhile, as soon as the speak-out ended, I rushed back to Columbia. Students, faculty, and staff had planned to assemble on campus and march down Broadway to Bryant Park on Forty-Second Street for a large rally. Kurt, Jack, Hazen, and I marched together. When we weren't chanting some version of "Two, four, six, eight, stop the war and smash the state," the thrill of filling Broadway with our bodies, stopping traffic, and joining hands as we marched brought a perpetual grin to our faces. At Bryant Park, marchers from throughout the city jammed the area.

That night, I described to Kurt the events at the museum. He was intrigued by the flyer we handed to people, asking them to write to members of Congress. "What if everyone opposed to the war did that?" he asked. "Congress would be swamped." After a pause during which I could see him thinking, he said, "We could start a chain letter! We give a letter to everyone we know and include a model letter they can send to Nixon and Congress. And we ask them to do the same with people they know." Within a couple of days, we had drafted the letters and mimeographed two thousand copies. I gave them to classmates; I brought copies that fall to the Regis alumni social; I circulated them at Berkey; Kurt and I slipped them under the doors of neighbors in our building.

When we went to DC for the national march in November, we distributed the letters to people assembling for the chartered buses that were taking us to the capital. As our bus got closer to Washington, the highway seemed filled with nothing but buses and cars converging for the same reason. The crowd that marched that weekend was bigger than anything I had ever seen. It was hard not to believe we were going to succeed.

. . . . . . . . . . . . .

The Moratorium events were exciting, but also exceptional. More immediate was the work at the draft counseling center. The center had begun reaching beyond Columbia students and making its services available to anyone facing the draft. I handed out flyers at City College, a mile north of Columbia in Harlem, describing the center's work. I brought flyers to neighborhood churches for ministers to distribute. Jeff, who seemed to generate most of the action plans at the center, asked several of us to go in shifts to the Selective Service office in Manhattan, on the far west side in Midtown. We were to give flyers to the men who were there and tell them about our services.

At some point, the core group at the counseling center decided to move beyond helping individuals. The plan was to put pressure on the local draft boards in Manhattan. Its members passed judgment on each draft-age man in their district. Jeff knew I was already going to the Selective Service office. He told me to ask for the names of all draft board members in Manhattan. When I made the request on my next visit, it drew a look of disgust from the woman staffing the reception desk, but she brought the lists and I copied the names. Once we had found addresses for some of them, we started picketing their apartment buildings. We informed residents of the building and others on the block that a neighbor was sending men to Vietnam. One draft board member owned a retail store in the West Village, and we picketed outside. We hoped to pressure them to resign. We wanted to cripple the system and make it impossible to draft enough men to keep fighting the war.

The demonstrations and picketing brought a good deal of satisfaction, but the heart of the counseling center's mission remained the work with individuals. Many guys were desperate. They had received the call for a physical and didn't know their options. In some cases, they had borderline conditions that, with a doctor's testimony, might get a deferment. More often they didn't. In a decade before obesity had become a common condition, many young men were thin enough that, if they starved themselves for a couple of weeks and went without liquids for two days before their physical, they might shrink below the threshold of an acceptable weight. Stories circulated about guys who were so underfed and dehydrated that they passed out during the physical. Of those I counseled, my experience with a graduating senior at City College captured the desperation of the times. As I read to him the physical conditions that exempted individuals, he held out his hands, looked at them, and asked, "How many knuckles would I have to lose to fail my physical?" A determination showed on his face and in his eyes, and I didn't know what to do other than to look through the regulations and answer his question.

...............

In the middle of all this activity, the Nixon administration announced it was abandoning the system of deferments and instituting a lottery. Nixon presented it as a matter of fairness: no exemptions for those privileged enough to attend college or for those in occupations that presumed the privilege of higher education. Instead, each calendar date would randomly receive a number from 1 to 365, and the number attached to one's birthday became one's place in the lineup of potential draftees.

There was some truth to the claims about fairness. A lottery was more equitable. But the shift to a lottery also involved a great deal of cynicism and vengeance. Since so much of the opposition to the war was coming from college campuses, eliminating student deferments worked as a form of payback. And by guaranteeing that those with high numbers would never be drafted, Nixon and his aides speculated that, for many, the motivation to protest would fade.

The lottery was held on the evening of December 1. The first year, it involved every male from eighteen to twenty-five. All activity seemed to stop at Columbia that night, and probably at most other campuses as well. Jack, Kurt, Hazen, and I sat together in our apartment riveted to the television. Over the next couple of hours, we watched officials pull individual capsules from a large container, each one containing a calendar date. Each pick determined the fate of thousands. As it turned out, the four of us were spread across the full range. Kurt's birthday came up almost immediately: his number was 5, which meant that he was certain to receive a call for induction. Jack came next: his birthday was in the low 100s, also certain to get a call to serve. Mine was in the low 200s, which made it unlikely I would be drafted. Hazen's was one of the very last to be picked. Two of us facing the draft, two of us safe: it didn't leave much room for celebration.

Even before the lottery became a certainty, I already knew that I was living through my last year of student deferment. Since the end of freshman year, I had wanted to file as a conscientious objector. But the enraged response it had produced from Dad made me back away and put my plans on hold. As senior year began, that was no longer an option. Before the lottery became definite, I had already begun asking the teachers who knew me best about writing letters that testified to my sincerity. With some hesitation about bothering someone of her importance, I also approached Dr. Mead, and she too promised a letter.

That fall, on one of my visits home, I raised the subject. I knew it might generate screams and threats, and I resolved to stay calm and not rouse them further. After dinner was over and Jimmy had retreated to the bedroom to watch television, I broached the subject. "I need to talk with you," I said. "My student deferment ends in June, and it's possible I'll get drafted. You know I don't intend to serve, and I want to register as a conscientious objector. I realize it isn't what you want, but I hope you'll support me and write letters that I can include with my application."

I could see the looks they were exchanging, looks I had come to recognize over these last years as saying, "Why are you putting us through this?" Finally, Mom turned to me and said, "We raised you to be an American. How can you do this? How are we going to explain this to the family and our neighbors? What if they send you to jail?"

"I don't think I'll be sent to jail, Mom. It's a possibility, but especially if you write for me, the chances are I'll get CO status, and that will just mean having to work at a community service job for two years."

"But why do you want to do this? It will bring the family shame. Your cousins Vincent and Donald served in the military. Why can't you?"

"They didn't have to fight in a war, Mom. I can't do it. This war is wrong, and it's made me realize that I couldn't fight in any war."

"What do you mean you couldn't fight in any war?" she shot back. "You wouldn't fight if there was another Pearl Harbor? What if the Russians dropped an atom bomb on us?"

"Mom, please," I said. She was pushing back as hard as I feared she would.

Dad hadn't spoken, which was interesting because the last time he had been the one who threatened to banish me forever. But now he intervened.

"Well, let me ask you this," he started. "Suppose your brother Jimmy was fighting in Vietnam. What if he got killed? You wouldn't feel you had to defend his honor? You wouldn't want to fight in his name?"

That did it. I lost it. Despite my best intentions, I found myself shouting. "That is the stupidest thing I have ever heard you say. If Jimmy were killed, what good could it do to kill someone else? It wouldn't even be the same guy who killed Jimmy! You're not making sense."

Mom was looking at Dad now, and he was just sitting there, staring at his hands. Finally, he said, "OK, I'll write a letter." His response caught me up short. All I could think to respond was, "You will? Why?"

"The question I asked you was the same question they asked me when I was in the service, and I told them the same thing, that I wouldn't fight even if my brother Doc was killed in the Pacific. And so they discharged me."

"What do you mean they discharged you because you wouldn't fight? I thought you got out of the army because you hurt your back and couldn't fight."

With that exchange began a dramatic revision of the family saga. During my childhood, for the adults in my family, World War II was an almost living presence. It came up often in conversation, even if the men never spoke directly about combat experiences. Uncles Phil and Doc and Tommy, as well as the male cousins in Dad's family, had all either served overseas or worked in a defense job. Dad was the only exception. The story I heard, and it was told often, was that after a few months of basic training, he was discovered to have a weak back and given a medical discharge. That was how he managed to get Sophie to go out with him, he explained, since her other boyfriends were fighting overseas. And then Dad would always laugh.

Now I heard a vastly different account. Apparently, army life had never agreed with Dad. After basic training in Arkansas, he came home on leave. When his leave was over, he refused to return and went AWOL. His family finally convinced him to go back, and the army court-martialed him and put him in a stockade for ninety days. Dad smiled as he told me that he got time off for good behavior, and he rejoined his troop in Arizona. But then, just as they received orders to go overseas, the one close buddy he had made in those months committed suicide. Dad, who never was good at making friends, was so upset that he took to his bed and refused to move. He tried to kill himself with an overdose of pills of some kind. But it didn't work, and the doctors sent him to an army psychiatrist. After several visits in which he didn't say much, the psychiatrist finally asked him the question that Dad posed to me, and soon two MPs were accompanying him on a train back to the Bronx and delivering him to his parents.

I listened quietly to his telling. Many in my generation were standing in solidarity with each other, boldly proclaiming our opposition to an unjust war and proud to accept the consequences. Refusing to fight was a mark of honor. Not in World War II. We had been attacked by Japan. Hitler was murdering Jews and trying to conquer the world. War resisters received no respect. They were traitors or cowards. Dad's refusal to fight promised shame. Fortunately, he had been able to live behind the protection that his medical discharge provided. Other than Mom, he never told anyone the truth. Not until now, that is, when my plea for support propelled him to reveal the story.

Mom was uncharacteristically silent, and I had no idea what to say other than to thank him for agreeing to write for me. Mom said she would write, too. A few weeks later, when I was home for dinner again, they gave me their neatly folded letters. Unlike the others that I had received, which were typed, Mom and Dad wrote theirs by hand, which made the content seem all the more real. They both attested to my sincerity. They described the seriousness with which I had always taken religion, from the time of my first communion. Mom described how, the Christmas that she and Dad had given me a toy gun and holster as a gift, I put the holster on and pulled out the gun, but then never played with it again. Dad explained that he believed me because, when he was my age, he had also felt that he couldn't kill another human being and had been discharged because of it. Later that night, as I read the letters in my apartment on Morningside Heights, I couldn't stop from crying.

. . . . . . . . . . . . .

The last semester at Columbia seemed to be about nothing but the war and the draft. Within days after the lottery, the draft counseling center was deluged by guys with low numbers wanting assistance. Through the winter and spring they came in droves.

Somehow, my expertise as a counselor didn't ease the anxiety of my own application for CO status. Through a series of questions on the Selective Service form, I basically had to tell my life story in a way that proved that my appeal was deeply rooted and undeniably sincere. Unlike a debate case, where I was arguing a topic completely removed from my own life, now I was having to make a case for myself. It was not an easy thing to do for a kid from a Sicilian family, one of whose basic values was never to draw attention to oneself, since attention only brought trouble. I don't think I ever felt more awkward than when I tried to describe the way the core messages of the life of Jesus—to love rather than hate, to be generous to enemy and friend alike, to turn the other cheek in the face of attack, to see everyone as a potential brother—were values that I tried to live by and that made it impossible to accept military service. But I pushed my way through each question and submitted it to my draft board. Within days, I received a notification to appear before the board.

The Bronx draft boards were all located on Arthur Avenue, a neighborhood that had once been filled with Italian immigrant families and that still housed some Italian businesses. The night of my appointment, I traveled there with Father Ridley (he had been ordained as a priest in the years since he taught at Regis), who agreed to come as a witness in support of me. Although the guidelines made it clear that I could bring a witness, the first thing the clerk for the board told me was that it was not hearing from anyone other than those under review. It didn't bode well.

The clerk took me into the office where the draft board members met. It was set up like a college seminar room, with four long tables arranged in a square. The chair of the board, a white-haired Irish-looking man probably in his sixties, was seated to my right, and three other board members were spread around the other two sides. They were all reviewing files and barely acknowledged my presence. The clerk gave the chairman my file and left.

I had brought copies of my statements and letters, and I passed them to the other board members. One of them asked why I was there, and I said I had applied for classification as a conscientious objector. As soon as I said it, another member looked at me with contempt and flung the pages across the room. I said nothing—how could I respond to that?—and sat waiting while the chair of the board read my application. Finally, he asked why they should grant my request. I began talking, trying to explain how being raised Catholic, even though Catholicism was hardly known for its pacifist leanings, had gotten me to this place. At one point, I must have used the phrase "my beliefs," because suddenly the board member who had thrown my materials on to the floor spit out, "We all have our beliefs." By this point I had broken into a sweat, and so I finished quickly and waited for questions. When none were forthcoming, the chairman told me I could leave.

The experience left me badly shaken. The chance of getting CO status suddenly seemed dim, and I felt at the mercy of a lottery that might, or might not, reach my number. A couple of days later, I was at the draft counseling office and described the experience to Jeff. He told me that I should write up a detailed description of the evening and bring it to the draft board for inclusion in my file, in case I had to appeal their decision. The next week, I was there with my typed account and told the clerk that I had something to add to my file. She brought out the file, opened it, and was about to take my summary when her phone rang. Leaving the file on the counter, she hurried to her desk. I quickly snuck a look. There it was, right on top, the form approving my request. A sense of relief like I had never experienced rushed through me. The fear of what would follow if I had to refuse induction was suddenly completely gone.

Not long after this, I received another notification from my draft board, this one telling me to report to Fort Hamilton in Brooklyn for my physical. This was standard procedure. All that winter and spring, notices were going out as Selective Service worked its way down the numbers in the lottery. Kurt and Jack had already received theirs. I knew from my counseling work that, as a CO, I did not have to take the physical. But I thought, why not? I'm counseling guys who are going for physicals. I'd be a more effective counselor if I had the experience.

Fort Hamilton was on the far edge of Brooklyn, and to get there on time, I had to leave Morningside Heights by dawn. Unlike the draft board experience, I was looking forward to this. Nothing was at stake.

The day began with a comprehensive questionnaire that asked for information on just about every physical and mental condition imaginable. I went through the questionnaire, checking "no" over and over. There was an item about "flat feet," which I did have, so I checked "yes" on that one, although I knew that it wasn't consequential. There was a question about "limitation of motion" of one's limbs. The surgery to repair my broken arm when I was eight had resulted in my not being able to turn my left arm the full 180 degrees. If I held both arms out, palms down, I could rotate my right arm around until the palm faced up, but my left arm only turned 90 degrees. It had never seemed like a big deal. The only activity I couldn't do was to eat soup with a spoon in my left hand. Along with flat feet, this was the only question to which I answered yes.

The form also asked about homosexual acts and tendencies. I knew the question would be there, and I knew it was a surefire veto on one's ability to serve. But I had long decided that I would not answer yes. I had struggled hard enough to feel comfortable with myself. I wasn't going to let the military decide there was something wrong with me, and I wasn't going to use it to save myself from the draft.

The questionnaire completed, we were all taken through a series of medical inspections. If anything showed up, the examining physician made a note on the questionnaire. Then, each of us met with a physician who went through the form and made a final recommendation. I waited as the army doctor flipped through my pages. When he came to the question about limitation of motion, he glanced at me quizzically. "What does this mean?" he asked. I told him about the broken arm and the surgery, and I explained about my inability to turn my left arm fully. When he said, "Show me what you mean," I held out both arms and demonstrated. He took my arm in his hand, carefully tried to turn it, and immediately felt the resistance in my limb. Suddenly, his whole demeanor changed. "You really can't turn your arm," he said almost gleefully. "You suffer from 50 percent limitation of motion in one of your main limbs." And he began scribbling a description on my form, all the while repeating, "Fifty percent limitation of motion!"

I had no idea what to make of this, but I took the form and made my way to the final stop, where an army officer reviewed it. When he got to the doctor's note, he looked straight at me and snarled, "What's this?" As I started to explain, he yelled, "Let me see!" I held out my left arm and was about to do the simple demonstration when he grabbed my arm and attempted to twist it the full way around. He couldn't do it, of course, but he almost flipped me over in the effort, and I screamed in pain. As I tried to recover my composure, he checked a box on the last page and sneered contemptuously, "We don't want you!"

Almost four years of worry, four years of preoccupation with how I would respond to the challenge of the war at the most personal level—it was over. I left Fort Hamilton, and when I reached the subway station to take me back to campus, I called home from a pay phone. When Mom answered, I practically screamed with delight, "I flunked my draft physical! The broken arm did it!" And Mom, the great patriot, the one who believed I should fight for my country, burst into tears of relief.

Nothing, not even discovering that my CO application had been approved, compared to the elation that coursed through my body. I could barely sit still on the long ride to Morningside Heights. A grin kept bursting across my face. Exiting at 110th Street, I ran the three blocks to the apartment to share the news with Jack and Kurt and Hazen. No one was home, so I ran from the apartment and headed to campus. I had to find someone, anyone, to share the news with. It was the end of the afternoon, and the campus walk on 116th Street was filled with people leaving for the day. I stood looking for a familiar face. And then, suddenly, I saw one of my professors who had written a letter for me, Sheila Biddle, walking in my direction, briefcase in hand. As I rushed toward her,

I shouted, "I flunked my draft physical." She dropped her briefcase, held out both her arms, and pulled me to her. "Oh, John," she said, as she hugged me. "That's wonderful! I'm so happy for you." Her reaction, as well as that of the doctor at Fort Hamilton, brought home how many adults were deeply concerned about those of us facing the draft.

...........

While my struggles with Selective Service were suddenly over, the war still seemed ever-present. Protests were happening constantly. The action was occurring on campus and off. When my Saturday shift at Berkey was over, I almost always headed for a rally or march somewhere in Manhattan. That spring, the trial in New Haven of a group of Black Panthers on charges of conspiracy and murder was scheduled to begin, and rallies supporting them were occurring steadily, adding to the sense of upheaval. Demonstrations were daily events at Columbia. One afternoon, a group broke off from a rally on Low Plaza and ran wildly around campus, jumping hedges, racing across fields, charging in and out of buildings as they disrupted classes with their shouting, and even smashing windows in Butler Library. As had happened before, the administration called in the police.

But all of this was nothing compared with what happened in May, at the start of my last month of classes. Nixon, who kept promising to bring our boys home, announced that US troops were invading Cambodia. The country was serving, he said, as a haven for Vietcong fighters, who used it as a base to launch attacks on US and South Vietnamese troops. Across the country, campus protests exploded beyond anything seen before. Students boycotted classes, marched in the streets, and seized campus buildings.

Then, in the middle of all this, the killing of student protesters at Kent State in Ohio and Jackson State in Mississippi blew the lid off everything. Students at hundreds of universities went on strike. At Columbia the student protests dwarfed what had happened in 1968. Rallies, picketing, the rushing of students off campus into the street to block traffic: the actions never stopped. With classes suspended, when I wasn't at the draft counseling center or working at Berkey or Dr. Mead's office, I had no reason not to be one of the faces in the crowd. One day, after a particularly tumultuous rally, I left campus early, exhausted. When I got to the apartment, Judy, Jack's girlfriend, was the only one there. She was sitting on the edge of the bed, looking as spent as I was feeling. I sat next to her and took her hand. We looked at each other, and suddenly we were holding one another tightly, sobbing.

...........

Through all this, my relationship with Billy was fading. After we returned from Europe, he had moved to Brooklyn to be nearer to his job and was never at Columbia anymore. He seemed to have no interest in the antiwar protests, and preoccupied as I was with the war, we had less and less to talk about. On my part, the prospect of leaving New York to go to graduate school added to the detachment I increasingly felt when we were together. Gay relationships were mysterious enough. But at a distance? Billy and I never broke up. We never had a conversation about how things were going between us. But as winter moved into spring, the phone calls became fewer and our time together less frequent until it evaporated into nothing. Going to visit him in the Village, spending the night, walking along Christopher Street with him: it had once seemed very compelling. Now, time together seemed an interruption from what my life was about.

The irony is that, as I received acceptances and fellowships to graduate school that spring, including to the program that would have sent me to Bologna, I could no longer imagine accepting any of them. Too much was happening for me to want to leave the United States. Even though I would be graduating, I knew that I could keep volunteering at the counseling center. Demonstrations were sure to continue. I wanted to remain part of it, to be one more body screaming no. And though I had the option to choose graduate school at Michigan or Minnesota, where there were certainly vibrant student movements, I also couldn't imagine saying goodbye to New York. Billy and I might no longer be a couple, but I had become familiar with the city's gay geography. I had a few friends who knew I was gay and with whom I could talk. Why start over? Why lose the little knowledge and safety that had taken so much to acquire? And so I turned down all the schools and fellowships. When Mom and Dad asked, I simply said that I wasn't sure graduate school was right for me and I didn't want to leave New York. Mom didn't come right out and say it, but the look on her face told me that she was glad. Italian sons were never supposed to stray far from family.

Graduation at Columbia came at the beginning of June. My housemates and I donned cap and gown for Class Day, a smaller event for seniors in the college. But with all the protests surrounding the invasion of Cambodia and the killings of students, radical leaders at Columbia called for a boycott of the main university-wide graduation ceremony. Naturally, I supported the boycott and was among those who picketed the ceremony rather than march in cap and gown. Mom was crushed. She and Dad had especially been looking forward to it—an event unlike any in our extended family's history. It was another sign that I was going about life my way, and it wasn't along the path traveled by the Scamporlino and D'Emilio clans.

# 21

..............

## A Door Opens

*Career.* It was not a word that had much meaning in my family. The adults had jobs. You worked to earn a living. If there was any goal, it was simply to earn a better living than the generation before you. I had aunts who worked in the garment industry; I had uncles who worked in a poultry market, in a pants factory, or as a janitor. My female cousins worked as secretaries; male cousins had jobs with the post office or as printers. The only job that made eyes widen was that of my Uncle Doc, but not because of its importance. As the check-in clerk in a theater district hotel, he frequently saw celebrities and was often the beneficiary of complimentary tickets to Broadway plays.

Except for Kurt, who was heading to Minneapolis for alternative service work as a conscientious objector, my small circle of friends at Columbia were all embarking on the next stage of training for a career. Jack was heading to a PhD program at Stanford and a guaranteed fellowship for two years of study in England. Hazen and Periconi were starting law school in the fall. The Regis buddies I had stayed in touch with who were not in seminary also had plans for graduate or professional school of one sort or another. And me? Having turned down all my graduate school acceptance offers, I was faced with the task of finding a job in order to, as Dad put it, "support yourself."

And so that May, while protests filled the campus and the streets, I began reading the ads in the city newspapers. Those in the *New York Times* were too straitlaced and professional, and those in the *Daily News* were aimed at its blue-collar readers. But the *Village Voice*, which very much seemed part of the world of protest, had ads for jobs that felt within my reach. I applied for several and, a couple of weeks before graduation, landed an interview for a position as assistant to the periodicals librarian at Long Island University in Brooklyn.

The librarian who interviewed me, Mr. Duchac, was friendly and relaxed, and quickly put me at ease. I could tell from comments he made that he, too, opposed the war and was one of those adults who had absorbed the spirit of those years. In fact, he mentioned that it was a time of change in the library. New magazines, journals, and newspapers, reflective of the oppositional politics of the 1960s, were being published, and he had a budget that allowed him to expand the collection. He needed someone to research these publications, recommend ones to add to the library's holdings, and then be ready to learn their contents well enough that students looking for material for research papers could be pointed to them. The job sounded like a wonderful extension of school. I would read and research and keep on top of current events in an environment that, from the look and sound of my prospective boss, seemed safe and welcoming. A few days later, when Mr. Duchac called and told me the job was mine, I said yes without hesitation. The salary was $105 a week, modest to be sure, but enough to live on. The frugality that Dad had inculcated in me from the days of my first allowance would serve me well.

On the next visit to Parkchester for dinner, I announced that I had gotten the job. Mom immediately began asking how long it would take to get there from Parkchester. As an unmarried son, I was expected to live at home, just as my older cousins and her and Dad's siblings had, without exception, all remained home until marriage. Sometimes even marriage wasn't reason enough to move away from parents. That's why Big Grandpa had purchased such a large house in the Bronx. When I told her I would be staying in the apartment on Morningside Heights, she began to argue, pulling out the phrases about family that I had heard so often as a child. But then Dad intervened. If I was earning my way and could support myself, he said, it was fine if I continued to live "downtown," as anywhere in Manhattan was referred to by a Bronxite. I could still come home for dinner, he said as he looked at Mom, just as I had while at Columbia. I appreciated what he said, though it didn't surprise me. How many times had I heard him say that, were it not for Sophie's wishes, he would have been perfectly content not to have any kids? My leaving home brought him closer to having Sophie all to himself.

And so it was settled. I would stay in the railroad flat at 400 Riverside Drive that I had shared with Jack, Kurt, and Hazen. The four years on Morningside

Heights had made the neighborhood seem like it was mine. The Gold Rail, Mama Joy's, the West End, Tom's Diner: all would still be there. The apartment, it was true, would not be the same. Jack and Kurt were heading out at the end of summer. But Hazen was starting law school at Columbia and would remain. We would find a new roommate or two to help with the rent. Meanwhile, the four of us still had a final summer together.

............

A week after graduation, I got up early on Monday morning, showered, ate breakfast quickly, put on my best clothes, and walked to the subway to make my way to downtown Brooklyn. The daily commute threw me back in time to when I started school at Regis. Riding the train every day, the way Dad had tutored me: here I was doing it again, learning a new route and set of stations to get me to my destination. But this time I was an adult going to work five days a week.

New York's subways in the 1960s were identified by a set of letters—IRT, BMT, and IND—that almost served as markers of identity for their respective riders. Parkchester, Regis, Columbia: all were on IRT lines, which served the Bronx. But now I was going to that other country—Brooklyn! The first week, I explored different routes, in search of the most efficient way to get to LIU. On Thursday morning, I exited the IRT at Times Square and transferred to the BMT line.

As I walked along the platform navigating the rush-hour crowd, I noticed a young guy carrying a bundle of books and waiting ahead of me. His hair was combed out in a large Afro. He had a beard with a thick black mustache, and his short-sleeve shirt revealed nicely muscled arms. I found myself riveted by his appearance, and I stopped on the platform nearby. When the train arrived, we entered through the same door. I scrambled to a seat, and he stood just a few steps away by the nearest door, facing me. Over the next several stops, I kept staring in his direction, but quickly averted my eyes when he returned my gaze. A few seconds later, I glanced back, only to have him shift his eyes in another direction. We played this noncommittal cruising game until the train pulled into Eighth Street. Then, as the doors opened, he stepped out of the train, immediately turned around, smiled broadly, and began indicating with head motions that he expected me to exit as well. But this was my fourth day at a new job, and I wasn't prepared to risk being late. The doors closed, the train slowly pulled away, and through the windows I could see him still standing there, his eyes remaining locked on me and his smile as broad as ever.

That day at work, I couldn't get my mind off him. Over dinner that night, I told Kurt, Jack, and Hazen that I had seen the man of my dreams on the subway that morning. They laughed, naturally, at the uncontained romanticism of my less-than-brief encounter. But I had decided. This stranger and I were meant for each other, and I was going to find him. Recalling that he was carrying a set of books, I concluded that he must be a student at NYU, since he had gotten off at Eighth Street, and that he was taking summer classes. I resolved to be at the same place at the same time on the BMT station the next morning, with the expectation that he would be there again.

He wasn't, but that didn't stop me. This gorgeous young guy and I were destined to spend our lives together. If he was waiting for the train at Forty-Second Street like I was, then he, too, must live somewhere on the Upper West Side. My weekend was wide open, with no plans, and so I spent much of Saturday and Sunday strolling the streets and avenues in the West Seventies, Eighties, and Nineties looking for my lover-to-be. When my efforts met with failure, on Monday morning I once again changed to the BMT train at Forty-Second Street and searched the platform, but to no avail. I repeated the routine on Tuesday, again without success. On Wednesday, though my hopes were admittedly dimming, I went back. As I came down the stairs to the platform, I saw him waiting ahead and reading one of the books he was carrying.

I headed quickly in his direction and, when I reached him, immediately said "Hello," with a big smile on my face. He looked at me, a little puzzled, but said hello back. I asked if he was going to class at NYU, and he confirmed my hunch. Pretty soon we were making small talk that continued after we boarded the train. As it approached Eighth Street I asked if he would like to come to dinner the next night. When he said yes, we each scribbled our name, address, and phone number on a sheet from the small pad I had in my briefcase, and then said goodbye as he left the train.

It took all the resolve I could muster not to spill out the story at work, but that evening when I got home, I announced with great joy that Carlos, the man who was sure to be my lover-for-life, would be coming over the next night. Determined to make the best possible impression, I went out to buy the ingredients for the dinner that always won me praise and spent the rest of the evening cooking a pot of thick tomato-based meat sauce and crafting a mass of fresh meatballs. Somehow, I managed to make it through another day of work without my expectations of a life of boundless happiness exploding forth. The moment the clock hit five, I was out of the office, running to the subway, and then rushing to my apartment on Riverside.

Carlos arrived—even a bit early, thank God!—and as I greeted him and he walked through the door, he immediately pulled me to him. Before I could walk him through the apartment and introduce him to my roommates, he began kissing me with an intensity I had never experienced. Soon we were in my room and out of control, stripping the cover from the bed and the clothes from our bodies. Sexual attraction will always remain a mystery to me, but within minutes it was obvious that the word *spark* barely did justice to the desire that was unleashed on my bed. His firm arms, the stockiness of his torso, the black hair on his legs and chest, and the smile that kept appearing between his beard and mustache whenever he pulled back for a moment from our kissing: all of it made the wanting pour out of me as I reciprocated every bit of his passion.

Eventually, we made it to the kitchen and soon were eating dinner. Jack and the others were kind enough to head out into the neighborhood after some quick hellos, so the apartment was ours as we shared the basics of our life stories. Carlos had grown up in the Puerto Rican neighborhood of East Harlem in a family that, compared with my own, was large—four brothers and a sister, among whom he was the oldest. The first surprise was to discover that, despite his status as an undergraduate at NYU, he was a good bit older than me. To my amusement, I learned that he was born in 1938, the same year as both Ron and Billy. For a stretch of time, he had lived in San Francisco, where he embraced a gay life, but then returned to New York. For several years, he had worked for an airline, checking in passengers at LaGuardia Airport. The job gave him the opportunity to travel for free, and he had made a number of trips around the United States and to the Caribbean. But two years earlier, drawn to the excitement that was erupting on campuses, he had landed an office position at NYU, which allowed him to attend college without paying tuition. When school and full-time work together had proved too much, he had gotten hired as manager of a single-room occupancy building on West Seventy-Third Street. The job wasn't especially demanding, and it came with the added benefit of free rent. To supplement his income, he sold weed "to hippies like me," an irresistible smile spreading across his face as he said that.

Conversation between us flowed easily, and it continued as I walked him to the subway at the end of the evening. Before he headed down the stairs, he pulled me to him one more time and gave me a quick kiss. A public display of affection like that wasn't something I had ever done. It was a bit of a shock, but also thrilling—proof that this was the start of a passionate and committed relationship.

We had made a second date for Saturday night, this time at his place, but as my workday ended on Friday, I could not imagine having to wait another whole day before seeing him. Getting home, I ate something quickly and then headed to the address that he had given me. Arriving on his block was a bit of a shock. Standing in front of each of the old brownstones was a sex worker—a prostitute, as I would have said then—and they were calling out to all the guys who were walking by, including me. I made my way to Carlos's building, which was unlocked, went up a flight of stairs to his apartment number, and knocked on the door. When he opened, a look of surprise washed across his face, but it didn't stop me. Following his example from the previous night, I stepped right in and immediately began kissing him. Soon, we were in his bed.

We were together every night after that, sometimes at my place, but more often at his. At the end of the summer, as Jack and Kurt headed out of town, I took my few possessions—a couple of bags of books, a suitcase packed with clothes, and a typewriter—and moved into Carlos's apartment. I had never lived with a lover before.

............

Living with Carlos was different in so many ways from anything I had experienced. On the most basic level, the space we occupied was so minimal. It made the one-bedroom apartment I had grown up in seem luxurious. Our toilet was in the hallway, shared with the three other SRO units on our floor. The apartment had the tiniest of kitchens, barely large enough for two people to stand in, and a bathtub was located along one wall of it. We ate, talked, relaxed, watched television, listened to music, made our telephone calls, and fell asleep in the one room that constituted the apartment.

But our living space was the least of the differences. Carlos had a kind of gay life that I had never seen before. Ron certainly had a group of gay male friends, but it was separated from every other part of his life. While Billy seemed comfortable navigating the gay streets of Greenwich Village, he had almost no close friends. His gayness served as a marker of his social isolation. But Carlos? It seemed as if everyone was aware that he was gay. Shockingly to me, his brothers and his sister knew, and after I moved in with him, we were treated like a couple. He was out to Robert, a close friend of his since childhood, and Robert had a younger gay brother, Raymond, with whom we hung out. Bill and Bob were two very good friends from Carlos's years as an airline employee. They lived in the neighborhood, and we were often there for dinner on a weekend night. There were many other friends as well, often former tricks who had morphed over time into buddies.

To use the language of the times, Carlos was not "in the closet." But he was not "out" in the political sense that a new cohort of activists that year was embracing. A few days before we met, I had learned that gay liberation groups were organizing a march to commemorate the Stonewall Riots of the previous year. When I mentioned it over dinner with Carlos, Bill, and Bob, they roared with laughter. The idea of "faggots marching in the street," as Bill described it, struck them all as hilarious. Comfortable as Carlos might be with his sexuality, marching in the streets was not a feature of his gay life.

I found myself absorbed into that life, even as we created something that was our own. Our time together was all ours. No longer a student, I didn't have course materials to read, papers to research, or exams to study for. I didn't have to prep a debate topic, and my weekends weren't spent at tournaments. When I got home from work each day, I could be fully there with Carlos. When the weekend arrived, we could do as we pleased. My time was "free," something I had rarely experienced since starting at Regis eight years earlier.

Some of that time was spent, of course, having sex. Sleeping with someone night after night was a new experience. As the end of an evening approached, the bed was there to bring us together in the most intimate way. Sex was happening in my living space, and certainly in that first year, it happened often. The sexual charge of our first nights continued to assert itself powerfully as we entwined our bodies together.

Music helped fuel the passionate love that seemed to grow with each passing week. It was a year when several singers who went on to have major careers were releasing the albums that first thrust them into the spotlight of popular culture. Elton John, James Taylor, Carole King: the words and rhythms of their songs seemed to be constantly playing in the background, encouraging the romantic bond between me and Carlos to keeping growing.

And then there were the drugs. At Columbia, my roommates and I smoked grass, but only occasionally, usually on a weekend night when there was no need to get up early the next morning for class. With Billy, I had dropped acid once; it was an intense experience, never repeated. But for Carlos, marijuana was as integrated into his daily life as was eating. On days when he didn't go to campus, he was stoned by midafternoon, and in the evening after I got home from work, a joint was on the small table where we ate our dinner. When we visited Bill and Bob, grass was always part of our time together. Being high, listening to music, hanging out with friends, having sex: all of it was woven into this life that we were creating.

Surprisingly, Carlos had never tried LSD or any other hallucinogens. My description of my one acid trip fascinated him; he even read the copy of Aldous Huxley's *Doors of Perception* that I gave him. Soon, we were tripping on weekends a couple of times a month and venturing out into the world while we were still hallucinating wildly. On one trip we made our way to Central Park, where a group of amateur musicians were playing Jefferson Airplane songs. Lying under a tree and listening to them with my eyes closed, I had a vision of Grace Slick sitting beside us on the grass, singing to me and Carlos, "Why can't we go on as three?"

Another time, we had made our way to Battery Park just after we took a dose of mescaline. As we wandered along the edge of Manhattan, the Statue of Liberty seemed to be waving at us in the distance. We rode the subway back to our neighborhood while still high, and I envisioned that the train roaring through the tunnels between stations was actually driving me down into the center of Mount Etna, the volcano that Mom had seen on her trip to Sicily as a child.

In these first months of dating and then living together, I felt so bound up with Carlos that I did something that would have seemed unimaginable to me even a couple of years earlier—I brought him home to the Bronx to meet my parents. Of course, I did not introduce him as my "lover." Instead, after I moved into his apartment at the end of the summer, I explained that he was a student at NYU whom I had met through a friend and that he had offered me free rent if I moved in to share his space, buy some of the groceries, help with the cooking, and do other things like that. When I brought Carlos to dinner that fall, Mom and Dad liked him immediately. He was a native New Yorker; he was raised Catholic; he had an extended family that he was close to; and he displayed not a hint of intellectual pretension. Over the next months, as we made occasional visits back to see them, I noticed Mom asking Carlos the kinds of questions about me and how I was doing that she might have posed to a son- or daughter-in-law. While the nature of our relationship would remain undisclosed for several years to come, Carlos had become, in effect, family. Mom's boy may have left home, but at least I was in good hands. Their embrace of Carlos brought me back to family. When I visited them in Parkchester, whether with Carlos or not, I experienced a peacefulness that I hadn't felt around them in years.

............

Thrilling as my time with Carlos was, it did not make me resent the hours I spent on the job away from him. If anything, working at LIU that year proved to be another form of fulfillment. Besides Joe, which is how my boss insisted on being addressed, I was the only full-time employee in the periodicals division, but there were several undergraduate student assistants. Joe created something of a family-like atmosphere in our work space, which was small and intimate. Everyone shared stories about what they had done since they were last in the library. I found myself talking freely about my activities with Carlos over the weekend, though once again without using the label *lover* to describe him and certainly without discussing sex.

But much more than the sociability kept me passionately engaged with my job. I was encountering a bracing new world of knowledge and political analysis that had somehow escaped my notice through four years in college.

At Columbia, though I didn't major in classics, I still focused my intellectual exploration on European history and culture, with things Italian occupying center stage. The last time I had taken a US history course was as a sophomore at Regis. SDS leaders and other student radicals might speechify about the corruption of the American system and the exploitation and oppression it generated, but to me these were simply words used to rouse the crowd. Rarely did I reflect upon them. My opposition to the war came not from a grand analysis of political economy but from a moral outrage stimulated by the values I had imbibed as a Catholic and reinforced by the Catholic antiwar activists I encountered.

But now, at the library, I was shelving—and reading—a spate of publications, most of them relatively young, filled with historical and political analyses of American capitalism—or imperialism, as it was commonly called. *New Left Review*, *Radical America*, *Socialist Revolution*, and other journals like them were filled with macro-interpretations of how capitalism worked and how empire was built into the very conception of the United States as a nation. Expansion westward wasn't simply a matter of hardworking families looking for opportunity. Rather, it was the making of a continental empire built on the displacement and annihilation of Native peoples. The Spanish-American War at the end of the nineteenth century was no longer a minor military engagement designed to disrupt the evil doings of a decaying European power. Instead, it was the beginning of an American imperialism that extended US power around the globe under the name of free trade. Seen in this framework, the war in Southeast Asia was not an aberration. Rather, it was another example in a long line of interventions.

This immersion in publications spawned by the radical movements of the sixties opened the door to activism of an intellectual sort. In the summer months after graduation, I continued to volunteer at the draft counseling center at Columbia. But the combination of the lottery system for choosing inductees and the gradual reduction in the number of American troops in Southeast Asia was leading to a noticeable decline in young guys coming to the center for assistance. In the meantime, my job at the library had alerted me to another new resource growing out of the era's radicalism. As a way of keeping track of the large number of publications emerging from this culture of protest, a group of activists connected to the world of journalism had launched something called the *Alternative Press Index*. It was meant to do for underground newspapers and magazines what the *Readers' Guide to Periodical Literature* did for the mainstream print media. I got in contact with those in charge, and soon I was reading from front to back a set of publications that I would index for them.

As I read through these journals that were changing fundamentally my understanding of the world, one name repeatedly surfaced. William Appleman

Williams was a historian with a long connection to left-wing intellectual circles. A historian of US diplomacy, he proposed a theory of American foreign policy as one of "informal empire." So many of the writers I was encountering in these journals paid homage to him that I felt compelled to read his work. Of the several books he had written, the one that received the most frequent reference was *The Great Evasion*. Its long subtitle suggests the appeal the book had for a new generation of young radicals: *An Essay on the Contemporary Relevance of Karl Marx and on the Wisdom of Admitting the Heretic into the Dialogue about America's Future.*

From the start, Williams framed his critique of American political economy as a story of community lost. Capitalism's centering of the individual broke the natural ties that human beings needed and expected. Instead, it constructed a society in which each person struggled alone, competing against one another, as everyone sought the security that the promise of individual success held out. This competitive reach for success fed into the expansionism that had characterized American life almost from the beginnings of colonization in the seventeenth century. And the competition among individuals existed in a magnified way among corporations. The corporate capitalism that Williams critiqued infused the national government with an expansionist philosophy. It had made Latin America a prime target of the quest for an ever-expanding informal empire, thus sparking a series of interventions over many decades. In this framework, Vietnam was simply the latest—and most egregious—example of American expansion. And given Williams's framework, it would not be the last.

Mixed in with this critical analysis of how capitalism had operated in the United States was the promise of an alternative. Throughout the book, Williams kept returning to the notion of community. Capitalism alienated individuals from one another. By challenging capitalism, by taking on the structures of corporate power, Americans would lay the groundwork for, as he phrased it, "a truly human community." We could become, over time, a society characterized by "cooperative community" in which life was organized "on principles of equity."

Williams's repeated invocation of "a moral, equitable, and cooperative community" triggered something in me. Two years earlier, my first summer in Europe had sparked a strong desire to study Italian history and culture as a way of connecting with a deep piece of my identity. Now, Williams's analysis of US history and his invocation of an alternative future that radicals might create was taking me back to values I associated with my Catholic heritage, whether it be the passion of Father Daley for a Catholicism rooted in social justice or the commitment of Catholic peace activists to resist violence. Suddenly, this revisionist history that Williams was setting forth seemed indispensable for those of us who had been protesting in the streets and on campuses. Its themes, its key events, its driving forces all needed to be accessible to the next generation of students and activists. Otherwise, we were never going to succeed in creating a world grounded in community, cooperation, and the natural human goodness that individualism and corporate capitalism had rendered so inaccessible. This Marxist historian even seemed to speak to the values that I learned from the Scamporlino and D'Emilio clans. Our strength comes from our ability to bond together, to be there for one another, to care not just about oneself but about each other.

I quickly found myself deciding that I wanted to be part of this recuperative effort to uncover and write the truth of the American experience. And so I applied to graduate school in history. Since I wasn't about to leave my new life with Carlos, Columbia was the only school I applied to. My teachers were happy to write another letter of recommendation for me, and I was well enough known as a successful undergraduate that I felt confident I would be admitted. When April came, the letter of acceptance arrived, as well as a notice that I would receive a fellowship to cover the cost of tuition and provide a modest stipend. I told Joe about my plans and that I would be leaving the job by late summer. We were both sad about my impending departure, since I had fit so easily and worked so well in the family atmosphere he created. But I was now going to become part of the effort to uncover and expose the history of corporate capitalism in the United States and its destructive impact on society. Joe deserved some of the credit for that decision. Had he never offered me the job at the library, I might not be taking this path into the future.

That summer, as the start of the semester approached, Hazen let me know that he and his girlfriend Kathy would be moving out of the apartment at 400 Riverside so that they could live in a smaller place of their own, without roommates. Did Carlos and I want to move in, now that I'd be coming back to Columbia? Unlike the free place that Carlos had, this would require a monthly rent. But the apartment was rent controlled, at $225 a month, and we could easily find ourselves two other roommates to cover the cost. The prospect of once again having a full kitchen, separate rooms for eating and socializing and for sleeping and sex, and being back in a neighborhood that was familiar to me was irresistible. At the end of August, we moved back to Morningside Heights, to what had been my first neighborhood away from home, and to the space where we had first made love.

The next month, I walked over to the campus that had so occupied me for four years of study and registered for my first US history courses. It was the beginning of a future whose shape and direction was still a mystery. But I had chosen it, and it felt right to me.

# Postscript

As those who know me can attest, that decision to study US history set me along a path that I have continued on for half a century. Though the campus radicalism and the antiwar movement of the 1960s were in steep decline by 1971, the ranks of graduate students studying US history were populated with individuals like myself who believed that a knowledge of history was a critical resource in the effort to build a society grounded in justice, equality, and inclusion. Books on working-class history, women's history, racial and ethnic history, and a history of corporate power and American imperialism were rolling off the presses in the years that I was a graduate student. They were allowing for a dramatically revised understanding of the nation's past.

In March 1973, two years into my graduate school experience, I went to a small, informal meeting of individuals interested in exploring how research and intellectual work could be a tool in the LGBTQ movement—or "gay liberation," as it was then commonly called—that was spreading rapidly across the United States in the early 1970s. As I described in previous chapters, I knew about the uprising that had occurred in 1969 after the police raided the Stonewall Inn in Greenwich Village. Later, I learned about the plans to hold a march and rally in June 1970 to commemorate that rebellion. But even though I was leading a fuller and more open gay life with Carlos, I had not participated in any of the movement activities that were occurring in the early 1970s.

That meeting, held in an apartment on Manhattan's Upper East Side, brought together eight individuals. Some, like myself, were connected to university life; others, like Jonathan Ned Katz, were independent researchers and writers who would come to be labeled "public intellectuals." The talk was so compelling and revelatory that we agreed to meet again in two weeks. Those meetings kept growing in size as more and more gay men and lesbians with an interest in history, culture, research, and knowledge production attended and spread the word among their networks. Six months of meetings led the core group, of which I was a part, to organize a conference that brought together more than three hundred people. By 1975, the annual conference of what we named the Gay Academic Union was attracting close to a thousand individuals.

Working with others involved with the Gay Academic Union created a sense of a deeply committed community that the years of grappling with my homosexuality had taken from me. These folks became like family. They helped revive in me the connectedness that I had enjoyed with my family in my earliest years and at Regis during my adolescence. And, above all perhaps, this engagement instilled a sense of purpose and direction in my life that the Catholic values that still shaped me had always called for. I made the decision to write a dissertation on gay and lesbian history, a commitment that involved a new level of coming out—to my teachers, to a professional world, and, eventually, to my family and really anyone who knew me.

Over the next years and decades, the decision to research and write LGBTQ history often put me on the front lines of change. It revived the public-speaking skills I had developed at Regis in high school debate, as I found myself giving presentations to LGBTQ community audiences in cities around the country. It helped open the academic world and the profession of history to a subject matter that would have been unimaginable a generation earlier. It put me in close touch with the growing world of full-time LGBTQ activists for whom my knowledge of history became a resource deployed in a range of campaigns for LGBTQ equality. My work was cited in a major Supreme Court decision that declared sodomy laws unconstitutional; a national annual award in LGBTQ history was named after me. And over the decades, my expertise in the history of sexuality, of LGBTQ life, and of social movements opened the eyes of a generation of students to histories they had never before encountered.

In 1971, I could never have imagined that the decision to enter a graduate program in US history would have propelled this boy from the Bronx on such a life course.

# Acknowledgments

This book has been a long time in the making. I composed the first pieces of it more than fifteen years ago, after I had coronary bypass surgery, an event that made me realize the preciousness of one's early memories. I began writing stand-alone essays on particular moments or events in my early life as an Italian boy in the Bronx. I never imagined when I started that these literary adventures into my past might coalesce into a full-blown narrative. But at a certain point, I was able to see a form and structure to it, and gradually the book took shape.

More than anyone, I owe thanks to Jim Oleson, who was my partner for thirty-four years, and who from the beginning encouraged me to keep writing. He was always happy to read early drafts of particular pieces, and his unbounded enthusiasm served as wonderful motivation for me to push forward. Jim passed away in 2015; I know he would have been thrilled to see the book in print.

The manuscript went through several stages of revision. Along the way, I benefited enormously from readings by friends and colleagues. Nan Enstad and Steven Lawson both read my early attempts at memoir writing, and their responses were supportive. Peter Nardi brought to his reading of a complete version his personal experience as an Italian boy from the Bronx, who also attended Regis and who later came out as gay. Robert Orsi read the manuscript not only from the vantage point of someone with personal experience as an Italian American but also with the depth of knowledge of a scholar who has studied the Italian American experience in New York. And Thomas LeBien's comments helped tremendously in pushing me to highlight particular themes and eliminate many unnecessary diversions from the memoir's main thread. Finally, Estelle Freedman, my dearest friend and frequent collaborator over a period of five decades, never stopped encouraging me and offered insightful commentary on the manuscript as a whole and on my late-stage efforts at revising.

Then there are those who figure in the narrative. In a sense, everyone whom I mention in the book contributed to it through the life experiences that we shared, but I want to mention four in particular. Jack Collins and Kurt Meyers, two of my college buddies and housemates, read the Columbia chapters and were helpful in their observations and support for the project. My dear Regis friend Vincent Hevern was kind enough to share with me all the letters I wrote to him while in college. Having those documents brought the experience of those years vividly back to life and allowed me to reconstruct the emotional and spiritual upheavals of that time. And then there is my mother, Sophie, who passed away in 2010. The family photo albums that she meticulously assembled and preserved over several decades kept alive for me my childhood as a member of the Scamporlino clan.

The road to publication owes everything to Duke University Press. Ken Wissoker, who has worked at Duke for decades, expressed excitement about the manuscript from the moment I sent it to him, and he shepherded it quickly and effectively through the approval process at the press. And Joshua Gutterman Tranen has been extremely helpful and encouraging in moving me through the production process.

Finally, a hug and thanks to Hal Watkins, who for the last three years has listened patiently to my expressions of doubt about whether I would ever succeed in completing this memoir.

I have dedicated this book to the memory of my parents, Sophie Scamporlino D'Emilio and Vincent D'Emilio. Without them, I would have had no stories to tell.